# AN APOLOGY FOR RAYMOND SEBOND

MICHEL EYQUEM, Seigneur de Montaigne, was born in 1533, the son and heir of Pierre, Seigneur de Montaigne (two previous children dying soon after birth). He was brought up to speak Latin as his mother tongue and always retained a Latin turn of mind; though he knew Greek, he preferred to use translations. After studying law he eventually became counsellor to the *Parlement* of Bordeaux. He married in 1565. In 1569 he published his French version of the *Natural Theology* of Raymond Sebond; his *Apology* is only partly a defence of Sebond and sets sceptical limits to human reasoning about God, man and nature. He retired in 1571 to his lands at Montaigne, devoting himself to reading and reflection and to composing his *Essays* (first version, 1580). He loathed the fanaticism and cruelties of the religious wars of the period, but sided with Catholic orthodoxy and legitimate monarchy. He was twice elected Mayor of Bordeaux (1581 and 1583), a post he held for four years. He died at Montaigne (1952) while preparing the final, and richest, edition of his *Essays*.

M. A. SCREECH is an Extraordinary Fellow of Wolfson College and an Emeritus Fellow of All Souls College, Oxford, a Fellow of the British Academy and of the Royal Society of Literature, and a Fellow of University College, London. He long served on the committee of the Warburg Institute as the Fielden Professor of French Language and Literature in London, until his election to All Souls in 1984. He is a Renaissance scholar of international renown. He has edited and translated the complete *Essays* for Penguin Classics and, in a separate volume, Montaigne's *Sceptical Apology for Raymond Sebond*. His other books include *Erasmus: Ecstasy and the Praise of Folly* (Penguin, 1988), *Rabelais, Montaigne and Melancholy* (Penguin, 1991), and, most recently, *Laughter at the Foot of the Cross* (Allen Lane, 1998); all are acknowledged to be classic studies in their fields. In Latin, he is the editor, with Anne Screech, of *Erasmus' Annotations on the New Testament* (in three volumes). Michael Screech was promoted Chevalier dans la Légion d'Honneur in 1992. He was ordained, in Oxford, deacon in 1994 and priest in 1995.

# MICHEL DE MONTAIGNE

# AN APOLOGY FOR RAYMOND SEBOND

Translated and edited
with an Introduction
and Notes by
M. A. Screech

PENGUIN BOOKS

## PENGUIN BOOKS

Published by the Penguin Group
Penguin Books Ltd, 27 Wrights Lane, London W8 5TZ, England
Penguin Putnam Inc., 375 Hudson Street, New York, New York 10014, USA
Penguin Books Australia Ltd, Ringwood, Victoria, Australia
Penguin Books Canada Ltd, 10 Alcorn Avenue, Toronto, Ontario, Canada M4V 3B2
Penguin Books (NZ) Ltd, Private Bag 102902, NSMC, Auckland, New Zealand

Penguin Books Ltd, Registered Offices: Harmondsworth, Middlesex, England

Published in Penguin Books 1987
Reprinted with corrections 1993

21

Printed in England by Clays Ltd, St Ives plc
Typeset in Linotron 202 Plantin

ISBN-13: 978-0-140-44493-3
ISBN-10: 0-140-44493-9

www.greenpenguin.co.uk

FOR
*the kindest of hosts:*
*the*
*Jesuit Fathers*
*of*
*Regina*

# CONTENTS

# CONTENTS

# INTRODUCTION

Montaigne enjoys a place apart among French Renaissance authors. Men and women of all sorts are fascinated by what they find in him. Many read him for his wisdom and humanity, for which he may be quoted in a newspaper as readily as in a history of philosophy. He writes about himself, but is no egocentric and is never a bore. He treats the deepest subjects in the least pompous of manners and in a style often marked by dry humour. His writings are vibrant with challenge; they are free from jargon and unnecessary technicalities. In the seventeenth century, Pascal, the great Jansenist author of the *Pensées* ('Thoughts' which owe much to Montaigne), was converted partly by reading him and was soon discussing the *Essays* at Port-Royal with his director, LeMaistre de Sacy (who had his reservations). Pascal gained, it is said, thirty years by reading Montaigne, thirty years of study and reflection.[1] Others, too, have felt the same. For Montaigne gives his readers the fruits of his own wide reading and of his own reflections upon it, all measured against his personal experience during a period of intellectual ferment and of religious and political disarray. Montaigne never let himself be limited by his office or station. As husband, father, counsellor, mayor, he kept a critical corner of himself to himself, from which he could judge in freedom and seek to be at peace with himself. He does not crush his reader under the authority of the great philosophers: he tries out their opinions and sees whether they work for him or for others. Traces of Plato, Aristotle, Plutarch, Cicero, St Augustine or of his own contemporaries can be found in every page he wrote, but they are skilfully interwoven into his own discourse, being renewed and humanized in the process. And he hardly ever names them.

*An Apology for Raymond Sebond* has all these qualities, despite its being the longest piece Montaigne ever wrote. In it, Montaigne remains triumphantly himself.

When his beloved father died (18 June 1568) he succeeded to the title and the estates at Montaigne, in South-West France. (Provisions were made for his mother.) He was thirty-five, and three years married. Soon he was able (1570) to sell his charge as counsellor in the *Parlement* of Bordeaux (a legal

---

1. Blaise Pascal, *Pensées et Opuscules*, ed. L. Brunschvicg, 1909, p. 120 – an old study, but still useful.

office). His plan was, like cultured gentlemen in Ancient Roman times, to devote himself to learned leisure. He marked the event with a Latin inscription in his château – he had a taste for inscriptions, covering the beams and walls of his library with some sixty sayings in Greek and Latin, many of which figure in the *Essays*. His rejoicing at leaving *negotium* (business) for *otium* (leisure) was tempered by grief for the death of his father and by his deep and lifelong sense of bereavement at the death of his friend, Etienne de la Boëtie (1563).[2] (His children all died young, too, except a daughter, Eléonore, who was deeply loved but could not, for a nobleman, replace a son and heir.)

Montaigne's project of calm study soon went wrong. He fell into an unbalanced melancholy; his spirit galloped off like a runaway horse; his mind, left fallow, produced weeds not grass. To shame himself, he tells us, he decided to write down his thoughts and his rhapsodies. That was the beginning of his *Essays*. But he was not a professional scholar: he had no 'subject' to write about. He was not a statesman or a general. He soon decided to write about himself, the only subject he might know better than anyone else. This was a revolutionary decision, made easier, no doubt, by his bout of melancholy, for that humour encouraged an increased self-awareness. No one in Classical Antiquity had done anything like it. In the history of the known world only a handful of authors had ever broken the taboo against writing primarily about oneself, as an ordinary man. St Augustine had done so in the *Confessions*; during the Renaissance, Girolamo Cardano wrote *On his Life* and *On his Books* and Joachim du Bellay lamented his Roman 'exile' in his poetic *Regrets*. But these works bear no resemblance to what the *Essays* were to become for Montaigne – 'tentative attempts' to 'assay' the value of himself, his nature, his habits and of his own opinions and those of others – a hunt for truth, personality and a knowledge of humanity through an exploration of his own reactions to his reading, his travels, his public and his private experience. The *Essays* are not a diary but are of 'one substance' with their author: 'I am myself the matter of my book.' In the case of a questioning and questing mind like his this study became not a book on a 'subject' but *Assays of Michel de Montaigne* – 'assays' of himself by himself.[3]

These *Essays* were first divided into two books (a third followed later). Each book contains many chapters and each chapter contains many 'assays'. He himself never referred to his chapters as essays: his chapters were convenient groupings of several assays – primarily 'assays' of a man called Michel

2. See Montaigne's chapter 'On affectionate friendships' (vol. I, chapter 28).

3. For fuller accounts of the genesis, aims and achievements of the *Essays* see the Introductions to volumes I and III of this translation (in preparation).

de Montaigne. Montaigne soon discovered that very short chapters did not allow him enough scope for all the essays he wanted to make. He let his chapters grow longer. In the process he discovered the joys of digression and freedom from an imposed order. And he found he could tackle deeper subjects more exhaustively.

But even judged by the length of the more developed chapters, *An Apology for Raymond Sebond* is in a class by itself. The very length of this twelfth chapter of Book II shows that it was for Montaigne a very special chapter indeed. He felt that the topic could afford him matter to write about for ever.

It is understandable that Montaigne should have written a considered defence of the *Natural Theology* of Raymond Sebond since he himself had translated it into French. In the opening pages of the *Apology* and in the dedication of the work to his father he tells us how he came to do so. Pierre Bunel, a Christian humanist from Toulouse (1499–1546) had once stayed at Montaigne and recommended Sebond's book as an antidote to the poison of 'Lutheranism' – a term often applied to Protestants generally. Bunel's visit may have occurred between 1538 and 1546; he was then living reasonably near Montaigne, first at Lavaur and later in Toulouse. If so, Michel de Montaigne was still a child, perhaps not yet in his teens.

That Bunel should offer such a book to Montaigne's father makes good sense. Raymond Sebond was a local figure, possibly a Catalan. Montaigne refers to him as a Spaniard professing medicine in Toulouse. In fact he was a Master of Arts who professed both Medicine and Theology. His *Natural Theology* was written in Toulouse in the 1420s or early 1430s. It seems to have circulated fairly widely in manuscript. By Montaigne's time it had been printed more than once, as well as being adapted to dialogue form – still in Latin – by Petrus Dorlandus under the titles of *Violet of the Soul* or of *Dialogues concerning the Nature of Man: Exhibiting Knowledge of Christ and of Oneself*.

Apart from these Latin books Raymond Sebond had fallen into oblivion. When inquiries about him and his *Natural Theology* were addressed to Adrian Turnebus (Montaigne's scholarly friend 'who knew everything') he could only say that the *Natural Theology* was a 'kind of quintessence drawn from Thomas Aquinas'. That may imply that Turnebus rightly considered it to have been influenced by another medieval Catalan theologian, Raymond Lull, the great *Doctor Illuminatus* who was himself held to be the Quintessence of Aquinas. Since Turnebus died in 1565, the *Natural Theology* of Sebond must have been in Montaigne's mind for several years before he published his translation.

In the *Apology* Montaigne tells us that he translated Sebond at the request of his father in the 'last days' of his life. In the epistle in which he dedicated the translation to his father, Montaigne lets it be understood he had been working on the task at least some months before that. Since the *Theologia Naturalis* runs into nearly a thousand pages, a year or more is certainly likely. The finished translation was Montaigne's tribute to his beloved parent. The dedicatory epistle is addressed from Paris 'To My Lord, the Lord of Montaigne'; in it, he wishes his father long life: yet it is dated from the very day of his father's death – hardly a coincidence but rather a fitting tribute to a son's feelings of piety at the death of the 'best father that ever was'. It may well imply that he wished he had translated and published the work more speedily, to give his father joy in his lifetime.

The works of Sebond had been appreciated by high-born ladies in France long before Montaigne wrote his *Apology* at the request of an unnamed patroness who may even have been Princess Margaret of France, the future wife of Henry of Navarre.[4] In 1551 Jean Martin had translated Dorlandus' version of Sebond's *Violet of the Soul* into highly latinate French for Queen Eleonora of Austria, the widow of King Francis I. In her absence from France the version was dedicated to the Cardinal de Lenoncourt; there we read that the *Viola animae* is a book which could 'bring back atheists, if any there be, to the true light, while maintaining the faithful in the good way'. Clearly Pierre Bunel had every reason to give the original and full version of such a book to an intelligent but not formally educated nobleman such as Montaigne's father, who wanted to find an 'antidote' to Lutheranism.

The Catholic credentials of the *Natural Theology* of Raymond Sebond may appear to need no defence or apology. In the fifteenth century the scholarly and saintly Cardinal Nicolaus of Cusa had possessed a copy: it may have contributed to his doctrine of 'learned ignorance' – that Socratic, Evangelical *docta ignorantia* of the Christian who is content to own that all human knowledge is as nothing, compared to that infinity who is God; learned ignorance never claims to know, or to aspire to know, anything beyond the saving law of Christ. In the sixteenth century the French Platonizing humanist Charles de Bouëlles also had a copy: he was a Christian apologist of real depth and power. But Montaigne was not mistaken in believing that the *Natural Theology* did need an apologist against criticisms arising within his own Church. In 1559 a work called the *Violetta del anima* appeared on a list of prohibited books drawn up by the Spanish Inquisitor Ferdinando de Valdés,

4. *Apology*, pp. 40 and 136.

Archbishop of Seville. It may refer to a Spanish version of the *Violet of the Soul*. More important, in 1558–9, the entry *Raymundus de Sabunde: Theologia Naturalis* appeared on the Index of Forbidden Books of Pope Paul IV.

So the Catholic Montaigne had translated a prohibited book! Or had he? His own translation was never condemned. On the contrary, it enjoyed a certain popularity well into the next century. After Montaigne's first and second editions in 1569 and 1581 (both in Paris) it was reprinted in Rouen in 1603, in Tournon in 1611, in Paris again, also in 1611 and finally in Rouen in 1641.

This fact can be easily explained. It was not the *Natural Theology* that the censors took exception to but to the short Prologue which accompanied it. That is shown by the definitive judgement of the Council of Trent; the Tridentine Index of Forbidden Books (1564) condemned the Prologue and nothing else. Shorn of the page and a half of Prologue, the Latin original of Sebond's *Natural Theology* circulated freely and was fully reprinted in Venice in 1581, in Frankfurt-on-the-Main in 1631 – with the Prologue – and finally in Lyons in 1648, by which time it was becoming dated. And even the Prologue was eventually removed from the Index in the nineteenth century. By then Raymond Lull was fully back in favour. But even at the worst Raymond Sebond needed to be expurgated, not obliterated.

This has not stopped Sebond's method of teaching the Catholic faith from being thought of as somehow dangerous. Even the New Catholic Encyclopedia (which ought to know better) calls it heretical. It is not. But it was clearly a disturbing book – a good defence againt heresy yet, for many, a work somehow not to be trusted. There were contemporaries of Montaigne who shared that opinion: hence his apology for it.

When Montaigne published his translation in 1569, he included with it a translation of the Prologue which proved quite acceptable to the Roman Catholic Church. No censor has ever said a word against it. He had clearly taken theological advice and had adapted the Prologue to meet the needs of the Faith. A comparison of his version and the original shows why the Latin Prologue appeared among the prohibited books, while the French version never did.

Sebond's original Prologue is dense and interesting. It is emphatic, trenchant and absolute. Its claims are such as were bound to appeal to intelligent Catholic ladies deprived of formal education and to laymen such as Montaigne's father. It claimed to 'illuminate' Christians with a knowledge of God and themselves. It required no previous knowledge 'of Grammar, Logic, nor any other deliberative art or science, nor of Physics nor of Metaphysics' – no Aristotle, therefore. It offered a method applicable to both clergy and laity.

It promised certain results, 'in less than a month, without toil and without learning anything off by heart. And once learned it is never forgotten.' The *Natural Theology* was said to lead not only to knowledge but to morality, making whoever studied it 'happy, humble, kind, obedient, loathing all vice and sin, loving all virtues, yet without puffing up with pride'.

Montaigne did not essentially lessen this appeal but introduced changes in the Prologue (and, indeed, in the work itself) which show a sensitivity to theological distinctions. Where the Prologue was concerned, his changes were few but vital enough to restore it to undoubted orthodoxy. For example, where Raymond Sebond had written of his art as '*necessary* to every man' Montaigne made it merely *useful*. When Sebond claimed that his method taught 'every duty' required of the student Montaigne changed that to 'nearly everything'. Sebond wrote:

In addition this science teaches everyone really to know, without difficulty or toil, every truth necessary to Man concerning both Man and God; and all things which are necessary to Man for his salvation, for making him perfect and for bringing him through to life eternal. And by this science a man learns, without difficulty and in reality, whatever is contained in Holy Scripture.

Montaigne tones that down:

In addition this science teaches every one to see clearly, without difficulty or toil, *truth insofar as it is possible for natural reason*, concerning knowledge of God and of himself and of what he has need for his salvation and to reach life eternal; *it affords him access to understanding what is prescribed and commanded* in Holy Scripture.

The words in italics are vital. In Montaigne's hands the work of Sebond is presented as a means of access to truths and duties prescribed in Scripture. Sebond's original Prologue could be taken to mean that his method stood alongside Scripture, independently. That of course would have been heretical if Sebond had been arguing from fallen natural reason. But he was not.

Today we are so used to commercialized religious charlatanism that the claims of Sebond risk sounding like some slick, patent road to an illusory salvation. That is far from the truth. The *Natural Theology* is a cogently written work in scholastic Latin seeking to anchor the reader firmly within the Roman Catholic Faith, free from all wavering and doubt. The Prologue (in both the original and in Montaigne's translation) ends with an uncompromising act of submission to the 'Most Holy Church of Rome, the Mother of all faithful Christians, the Mistress of grace and faith, the Rule of Truth'.

The method of Raymond Sebond is sufficiently complex to be misunderstood, not least by the many who were long deprived of his Prologue by the folly of censorship. Obviously even quite a few moderns writing on Montaigne have never been able to study it.[5]

Sebond firmly bases his method on 'illumination'. He does not claim that human reason by itself can discover Christian truths. Quite the reverse. Without 'illumination' reason can understand nothing fundamental about the universe. But, duly illuminated, Man can come to know himself and his Creator as well as his religious and moral duties, which he will then love to fulfil. It is a method of freeing Man from doubts; it reveals the errors of pagan antiquity and its unenlightened philosophers; it teaches Catholic truth and shows up sects as errors and lies. It does all these things by teaching the Christian the 'alphabet' which must be acquired if one is to read Nature aright. This science 'teaches Man to know himself, to know why he was created and by Whom; to know his good, his evil and his duty; by what and to Whom he is bound. What good are the other sciences to a man who is ignorant of such things?'

'The other sciences', when this basis is lacking, are but vanity. They lead to error, men not knowing 'whither they are going, whence they came' nor where he is. Sebond shows Man how far he has fallen and how he can be reformed.

Raymond Sebond believes that God has given Man two Books, a metaphorical one and a real one. The first is the 'Book of all Creatures' or the 'Book of Nature'. The second is Holy Scripture. The first Book to be given Man – at the Creation – was the Book of Nature. In it all created things are like letters of the alphabet; they can be combined into words and sentences, teaching Man truths about God and himself. But with the Fall, Man was blinded to the sense of the Book of Nature. He could no longer read it aright. Nevertheless, that book remains common to all.

The Second Book, Holy Writ, is not common to all – 'to read the second book one must be a clerk'. Yet (unlike Scripture) the Book of Nature cannot be falsified; it cannot lead to heresy. Yet in fact both Books teach the same lesson (since the same God created all things in due order and revealed the Scriptures). They cannot contradict each other, even though the first is natural – of one nature with us Men – while the other is above all Nature, supernatural.

Now, Man was created in the beginning as a reasonable creature, capable of learning. But at his creation, Man – Sebond means Adam – knew nothing whatever. 'Since no doctrine can be acquired without books', it was most

5. A translation of Montaigne's version of the *Prologus* is given after this Introduction in an Appendix.

appropriate that Divine Wisdom should create this Book of Creatures in which Man, on his own, without a teacher, could study the doctrines requisite for him. It was the visible 'letters' of this Book – the 'creatures' placed in God's good order, not our own – that Man was intended to read, not with human will but aided by God's judgement.

But since the Fall all that has changed. Man can no longer find God's truths in Nature, 'unless he is enlightened by God and cleansed of original sin.[6] And therefore not one of the pagan philosophers of Antiquity could read this science, because they were blinded concerning the sovereign good, even though they did read some sort of science in this Book and derived whatever they did have from it.' But the solid, true science which leads to life eternal – even though it was written there – they were unable to read.

In Montaigne's hands Raymond Sebond's method shows enlightened Christians that the revealed truths about God and man are consonant with the Book of Nature properly read. It reconciles observed nature with revealed truth and so can lead men to accept it without doubt or hesitation.

Montaigne's *Apology* is a defence of this doctrine, and corresponds to the two assertions of Sebond: i: Man, when enlightened, can once again read the Book of Nature aright; ii: Man when not enlightened by God's grace can never be sure he has read it aright: Mankind has read 'some sort of science' in this Book of Nature but is 'unable to read' that 'true science which leads to life eternal'. This means that unenlightened Man, Man left to his own devices, can no longer 'read' God's creatures – and *creatures* covers not only plants and animals but everything within the Universe – the letters of that alphabet appear all jumbled up. No longer can Man be sure he has any knowledge of himself or of any created thing or being, from the highest heavens to the tiniest ant.

The two main sections of the *Apology* are of widely different lengths. Montaigne dismisses fairly curtly, though courteously, the first of the two criticisms made of Sebond.

The first charge is . . . that Christians do themselves wrong in wishing to support their belief with human reason: belief is grasped only by faith and by private inspiration from God's grace.

Montaigne's reply is to accept 'that purely human means are not enough; had they been so, many choice souls in ancient times' would have succeeded in reaching truth. But despite their integrity and their excellent natural faculties, the Ancients all failed in their ultimate quest: 'Only faith can embrace, with lively certainty, the high mysteries of our religion' (*Apology*, p. 3).

6. This is the conviction of Pascal, *Pensées*, Brunschvicg no. 244.

That is quite orthodox. At least from the time of Thomas Aquinas it was held that natural reason ought to bring Man to the preambles of the Faith – that there is one God, that he is good, that he can be known from revelation – but that specifically Christian mysteries are hidden until revealed.[7] Montaigne may seem to put even those preambles in doubt, only to vindicate them triumphantly at the end of the *Apology* with the aid of Plutarch.

But Montaigne contrasts the routine practising Christian, merely accepting the local religion of Germany or Périgord in casual devotion, with what illuminated Christians are really like when 'God's light touches us even slightly'. Such Christians emanate brightness (*Apology*, p. 4). The apprentice Christian may not rise so high but, once his heart is governed by Faith, it is reasonable for Faith to draw on his other capacities to support him. Sebond's doctrine of illumination helps us to do so effectively and to draw religious strength from a knowledge of God's creation:

God has left within these lofty works the impress of his Godhead: only our weakness stops us from discovering it. He tells us himself that he makes manifest his unseen workings through the things which are seen. (*Apology*, p. 1)

Montaigne turns to a key text of Scripture which he suitably cites. Sebond could toil to show that, to the enlightened Christian, 'no piece within this world belies its Maker' precisely because Scripture gives Man that assurance:

All things, Heaven, Earth, the elements, our bodies and our souls are in one accord: we simply have to find how to use them. If we have the capacity to understand they will teach us. 'The invisible things of God,' says St Paul, 'are clearly seen from the creation of the world, his Eternal Wisdom and his Godhead being perceived from the things he has made.' (*Apology*, p. 10)

That quotation, adapted from the Vulgate Latin text of Romans 1:20, is the foundation of all natural theology in the Renaissance. That can be seen from author after author, since Montaigne had chosen his Scriptural authority well. He had selected the obvious text. In 1606, for example, George Pacard published his own *Théologie Naturelle* and placed Romans 1:20 firmly on his title page, lending its tone to his whole book. A generation later Edward

---

7. Thomas Aquinas, *Summa Theologica*, II[a], II[ae], Q.1 ad 5. Later, this theme is briefly treated in ways relevant to Montaigne in Daniel Huët, Bishop of Avranches, *De imbecillitate mentis humanae*, 1738, Bk. 2, chapter 1, or in the same chapter of the French original, *Traité philosophique de la foiblesse de l'esprit humain*, 1723. (It was already a standard doctrine long before Montaigne's time.)

Chaloner could defend the general thesis of Montaigne here, with precisely this verse, in a sermon preached at All Souls College in Oxford.[8]

To make his point clear, Montaigne uses an analogy taken from Aristotelian physics, in which any object is composed of inert *matter* and a *form* which gives it its being.

Our human reasonings and concepts are like matter, heavy and barren: God's grace is their form, giving them shape and worth. (*Apology*, p. 11)

Since men such as Socrates and Cato lacked God's grace, even their most virtuous actions are without shape or ultimate value; in the context of salvation they 'remain vain and useless'. So too with the themes of Sebond. By themselves they are heavy and barren. When Faith illuminates them, they become finger-posts setting man on the road which leads to his becoming 'capable' of God's grace.[9] In the light of the closing words of the *Apology* that is a vital consideration.

The Renaissance thinker, like his forebears from the earliest Christian times, had to decide what to do about the great pious men of Ancient days. Were they saved by their loyalty to the Word (the *Logos*) before he was incarnate in Christ? – one of the earliest theologians, Justin Martyr, thought they were. Or were they inevitably destined to eternal reprobation, since even their good actions were not directed to the right End? Were some, such as Socrates or Plato, vouchsafed special saving grace? Erasmus would like to think that God would make the same kind of understanding, graded concessions that he himself made to those Ancients who were pious, moral and sensitive to metaphysical realities.

Montaigne's admiration for the virtuous heroes of Antiquity was boundless: the moral system he was teasing out for Christian laymen like himself to supplement the Church's teaching owed nearly everything to them. He insisted nevertheless that they were great with human greatness only and in

8. Edward Chaloner, *The Gentile's Creede*, or *The Naturall Knowledge of God*, in *sixe sermons*, 1623, p. 223: 'The doctrine therefore which our *Apostles* in my Text doe insinuate unto us, when they say, that God left not himselfe to the Gentiles without witnesse, must needs be this. *That so much may be knowne of God by the Witness of Nature, as is sufficient to confirme unto us, though not his Persons, or workes of Redemption, yet his Godhead,* and also his *handie-worke in creating and governing the World.* God is himself invisible, and yet *The invisible things of him* (sayth the Apostle, Rom. I.20) *that is, his Eternall Power and Godhead, are seene by the creation of the World, being considered in their workes.* To resolve the members of which Verse, were to propose unto you a whole systeme of naturall Divinitie . . .' Cf. Sir Walter Raleigh, *Historie of the World*, I, 1, cited by E. M. W. Tillyard, *The Elizabethan World Picture*, p. 36.

9. *Apology*, p. 11; cf. my book, *Montaigne and Melancholy*, p. 49.

no wise proto-Christians. Yet the *Apology* also shows by the careful use of theological language that Montaigne did not look on all the Ancients as an undifferentiate 'mass of damnation'. This is brought out by the way he cited Romans 1:20, without the final clause, '*so that they [the pagans] are inexcusable*'.

Many did attach this clause to St Paul's assertion that the invisible things of God are accessible through the visible: George Pacard did precisely that in the title page of his *Théologie Naturelle*. But many did not; to cite only one example: Allessandro della Torre, Bishop of Sittià, cited this text of Romans three times in his Italian work, *The Triumph of Revealed Theology* (Venice, 1611): each time he omits that damning clause. By doing the same Montaigne and others could stress the human limitations of Socrates or Plato, while avoiding the Jansenist rigour which Pascal read back into the *Apology*:

There is enough light [Pascal wrote] to lighten the Elect and enough darkness to make them humble. There is enough darkness to blind the Reprobate and enough light to damn them and render them inexcusable. *St Augustine, Montaigne, Sebond.*[10]

Montaigne follows Sebond in dwelling on the errors and the chaotic jumble of ideas expounded by those unenlightened wise men, vainly seeking certain truth with their human reason from the Book of Creatures: but he does not consider their opinions to be all equally 'inexcusable'. Nevertheless he asserted that 'human reason goes astray everywhere, but especially when she concerns herself with matters divine' (*Apology*, p. 90). Christian mysteries they never grasped as Christians can. But what about God's 'Eternal Wisdom and his Godhead'?

A standard doctrine was, that a grasp of the elements of good morality was possible for all men, Christian or otherwise, though grace was always required for Salvation (even the Mosaic Law would not suffice by itself). That good morality was achieved by pagans is shown by Socrates or by other heroes of Montaigne, such as Epaminondas. (The great moral platitudes are never put in doubt anywhere in the *Essays*.)

Montaigne specifically finds pagan monotheism at its best not 'true' (in the sense of attaining with certainty to the Christian revelations) but nevertheless 'most excusable'. This is not a correction to St Paul's teaching in Romans 1:20, but a gloss on it.[11]

10. *Pensées*, Brunschvicg no. 578.
11. *Apology*, p. 82; this can be conveniently seen from the gloss of a later scholar, Estius: in one sense even good pagans were 'not excusable' because of their ignorance; yet 'they can in some way be said to be excusable' by comparison with others who did less well. A hyper-orthodox preacher, Father Boucher, was to condemn Montaigne

Montaigne touches so lightly on some crucial theological points that readers may miss their import. Yet they can be vital, not least in the *Apology*, which is centred on religious knowledge and doubt. In at least one respect, Montaigne's conception of God was that of St Augustine, of many medieval and Renaissance thinkers, and of Pascal: God is a Hidden God, a *Deus absconditus* who hides himself from Man and therefore can only be known from his self-revelation. Montaigne lightly but specifically attributes that concept to St Paul. When in Athens, Paul saw an altar dedicated to 'an unknown God' – Athenian philosophers could get that far. In the *Apology* those words appear as 'a *hidden*, unknown God'. That enables Paul (in the *Apology*) to find the Athenian worshippers to be 'most excusable' (Apology, p. 82). The same doctrine appears in the medieval theologian Nicolas of Lyra.[12]

Such deft and telling use of words should scotch the notion that Montaigne was theologically naïve. (No theologian who had studied his translation of Sebond could make such a gaffe.) And in this case it should help to undermine the curiously coarse interpretation of the *Apology* as a work championing 'fideism', one, that is, which denies that there ever can be any rational basis for Christianity since all depends on unfettered faith – faith as trust and faith as credulity. For Montaigne there is a hierarchy of religious opinion among the pagans. (The *Apology* ends with one of the most impressive of them all: Plutarch's.) Yet Montaigne held with Sebond that even the best of pagans failed to penetrate through to most of the vital truths contained in the Book of Creatures.[13]

The defence of Raymond Sebond against the second charge – that his arguments are weak – falls into several parts, all marked by varying degrees of scepticism. By turning his sceptical gaze on Man and his cogitations, Montaigne denies that it is possible to find better arguments than Sebond's any-

over this, but could only do so by distorting his thought. Cf. his *Triomphes de la Religion Chrestienne*, 1638, pp. 128–29; Boucher believed that Montaigne was advocating the pagan religion he was seeking to 'excuse'. That was because he was distressed to see Montaigne so influential over 'the *beaux esprits* of these times' that he attributed to him ideas he believed to be held by free-thinkers in his own day.

12. The expression *Hidden God* derives from Isaiah 45:15. Christians of many persuasions used the term to emphasize the need of grace and for revelation from God, who is his own interpreter. It was associated by Nicolas of Lyra with Romans 1:20 in his gloss.

13. In this he remains orthodox. The notion of a Book of Nature (or of Creatures) in Sebond's and Montaigne's sense became quite common among theologians: cf. those mentioned in Reginald Pole's *Synopsis criticorum*, 1686, vol. 5, col. 21, line 45 f.; it was also pleasing to Francis Bacon, *Advancement of Learning* I, vi, 16.

where whatsoever. This assertion is governed (as are all the long answers to
the second objection) by a declaration of intent which applies to all the many
pages which are to follow:

> Let us consider for a while Man in isolation, Man with no outside help, armed with
> no arms but his own and stripped of that grace and knowledge of God in which consist
> his dignity, his power and the very ground of his being. (*Apology*, p. 13)

Today the very word *scepticism* implies for many a mocking or beady-eyed
disbelief in the claims of the Church to intellectual validity. It did not do so
then. You can be sceptical about the claims of the Church: or you can be
sceptical about rational attempts to discredit them . . .

The unenlightened rivals to Sebond have both their hands tied firmly
behind their back. Sebond has grace and illumination: they have not. In this
second, longer part of the *Apology*, comments are occasionally addressed to
this unilluminated ignorance on the basis of revealed wisdom, but the ignorance remains unilluminated and so can only fortuitously, randomly and hesitantly ever arrive at the goal gracefully reached by Sebond's natural theology.
That is what makes it so interesting. Instead of calmly orthodox certainty,
we are exhilarated by following all the highways and byways and side-tracks
travelled along by Man's questing spirit in his search for truth about God,
Man and the Universe. Montaigne did his job thoroughly: that is why all of
this section was pillaged for anti-Christian arguments by the *beaux esprits* of
later centuries.

Montaigne is so lightly untechnical that it is easy to overlook that, in a
fascinatingly personal and idiosyncratic way, he is saying what learned Latin
treatises also taught about the opinions of fallen man. Since sixteenth-century
Jesuits appreciated Montaigne, one could cite Cardinal Bellarmine, S.J., who
(with the help of St Augustine's *City of God*) was struck by the 'monstrous
opinions' of those unenlightened pagans who 'even went so far as to make
gods of vines and garlick'.[14] But where Bellarmine finds bleak error Montaigne finds – also – fascinating and inevitable variety.

Montaigne answers the second lot of criticism of Sebond by first crushing
human pride: no purely human reasons can show conclusively (as Sebond
can) that Man – for all his 'reason' – is in any way higher than the other
animals. They, too, like us, have reasoning powers. They have instincts, it
is true, but so do we. For this crushing of Man's pride Montaigne first drew
mainly on his favourite writer: Plutarch (as translated into French by Bishop

14.  Robert Bellarmine, S.J., *De Controversiis Christianae Fidei, adversus hujus temporis haereticos (Opera*, 1593, III; 'On the Loss of Grace and the State of Sin', col. 487
B; cf. p. 107).

Amyot, who presented his author as an excellent moral guide for Christian
noblemen). It seems that Plutarch so dominated the first outline of the *Apology* that Montaigne could even assert that it owed everything to him, a remark
he removed once he realized how far he had moved in indebtedness to Sextus,
to Cicero, to Aristotle and to Plato (*Apology*, p. 137 note 331).

Parts of this praise of the beasts to humble Man's pride have acquired a
certain quaintness: zoology has been revolutionized since the Renaissance.
Moreover, Montaigne, by long-established convention, cited the weeping
war-horses of the poets or the tale of Androcles and the Lion as though they
were zoological and historical fact. His loyal dogs commit suicide or haunt
their masters' tombs. In his own day, however, his animal science was powerfully persuasive. (Well into the next century, his elephant lore is repeated by
authors such as Salomon de Priezac in his *Histoire des Eléphants*, Paris, 1650.)
As codified by his learned clerical disciple, Pierre de Charron, in his book
*On wisdom*, Montaigne's attitude to the beasts became central to some of the
great controversies among the most famous philosophers and theologians of
the seventeenth century. In its own way it even had something of the appeal
of Darwin. By a very different route it forced people to re-examine in anger
or humility what place Man occupied in the Book of Nature among all the
other creatures. And Montaigne emphasizes that the common examples of
ants, bees and guide-dogs are just as persuasive as exotic rarities.

Pride is the sin of sins: intellectually it leads to Man's arrogantly taking mere
opinion for knowledge. In terms which were common to many Renaissance
writers, Montaigne emphasized that 'there is a plague (a *peste*) on Man: the
opinion that he knows something.'[15]

This pride and this trust in opinion are all part of Man's vanity (of that
vain emptiness evoked by Ecclesiastes, the Old Testament book from which
were derived several sceptical inscriptions in Montaigne's library). The *Apology* briefly contrasts such 'vanity' with the assurance supplied by Christian
'Folly' (which proclaims that God's true wisdom is to be found in the lowly,
the simple, the humble and the meek).[16]

'Christian folly' was a major theme in Renaissance thought and had been

15. Cf. Melanchthon, *De Anima*: 'Hence arises other plagues (*pestes*): the soul loves
itself and admires its own wisdom, fashions opinions about God and delights in this
game and, in its distress, rails against God.' A century later Father Boucher is still
using the same phrases: 'Presumptuousness of mind is the mother of error, the nurse
of false opinions, the scourge of the soul, the plague (*peste*) of Man.'

16. Erasmus played a major role in spreading the doctrine of Christian Folly in the
Renaissance. It was widely accepted by Christians of many persuasions.

long allied to scepticism. Montaigne was not writing the *Apology* in a void. More specifically, the general thrust of his defence of Sebond would have been evident to any reader of Henry Cornelius Agrippa's declamation *On the Weakness and Vanity of all Sciences and on the Excellence of the Word of God* (Cologne, 1530). It was reprinted in Montaigne's time; he drew on it heavily. It continues a tradition of Christian scepticism to be found in a fifteenth-century scholar such as Valla, who influenced Erasmus, but which is more fully developed in Gian-Francesco Pico della Mirandola's *Examination of the Vanity of the Doctrines of the Pagans and of the Truth of Christian Teachings* (Mirandola, 1520).[17]

These were major and successful books; Montaigne also drew heavily on a work of 1557, unsuccessful enough to be remaindered (freshened up with a new title page in 1587): the *Dialogues* of Guy de Brués. The magic of Montaigne's art in the *Essays* and the originality of his thought enabled him to take ideas and matter lying about in Latin tomes or even in unsaleable treatises and then metamorphose them into the very stuff of his most readable pages.[18]

That certainly applies to his scepticism.

Scepticism is a classical Greek philosophy. Its full force was rediscovered towards the end of the sixteenth century. As such it plays a vital role in Renaissance thought; but the essential doctrines of scepticism (including some of the basic arguments and examples which appear in the *Apology*) were known much earlier, from Cicero's *Academics* and from critical assessments of scepticism (sometimes associated with judgements on the proto-Sceptic Protagoras) in both Plato and Aristotle. Cicero's *Academics* is the easiest to read for lovers of Montaigne (who find that whole passages have been integrated into the *Apology*). So are major borrowings from other works of Cicero, including *On the Nature of the Gods* and the *Tusculan Disputations*. But the influence of Plato and Aristotle goes far deeper.

Up to a point Cicero was a good guide, but less exciting than Sextus Empiricus and the intellectual stimulus of Plato and Aristotle.[19] Clearly,

17. Fundamental scepticism, typified by the work of François Sanchez, a doctor in Toulouse, *Quod nihil scitur* ('That Nothing is Known', 1581), was also accessible to Montaigne. He may even have read this particular book in manuscript. (It is being edited by Elaine Limbrick.)

18. The *Dialogues* of Guy de Brués were aimed against 'the new Academics' and sought to show 'that all does *not* consist in opinion'. The sceptics are allowed to state their case fairly.

19. Montaigne was irritably aware that Cicero was not an original thinker. More provocative for him were, say, Plato's hostility towards relativism, in the *Theaetetus* and similar passages in Aristotle, as well as his brief indirect account of scepticism

Sextus' *Pyrrhonian Hypotyposes* dominates parts of the *Apology*, yet appears in no other chapter of the *Essays*. (This has helped support the contention that, when writing the *Apology*, Montaigne went through an acute crisis of scepticism, symbolized by his device of the poised scales with *Que sçayje?*; *What do I know?*) By any standards the publication in 1562 by Henri Estienne of the first edition of the original Greek text of Sextus' account of Pyrrho's scepticism was a major event. (Montaigne probably relied chiefly on his Latin translation – also found in the second edition of 1567, but quotations from the original Greek enlivened his library.) Gentian Hervet in his introduction to Sextus' other work, *Against the Mathematicians* (or *Against the Professors*) (1569) helps us to read Montaigne in context. For Hervet, too, the works of Sextus are an excellent weapon against heretics: Pyrrho's scepticism, by reducing all Man's knowledge to opinion, deprives heretics of any criterion for truth. Montaigne did the same in the pages of the *Apology* which follow upon his address to his patroness (p. 136).

However thorough-going the Pyrrhonism in these final pages, scepticism remained for Montaigne – as for many others – a weapon of last resort: a way of demolishing the arguments of would-be infallible adversaries. There was a price to pay, though. The Pyrrhonian method leaves *you* with no purely human certainties either! But only much later did that worry many Roman Catholics. Among writers variously attracted to Pyrrhonism were St Francis of Sales (who admired Montaigne's uprightness) and Maldonat (Montaigne's Jesuit friend).

Opinion is not knowledge. Pyrrhonist sceptics revelled in that fact. Sextus Empiricus systematized that contention into a powerful engine of doubt which helped a wise man to suspend his judgement and so to attain tranquillity of mind.

The rediscovery of the works of Sextus gave a fresh impetus to Renaissance scepticism, but it did not create it; Sextus fell on welcome ears: already in 1546 Rabelais has his wise old evangelical King delighted to find that all the best philosophers are Pyrrhonists nowadays.

It is deliberately paradoxical that the poet who dominates the Pyrrhonist pages of the *Apology* should be Lucretius. This Latin poet of the first century BC was a follower of Epicurus and remains our principal source for Epicurean doctrine in the realm of physical nature. But Epicureanism is flatly opposed to Pyrrhonist scepticism. Far from asserting that all man's boasted

---

and its arguments (*Metaphysics*, 1010 b), which placed scepticism within the major philosophical contexts of the Renaissance, which was anchored in Aristotle.

knowledge is mere opinion, it holds that the senses give Man access to
infallible certainty. The point is made clearly and sharply in Denis Lambin's
edition of Lucretius, which Montaigne read with marked attention. For
Lucretius, truth about things must be accessible to our minds from sense-
impressions: if they are not, all claims to know truth collapse. So even the
Sun can be only a trifle larger than appears to our sight. If we cannot explain
why, we must nevertheless make no concessions to those who deny this. Such
a view flew in the face of traditional and solid scientific knowledge. Montaigne
delights in citing Lucretius' own words to undermine Epicurean assertions.[20]
But Lucretius also serves to undermine other ideas widely supposed to be
true – and to warn against superstition.

Montaigne was perhaps first attracted to Lucretius by his arguments
against that fear of dying which haunted his youth and young manhood. In
the *Apology*, however, he chiefly cites him in order to reveal yet another
source of darkness and error or, at best, of the kind of partial truths reached
by unenlightened sages.

Particularly effective are his exploitations of precisely those verses in which
Lucretius tried to refute those who hold that 'we can know nothing'. Denis
Lambin in his edition praised Lucretius for his solid opposition to the
doctrine that 'nothing can be known'. Montaigne eventually succeeds in
exploiting the principal opponent of scepticism for sceptical ends![21]

On many matters, Montaigne and Lambin were in agreement. Especially
interesting for the *Apology* is Lambin's dedication of Book III of Lucretius'
poem to Germain Valence. It shows that the very failure of even Lucretius
and the Epicureans to reach Christian certainties about the nature of the Soul
can be turned into yet another argument in favour of Christian revelation:

Not unjustly we despise their unwise wisdom. We should congratulate ourselves that
we have been taught by JESUS CHRIST . . . (without being convinced or coerced by
any human reasons or by any arguments, no matter how well demonstrated – not even
by the Platonists) and so are persuaded that no opposing reasons, however sharp or
compelling, however probable or verisimilitudinous, however firm or strong (let alone
those of Lucretius, which are light and weak) could ever dislodge us from this judgement.[22]

The Renaissance was a period of new horizons: one was a vast increase in

20. Cf. *Apology*, p. 147f.

21. This section begins with line 469 of Book IV of Lucretius: 'Moreover if anyone
thinks nothing is to be known, he does not even know whether that can be known, as
he says he knows nothing.' (Cf. ed. Lambin, 1563, p. 308 ff.)

22. Lucretius, p. 190.

knowledge of the world and its inhabitants, as Europeans sailed the seas and
discovered new lands and new peoples; another was the rediscovery of Greek
literature in its fullness. New horizons make local certainties seem wrong or
parochial: they also open up whole treasure-houses of new facts and facets to
the sceptic, who with their aid can increase the sense of the relativity of all
Man's beliefs about himself and the universe in which he lives. Montaigne
exploited Sextus Empiricus, but he also devoured the writing of the Spanish
historians, including those who told of the horrors of the conquest of the
New World. There were also compendia such as Johannes Boemus' *Manners
of all Peoples* (Paris, 1538), as well as standard works such as Ravisius Textor's
*Officina* ('Workshop') which contains chapters with such titles as *Various
opinions about God* and *Divers morals and various rites of peoples* (Montaigne
would have read in it a full account of Androcles and the Lion). New books
gave him and the *Essays* a dimension and an actuality lacking to Agrippa and
Pico. His universe was open to immense variety. He knew of Copernicus. If
he wanted noble savages he could draw on the Indies as well as on the Golden
Age; or he could try and talk to American Indians for himself (in Rouen) or
question sailors.

But he did not stop there. If he had, he might indeed have been a fideist,
claiming that only an arbitrary act of faith could make an irrational leap from
a boundless sea of doubt to the rock of certain truth: the Church. Such a
theology, never really convincing, was rarely less convincing than in the
Renaissance and the nascent scientific world of the following century. If the
leap is irrational, why leap to Catholicism and not to a sect or to any other of
the teeming religions of the world? Truth must be the same everywhere.

This infinite variety of the world can be put to the service of Pyrrhonism
and its universal doubt: it can also be put to the service of Catholic orthodoxy
against sect and schism. If Catholic Christianity is true at all it must be
universally true, not merely true for Périgordians, Germans or successive
English parliaments. Otherwise it is just one opinion among many. Ever since
St Vincent of Lérins in the fifth century, Catholic truth was categorized as
being *Quod semper, quod ubique, quod ab omnibus* ('What has been held always,
everywhere and by all'). In the Renaissance the aspiration to make that a
reality lay behind the vast, world-wide evangelism by Rome (which con-
trasted sharply with the local concerns of the rival Churches seeking to reform
one City or one Kingdom). The Roman Catholic faith could indeed claim to
be taught universally. Therein lay its strength for minds like Montaigne's.

For Montaigne, the strength of Raymond Sebond's *Natural Theology* also
lay in universality. He believed that Sebond's illumination of the universal

Book of Nature showed that all Nature everywhere was in strict conformity with Catholic truth.

At the end of Montaigne's Pyrrhonist pages we are brought to the very brink of uncertainty. Reason has been shaken. So have the senses. If sense-data are unsure, uncertain and often plainly misleading, that does not simply cut us off from any sure and solid knowledge of phenomena: it cuts us off from any sure and certain knowledge of 'being'. And so 'we have no communication with Being' – other than our own transient one (perhaps).

To conclude: there is no permanent existence either in our being or in that of objects. We ourselves, our faculty of judgement and all mortal things are flowing and rolling ceaselessly. Nothing certain can be established about one from the other, since both judged and judging are ever shifting and changing.[23] (*Apology*, p. 186)

But this – despite the words 'to conclude' (*finalement*) – is not the end of the *Apology*: it is the end of a chain of arguments which can leave man ignorant, or, on the contrary, show him a new way to proceed. If it had been Montaigne's conclusion, then Sextus Empiricus would literally have had the last word, for the Pyrrhonist basis is evident. But it is precisely here that Pyrrhonism joins Plato and Aristotle in joint hostility to a sophistical trust in individual subjectivity.

At the end of the long section which immediately precedes Montaigne's address to his Royal patroness, just as he was about to embark on his Pyrrhonian arguments, Montaigne added an important comment in the margin of the Bordeaux copy of his works he was preparing for the press. It concerns Protagoras, the arch-Sophist who was trounced by Sextus, Plato and Aristotle in very similar terms and for identical reasons:

And what can anyone understand who cannot understand himself? . . . Protagoras was really and truly having us on when he made 'Man the measure of all things' – Man, who has never known his own measurements.

Protagoras meant – that is what shocked Plato, Aristotle and Sextus Empiricus – that there is no universal standard of truth: each human being is severally and individually the sole criterion; all is opinion, and all opinions are equally true or false.

For Montaigne, Protagoras' 'measure of Man' is 'so favourable' to human vanity as to be 'merely laughable. It leads inevitably to the proposition that the measure and the measurer are nothing.'

23. Sextus, *Hypotyposes*, I, 217–19 (criticizing Protagoras for dogmatism and relativism). Some excellent reflections on this topic in Jean-Paul Dumont, *Le scepticisme et le phénomène* (especially chapter 3); see also M. Burnyeat, *The Skeptical Tradition*.

Montaigne countered Protagoras, immediately, by citing Thales (the Greek sage to whom he himself had been likened): 'When Thales reckons that knowledge of Man is hard to acquire, he is telling him that knowledge of anything else is impossible' (*Apology*, p. 136).

In the *Theaetetus*, Socrates treated Protagoras and his 'measure' as a clever man talking nonsense – otherwise how can the same wind seem hot to one and cold to another? Nor would anyone maintain that a colour appears the same to a dog, to other animals and to ourselves.[24]

Montaigne made good use of such notions in the *Apology*: they can serve to show the fallibility of sense-data and also to place man where his unaided natural reason ought to place him: among the other creatures. But to go from there and make Truth itself the plaything of individual subjectivity, he never did.

Aristotle similarly mocked Protagoras and his Man-as-measure: his demonstration was adapted by Montaigne.[25]

Montaigne knew, before he had read a word of Sextus – probably in his days at school in Bordeaux – that in the world of creation nothing ever *is*; it is only *becoming*. Plutarch reinforced this.[26] But neither Plutarch nor Plato held that such doctrines cut Man off from a knowledge of God or obliged each person to plunge into pure subjectivism. There were, for Plato, divine revelations; and there was wisdom arising from knowing oneself as Man.

Within the flux of the created universe, Montaigne strove to follow the Delphic injunction, *Know Thyself*. He sought to 'discover the personal, individual, permanent strand in the transient, variegated flux of his experience and sensations'. He was not seeking to know a static soul in a static body but to isolate his *forme maistresse*, his 'master mould' which alone gave continuity to his personality – to his 'being' as a Man.[27]

But this was not a merely subjective indulgence. By studying his own *form* (his soul within his body) he aspired to know Man – not just one odd individual example of humankind. For each Man bears within himself (he asserted with the scholastics) the 'entire form' of the human condition.[28]

24. Plato, *Theaetetus*, 152B; again, 152 CD. (Was this saying of Protagoras' only meant for the mob?) Arguments drawn from 153–54 are used by Montaigne (p. 182).

25. Aristotle, *Metaphysics*, 1053b (misunderstanding Protagoras): 'Thus, seeming to say something unusual, he is really saying nothing.' More relevant to Montaigne (who uses some of the arguments) are *Metaphysics*, 1062b–1063a.

26. In his studies of Plato, e.g. *Timaeus*, 37D–38B; *Theaetetus*, 152DE, etc. (For Plutarch, see p. 186ff.)

27. Cf. *Montaigne and Melancholy*, p. 125; 101 f.

28. *Ibid.*, p. 104 (see Introduction to vol. I of the *Essays*, in preparation).

The *Essays* as a whole do not end with the last words of the *Apology*: much exploration of self and of Man remained to be done, but Montaigne had clearly seen that the characteristic property of the creature is impermanence. No creature ever *is*: a creature is always shifting, changing, *becoming*.

The Platonic background to such a conclusion – unlike the purely Pyrrhonian one – enabled Montaigne to pass from the impermanence of the ever-changing creature to what he presents as a 'most pious' concept of the Godhead, accessible to purely human reason: the Creator must have those qualities which Man as creature lacks: he must have unity, not diversity; absolute Being not mere 'becoming'. And since he created Time he must be outside it and beyond it.

It is strikingly right that this natural leap to the Eternal Being of God should be given not in Montaigne's own words – he is not a pagan – but in a long and unheralded transcription from Plutarch. Montaigne took it from the dense mystic treatise *On the E'i at Delphi*.

In this powerful work Plutarch grappled with the religious import of the word *E'i* inscribed on the temple of Apollo at Delphi. In Greek it can mean 'Five'; it can mean 'If': but above all it means 'Thou Art'. As such it declares that God has eternal Being. He is the eternal *THOU* to our transient *I*. Each individual human being is relative, contingent, impermanent. But each 'I' can know itself; it can know Man through itself; and it can stretch out to Reality and say THOU ART.

In doing so, it recognizes God.[29]

The *Natural Theology* of Sebond taught each man to know himself *and* God. It is, in a sense, the key to that Delphic utterance: *Know Thyself*. Montaigne's translation of the *Natural Theology* is all of a piece with the self-exploration of the *Essays*. For both Plutarch and Raymond Sebond 'knowing oneself' is, properly understood, a complement to knowing God. Sebond says so on his title pages: Plutarch does so in the closing words of *On the E'i at Delphi*:

Meanwhile it seems that this word *E'i* [THOU ART] is in one way an antithesis to that precept KNOW THYSELF, yet in another it is in agreement and accord with it. For one saying is a saying of awe and of adoration towards God as Eternal, ever in Being; the other is a reminder to mortal man of the weakness and debility of his nature.

29. There is a striking parallel between Plutarch's conception of God and the Christian scholastic doctrines based upon God as revealed to Moses in the burning bush. (Where in English God says I AM THAT I AM, in the Greek and in scholastic theology he says I AM EXISTENCE or I AM THE EXISTING ONE.) Montaigne does not emphasize this: he lets it sink in.

Plutarch could reach that pious height: a Roman Stoic could also assert that if a man is to aspire towards God he must 'rise above himself'. So far so good.

We are doubtless stirred by such eloquent aspirations. But the final words of the chapter tip over the house of cards. If any human being is to rise up towards that Eternal Being glimpsed by Plutarch, it will not be through Greek philosophy or proud Stoic Virtue: it will be 'by grace' or, more widely, 'by purely heavenly means'. That will be an event 'extraordinary' – outside the natural *order* of the universe. In the process, the individual human being will not raise himself but *be* raised to a higher form. He will (in the last word of the chapter) be 'metamorphosed': transformed and transfigured.[30]

This leaves Montaigne free as always to continue to explore his 'master-mould'; to examine his relative 'being' – his body-and-soul conjoined.

Nowhere else in the *Essays* does Pyrrhonian scepticism make the running – it does not make all of it even in the *Apology*. But to the solid bastion of his faith Montaigne added a shield of last resort, ever ready in reserve to use against those who sought to oppose his Church's infallibility by a rival one. As Edward Stillingfleet, Dean of St Paul's, perceived in the following century, Pyrrhonism comes into play only when men are not content to 'take in the assistance of Reason, which, though not Infallible, might give such Evidence, as afforded Certainty, where it fell short of Demonstration'. But as soon as 'Epicurus thought there could be no Certainty in Sense, unless it were made Infallible', he could only defend his hypothesis with absurdity: 'the Sun must be no bigger than a bonfire.'[31]

Of course Pyrrhonian scepticism shocked many. It always does. When Montaigne's *Essays* were examined by a courteous censor in Rome, such little fuss there was at the time came from factions among the French. The Maestro del Sacro Palazzo, Sisto Fabri, told him to take no notice and do what he thought fit.[32]

In the following century Montaigne's respect for the beasts and his distrust of unaided human reason brought him many enemies among dogmatic philosophers and theologians; they brought him many friends as well, ranging from Francis Bacon to Daniel Huët, Bishop of Avranches. In his *Philosophical Treatise on the Weakness of the Human Spirit* (1723) Huët reminded his readers

30. *Apology*, p. 190. The full implications of this are not revealed until the last pages of the final chapter of the *Essays*: vol. III, chapter 13, 'On Experience'.
31. Edward Stillingfleet, *Nature and Grounds of the Certainty of Faith*, 1688, p. 35.
32. Montaigne, *Journal de voyage en Italie*, ed. Pierre Michel, 1974, pp. 287–88, 310. (Further details in the Introduction to vol. I of these *Essays*, in preparation.)

that when Pyrrhonism was rejected in Ancient times, it was nothing to do with Christians fearful for the Faith but of pagans fearful for their Science. What is dangerous to Christianity, he added, is not Pyrrhonism but Pride.[33]

But Montaigne had done his job well – well enough for many free-thinkers including those of the Enlightenment to see him as a forerunner of their sceptical Deism or atheistic naturalism. This was in part inevitable: truth is one and unchanging while men are ever-changing. Truth cannot be set finally in words. It was a sound theologian, Bishop Wescott, who said, 'No formula which expresses clearly the thought of one generation can convey the same meaning to the generation which follows.' In a different climate of opinion, Montaigne's protestations of loyalty to his Church were taken to be moonshine. Allusions to 'Christian folly' were interpreted as smirking and knowing acknowledgements that Christianity was silly or stupid, fit for fools. Read in this way, selectively, the *Apology* could, did and does provide weapons and delight to a variety of readers. This became more easily possible after Hellenistic philosophy lost its hold on many in the eighteenth century. Hellenistic Christianity (like Hellenistic Philosophy) accepts that the true nature of things lies behind their visible appearances, and beyond time and space. It holds with Plotinus that nothing that *is* can ever perish.[34] Such a conviction dominated the thought of Renaissance Christians including Ficino, Erasmus, Rabelais and Montaigne. Without such a conviction and a respect for its roots in Platonism, the end of the *Apology* may seem purely arbitrary – arbitrary and ironic, or a meaningless tactical bow to authority.

But we know from Montaigne's Journal (discovered in 1772 and never intended for publication) that he was a practising Christian whose devotion was as superstitious as Newman's. He could attach great importance to the pious family ex-voto which he paid to be displayed in the Church of Santa Maria de Loreto (in the shrine of the Holy House of the Virgin, transported by angels to Loretto was it not, on 2 December 1295) and to the miraculous cure there of Michel Marteau.[35]

33. Daniel Huët, *Traité philosophique*, 1723, III, 16. Cf. II, 6: 'What is the End Proposed by the Art of Doubting?' There are two ends. 'The proximate end is to avoid error, stubbornness and arrogance. The eventual end is to prepare one's spirit to receive Faith.' These are the professed aims of Montaigne.

34. W. R. Inge, Dean of St Paul's, in *Faith and Knowledge*, 1905, p. 245; *The Church and the World*, 1927, p. 191; *More Lay Thoughts of a Dean*, 1931, p. 160, aphorism no. 37: '*Know Thyself* is really the sum of wisdom; for he who knows himself knows God.'

35. *Journal*, pp. 325–26; 330. Newman similarly puzzled and irritated many by his respect for the shrine of Our Lady at Walsingham.

This was a great shock to those *philosophes* and wits who had grown used to exploiting the *Essays* as an anti-Christian weapon-house. They had done so all the more mockingly after the *Essays* had been put on the Index in 1697. But this act of absurdity can be better attributed not to the *Essays* as such as to Jansenist zeal and to horror at the use made of them by the free-thinking *libertins*.[36]

In Montaigne's own day Rome knew better – and presumably does so now. The Vatican Manuscript No. 9693 records the granting of Roman citizenship to Montaigne. It states that it was granted to 'the French Socrates'.

And that Christian Socrates died in the bosom of his Church. (But, even then, André Gide persuaded himself that he only pretended to do so because of moral blackmail from his wife . . .)

Citing Plutarch at the end of the *Apology* does more than vindicate Raymond Sebond: it vindicates St Paul. In retrospect it can be seen that Romans 1:20 gave authority not only to Montaigne's defence of natural theology in his reply to the first charge against the book he had translated: it governs the long reply to the second charge. St Paul declared that what can be grasped by natural theology ('from the things that are made') are God's 'eternal power' and his 'divinity'. Plutarch shows that that is true: Plutarch did so. But Plutarch is nevertheless only one pagan voice among many, one ray of light in confused darkness.

Montaigne is exemplifying a tradition codified at least as early as Nicholas of Lyra, the thirteenth-century Scriptural commentator who suggested that by the words *from the creation of the world* (in the Vulgate Latin, *a creatura mundi*) Paul meant *from Man* (who is the 'creature of the world' *par excellence*). Montaigne does not say this explicitly, but his whole enterprise in the *Essays* is driven forward by a desire to know Man and his place in the Universe (not simply one example of Mankind, himself, though that is his means to the greater end). The seeking of God 'from the things that are made' is explained by Nicolas of Lyra to mean *per creaturas* ('through the creatures' – through all that God created). And what Man can discover concerns 'the divine Essence': 'from the creatures a man can learn that that eternal Essence is "One, Uncompounded and Infinite".'[37]

36. *Ibid.* (note by Pierre Michel, p. 310, n. 184); and his Introduction.

37. Cited from *Biblia Maxima*, vol. XV. This exegesis was accepted by scholars of many schools and Churches: cf. for example Matthew Henry, *Exposition of the New Testament*, 1738, vol. 5, commentary on this verse.

Of course, none of this 'natural theology' brings fallen Man effectively to the Triune God: that needs grace.[38]

One of the many achievements of Montaigne in the *Apology* is to breathe living controversy into these dry old contentions. We can see the Counter-Reformation at work in a layman of genius. And since he is fairness personified he still provides his opponents with sound arguments to use against him – if they ignore or discount his Christian context.[39]

**ALL SOULS COLLEGE**
**OXFORD**
**EASTER 1986**

---

38. Cf. Nicolas of Lyra on Romans 3:10 (*Biblia Maxima*, vol. XV: index, s.v. *natura*): a man can perform moral acts without grace: he cannot be justified.

39. I am most grateful to those readers who have suggested corrections or improvements, many of which have been included in this 1993 reprinting. A special word of thanks is due to Mr Jan Stolpe, the distinguished translator of Montaigne into Swedish, and to an excellent classicist, Donald Upton, Esq.

# NOTE ON THE TEXT

There is no such thing as a definitive edition of the *Essays of Michel de
Montaigne*. One has to choose. The *Essays* are a prime example of the expand-
ing book.

The text translated here is an eclectic one, deriving mainly from the corpus
of editions clustering round the impressive *Edition municipale* of Bordeaux
(1906–20) edited by a team led by Fortunat Strowski. This was further edited
and adapted by Pierre Villey (1924); V.-L. Saulnier of the Sorbonne again
revised, re-edited and adapted the work for the Presses Universitaires de
France (1965). Useful editions were also published by J. Plattard (Société
'Les Belles Lettres', 1947) as well as by A. Thibaudet and M. Rat for the
Pléiade (1962).

I have also used the posthumous edition of 1595, that of 1598 and, since
it is good and readily available at All Souls, the *Edition nouvelle* procured in
1617 by Mademoiselle Marie de Gournay, the young admirer and blue-
stocking to whom Montaigne gave a quasi-legal status as a virtually adopted
daughter, a *fille d'alliance*.

# EXPLANATION OF THE SYMBOLS

[A] all that follows is (ignoring minor variations) what Montaigne published in 1580 (the first edition).

[A1] all that follows was added subsequently, mainly in 1582 and in any case before [B].

[B] all that follows shows matter added or altered in 1588, the first major, indeed massive, revision of the *Essays*, which now includes a completely new Third Book.

[C] all that follows represents an edited version of Montaigne's final edition being prepared for the press when he died. The new material derives mainly from Montaigne's own copy, smothered with additions and changes in his own hand and now in the Bibliothèque Municipale of Bordeaux. The editions of 1595 and 1598 (as well as subsequent ones such as that of 1617) give what is essentially the same text, but with interesting variations.

### Summary

[A] 1580

[A1] 1582 (plus)

[B] 1588

[C] text of the manuscript edition being prepared by Montaigne when he died, interpreted in the light of the posthumous printed editions.

In the notes there is given a selection of variant readings, including most abandoned in 1588 and many from the *printed* posthumous edition of 1595 (prepared by Montaigne's widow and Marie de Gournay and subsequently corrected by them).

By far the most accessible account of the text is that given in R. A. Sayce, *The Essays of Montaigne: A Critical Exploration*, 1972, chapter 2, 'The Text of the *Essays*'.

MICHEL DE MONTAIGNE

## The Annotations

Marie de Gournay first contributed to the annotation of Montaigne by tracing
the sources of his verse and other quotations, providing translations of them,
and getting a friend to supply headings in the margins.

From that day to this, scholars have added to them. The major source has
long been the fourth volume of the Strowski edition, the work of Pierre
Villey. It is a masterpiece of patient scholarship. Most notes of most subsequent editions derive from it. This translation is no exception, though I
have made quite a few changes and added my own.

Plutarch's *Moralia* are cited from Amyot's French translation, which plays
a quite exceptional role in Montaigne's thought and art.

The Latin quotations in the text are given as they appear in the Villey/
Saulnier edition (with minor corrections) as they may help readers who wish
to compare text and translation.

# NOTE ON THE TRANSLATION

I have tried to convey Montaigne's sense and something of his style, without archaisms but without forcing him into an unsuitable, demotic English.

Modern critical editions of Montaigne have imposed modern French punctuation on to his text: that gives a sense of grammatical order sometimes foreign to the original. It can also pervert the sense. Montaigne's sentences are often very long; where the sense does not suffer I have left a few of them as they are. It helps to retain something of his savour.

It is seldom possible to translate one word in one language by one only in another. I have striven to do so in two cases vital for the understanding of Montaigne. The first is *essai, essayer* and the like: I have rendered these by *essay* or *assay* or the equivalent verbs. The second is *opinion*. In Montaigne's French, as often in English, *opinion* does not imply that the idea is true: rather the contrary, as in Plato.

Montaigne's numerous quotations are seldom integrated grammatically into his sentences. However long they may be we are meant to read them as asides – mentally holding our breath. I have respected that. To do otherwise would be to rewrite him.

When in doubt, I have given priority to what I take to be the meaning, though never, I hope, losing sight of readability.

Of versions of the Classics Jowett remarked that, 'the slight personification arising out of Greek genders is the greatest difficulty in translation.' In Montaigne's French this difficulty is even greater since his sense of gender enables him to flit in and out of various degrees of personification in ways not open to writers of English. Where the personification is certain or a vital though implied element of the meaning I have normally used a capital letter and personal pronouns, etc., to produce a similar effect.

# FURTHER READING

❧

(A fuller bibliography will appear in Vol. 3 of this translation, in preparation)
The Studies listed all contain suggestions for further reading in their bibliographies.

Annas, J., and Barnes, J., *The Modes of Scepticism*, Cambridge, 1985.

Aulotte, Robert, *Montaigne: Apologie de Raimond Sebond*, Société d'Edition d'Enseignement Supérieure, Paris, 1979. A sound introduction, giving opposing views and a good bibliography.

Battlori, Miquel, 'Sur le Lullisme en France au XVIe siècle', in André Stegmann (ed.), *L'Humanisme en France au début de la Renaissance*, Colloque International de Tours, XIVe stage, Paris, 1973.

Bujanda, J. M., *L'Influence de Sebond en Espagne au XVIe s.*, *Renaissance & Réformation*, Toronto, X, 1974, 78–84.

Burnyeat, M. (ed.), *The Skeptical Tradition*, Berkeley, 1983.

Carreras Artau, T. and J., *Historia de la Filosofía Española. Filosofía cristiana de los siglos XIII al XV*, Madrid, 1943.

Cave, T., *The Cornucopian Text*, Oxford, 1979.

Conché, M., *Pyrrhon et l'Apparence*, Villers s/Mer, 1973.

Coppin, J., *Montaigne traducteur de Raymond Sebond*, Lille, 1925.

Dréano, M., 'L'Augustinisme dans l'*Apologie de Raymond Sebon*', *Bibliothèque d'Humanisme et Renaissance*, XXIV, pp. 559–75, 1962.

Dumont, J.-P., *Le Scepticisme et le Phénomène*, Paris, 1972.

Janssen, H., *Montaigne fidéiste*, Nijmeghen, 1930.

Limbrick, E., 'Montaigne and St Augustine' and 'Montaigne and Socrates', *Renaissance & Réformation*, Toronto, 1972, 49 ff.; 1973, 46 ff. 'Was Montaigne really a Pyrrhonian?', *Bibliothèque d'Humanisme et Renaissance*, 39, 1977.

Morphos, P. P., *The Dialogues of Guy de Brués: A Study in Renaissance Scepticism and Relativism*, Baltimore, 1953.

Muller, A., *Montaigne (Les Ecrivains devant Dieu)*, Bruges, 1965.

Popkin, R. H., *The History of Skepticism from Erasmus to Descartes*, 1960 (2nd edition, revised, 1964).

Regosin, R. L., *The Matter of My Book: Montaigne's 'Essais' as the Book of the Self*, Berkeley, 1977.

Rice, E., *The Renaissance Idea of Wisdom*, Cambridge, Mass., 1958.

Sayce, R. A., *The Essays of Montaigne. A Critical Exploration*, London, 1972.

Scaduto, M., 'Lainez e l'Indice del 1559: Lullo, Sabunde, Sabanarola, Erasmo', *Archivum Historicum Societatis Jesu*, 24, pp. 3–32, 1955.

Schmitt, Charles B., *Cicero Scepticus; A Study of the Influence of the* Academica *in the Renaissance*, The Hague, 1972.

Sclafert, C., *L'Ame religieuse de Montaigne*, Paris, 1957.

Screech, M. A., *Montaigne and Melancholy: The Wisdom of the 'Essays'*, London, 1983.

*Ecstasy and the Praise of Folly*, London, 1980. To be reprinted in Penguin.

Smith, Malcolm, *Montaigne and the Roman Censors*, Geneva, 1981.

Stegmüller, Friedrich (ed.), *Raimundus Sabundus: 'Theologia Naturalis'*, Stuttgart-Bad Cannstatt, 1966.

Tillyard, E. M. W., *The Elizabethan World Picture*, London, 1963 (contains a résumé of Sebond's *Viola animae*).

Wade, I. O., *The Intellectual Origins of the French Enlightenment*, Princeton, 1971.

Lucretius is cited from the edition of Denis Lambin, Paris and Lyons, 1563; the *Moralia* of Plutarch are cited from the translation made by Bishop Jacques Amyot (*Les Œuvres morales et meslées*, Paris, 1572; reprint S. R. Publishers, Johnson Reprint Corporation and Mouton, 1971). The various books of Rabelais are cited from the TLF editions (*Textes Littéraires Français*, Droz, Geneva), which are useful for their annotations.

# APPENDICES

## I

*Montaigne's dedication of his translation of Raymond Sebond's* Natural Theology *to his father.*

### TO MY LORD, MY LORD OF MONTAIGNE

My Lord, following the task you gave me last year at Montaigne, I have tailored and dressed with my hand a garment in the French style for Raymond Sebond, the great Spanish Theologian and Philosopher, divesting him (in so far as in me lay) of his uncouth bearing and of that barbarous stance that you were the first to perceive: so that, in my opinion, he now has sufficient style and polish to present himself in good company.

It may well be that delicate and discriminating people may notice here some Gascon usages or turns of phrase: that should make them all the more ashamed at having neglectfully allowed a march to be stolen on them by a man who is an apprentice and quite unsuited to the task.

It is, my Lord, right that it should appear and grow in credit beneath your name, since it is to you that it owes whatever amendment or reformation it now enjoys.

And yet I believe that if you would be pleased to reckon accounts with him, it will be you who will owe him more: in exchange for his excellent and most religious arguments, for his conceptions lofty and as though divine, you, for your part, have brought only words and language – a merchandise so base and vile that who has most is perhaps worth least.

My Lord, I beg God that he may grant you a most long and a most happy life.

From Paris: this 18th of June, 1568.
Your most humble and obedient son,
MICHEL DE MONTAIGNE.

## II

*Montaigne's translation and adaptation of the* Prologus *of Raymond Sebond.*

Book of the Creatures of Raymond Sebond.
Translated from the Latin into French. Preface of the Author.

To the praise and glory of the most high and glorious Trinity, of the Virgin Mary, and of all the heavenly Court: in the name of our Lord Jesus Christ, for the profit of all Christians, there follows the doctrine of the Book of the Creatures (or, Book of Nature): a doctrine of Man, proper to Man insofar as he is Man: a doctrine suitable, natural and useful to every man, by which he is enlightened into knowing himself, his Creator, and almost everything to which he is bound as Man: a doctrine containing the rule of Nature, by which also each Man is instructed in what he is naturally bound towards God and his neighbour: and not only instructed but moved and incited to do this, of himself, by love and a joyful will.

In addition this science teaches every one to see clearly, without difficulty or toil, truth insofar as it is possible for natural reason, concerning knowledge of God and of himself and of what he has need for his salvation and to reach life eternal; it affords him access to understanding what is prescribed and commanded in Holy Scripture, and delivers the human spirit from many doubts, making it consent firmly to what Scripture contains concerning knowledge of God and of oneself.

In this book the ancient errors of the pagans and the unbelieving philosophers are revealed and by its doctrine the Catholic Faith is defended and made known: every sect which opposes it is uncovered and condemned as false and lying.

That is why, in this decline and last days of the World it is necessary that Christians should stiffen themselves, arm themselves and assure themselves within that Faith so as to confront those who fight against it, to protect themselves from being seduced and, if needs be, joyfully to die for it.

Moreover this doctrine opens up to all a way of understanding the holy Doctors [of the Church]; indeed, it is incorporated in their books (even though it is not evident in them) as an Alphabet is incorporated in all writings. For it is the Alphabet of the Doctors: as such it should be learned first. For which reason, to make your way towards the Holy Scriptures you will do well to acquire this science as the rudiments of all sciences; in order the better to reach conclusions, learn it before everything else, otherwise you will hardly manage to struggle through to the perfection of the higher sciences: for this is the root, the origin and the tiny foundations of the doctrine proper to Man and his salvation.

Whoever possesses salvation through hope must first have the root of salvation within him and, consequently, must furnish himself with this science, which is a fountain of saving Truth.

And there is no need that anyone should refrain from reading it or learning it from lack of other learning: it presupposes no knowledge of Grammar,

Logic, nor any other deliberative art or science, nor of Physics nor of Metaphysics, seeing that it is this doctrine which comes first, this doctrine which
ranges, accommodates and prepares the others for so holy an End – for the
Truth which is both true and profitable to us, because it teaches Man to know
himself, to know why he has been created and by Whom; to know his good,
his evil and his duty; by what and to Whom he is bound.

What good are the other sciences to a man who is ignorant of such things?
They are but vanity, seeing that men can only use them badly to their harm,
since they know not where they are, whither they are going nor whence they
came. That is why they are taught here to understand the corruption and
defects of Man, his condemnation and whence it came upon him; to know
the state in which he is now: the state in which he originally was: from what
he has fallen and how far he is from his first perfection; how he can be
reformed and those things which are necessary to bring this about.

And therefore this doctrine is common to the laity, the clergy and all
manner of people: and yet it can be grasped in less than a month, without
toil and without learning anything off by heart; no books are required, for
once it has been perceived it cannot be forgotten. It makes a man happy,
humble, gracious, obedient, the enemy of vice and sin, the lover of virtue –
all without puffing him up or making him proud because of his accomplishments.

It uses no obscure arguments requiring deep or lengthy discourse: for it
argues from things which are evident and known to all from experience –
from the creatures and the nature of Man; by which, and from what he knows
of himself, it proves what it seeks to prove, mainly from what each man has
assayed of himself. And there is no need of any other witness but Man.

It may, meanwhile, at first appear contemptible, a thing of nothing,
especially since its beginnings are common to all and very lowly: but that does
not stop it from bearing great and worthwhile fruit, namely the knowledge of
God and of Man. And the lower its starting-point, the higher it climbs, rising
to matters high and celestial.

Wherefore, whosoever wishes to taste of its fruit, let him first familiarize
himself with the minor principles of this science, without despising them:
for otherwise he will never have that taste, no more than a child ever learns
to read without a knowledge of the alphabet and of each individual letter.
And, finally, let him not complain about this labour by which, in a few
months, he becomes learned and familiar with many things, to know which
it would be proper to spend long periods reading many books.

It alleges no authority – not even the Bible – for its end is to confirm what
is written in Holy Scripture – and to lay the foundations on which we can

build what is obscurely deduced from them. And so, in our case, it precedes the Old and New Testaments.

God has given us two books: the Book of the Universal Order of Things (or, of Nature) and the Book of the Bible. The former was given to us first, from the origin of the world: for each creature is like a letter traced by the hand of God: this Book had to be composed of a great multitude of creatures (which are as so many 'letters'); within them is found Man. He is the main, the capital letter.

Now, just as letters and words composed from letters constitute a science by amply marshalling different sentences and meanings, so too the creatures, joined and coupled together, form various clauses and sentences, containing the science that is, before all, requisite for us.

The second Book – Holy Scripture – was subsequently given in default of the first, in which, blinded as he was, he could make out nothing, notwithstanding that the first is common to all whereas the second is not: to read the second book one must be a clerk. Moreover, the Book of Nature cannot be corrupted nor effaced nor falsely interpreted. Therefore the heretics cannot interpret it falsely: from this Book no one becomes an heretic.

With the Bible, things go differently. Nevertheless both Books derive from the same Author: God created his creatures just as he established his Scriptures. That is why they accord so well together, with no tendency to contradict each other, despite the first one's symbolizing most closely with our nature and the second one's being so far above it.

Since Man, at his Birth, did not find himself furnished with any science (despite his rationality and capacity for knowledge) and since no science can be acquired without books in which it is written down, it was more than reasonable (so that our capacity for learning should not have been given us in vain) that the Divine Intelligence should provide us with the means of instructing ourselves in the doctrine which alone is requisite, without a schoolmaster, naturally, by ourselves.

That is why that Intelligence made this visible world and gave it to us like a proper, familiar and infallible Book, written by his hand, in which the creatures are ranged like letters – not in accordance to our desires but according to the holy judgement of God, so as to teach us the wisdom and science of our salvation. Yet no one can [now] see and read that great Book by himself (even though it is ever open and present to our eyes) unless he is enlightened by God and cleansed of original sin. And therefore not one of the pagan philosophers of Antiquity could read this science, because they were all blinded concerning the sovereign good; even though they drew all their other sciences and all their knowledge from it, they could never perceive nor dis-

cover the wisdom which is enclosed within it nor that true and solid doctrine
which guides us to eternal life.

Now, in anyone capable of discernment, there is engendered a true understanding from a combining together of the creatures like a well-ordered tissue
of words. So the method of treating this subject in this treatise is to classify
the creatures and to establish their relationships one with the other, taking
into consideration their weightiness and what they signify and, after having
drawn forth the divine wisdom which they contain, fixing it and impressing
it deeply in our hearts and souls.

Now, since the Most Holy Church of Rome is the Mother of all faithful
Christians, the Mother of Grace, the Rule of Faith and Truth, I submit to
her correction all that is said and contained in this my work.

## II:12 AN APOLOGY FOR RAYMOND SEBOND

[A] Truly, learning is a most useful accomplishment and a great one. Those who despise it give ample proof of their animal stupidity. Yet I do not prize its worth at that extreme value given to it by some, such as the philosopher Erillus who lodged Supreme Good in it, holding that it was within the power of learning to make us wise and contented.[1] That, I do not believe – nor what others have said: that learning is the Mother of virtue and that all vice is born of Ignorance. If that is true, it needs a lengthy gloss.[2]

My house has long been open to erudite men and is well known to them, since my father, who had the ordering of it for fifty years and more, all ablaze with that new ardour with which King Francis I embraced letters and raised them in esteem, spent a great deal of trouble and money seeking the acquaintance of the learned, welcoming them into his house as holy persons who had been granted private inspiration by Divine Wisdom; he collected their sayings and their reasonings as though they were oracles – with all the more awe and devotion in that he had less right to judge: he had no acquaintance with literature, [A1] any more than his forebears did. [A] I like learned men myself, but I do not worship them.

Among others there was Pierre Bunel, a man who, in his own time, enjoyed a great reputation for learning.[3] He and other men of his kind stayed several days at Montaigne in my father's company; when leaving, Bunel gave him a book called *Theologia Naturalis sive Liber creaturarum magistri Raymondi de Sabonde – Natural Theology, or, The Book of Creatures by Master Raymond Sebond*. My father was familiar with Italian and Spanish and so, since the book is composed in a kind of pidgin – Spanish with Latin endings – Bunel hoped that my father could profit by it with only very little help. He

1. Commonplace; cf. Cicero, *De fin.*, II. xiii. 43; Erillus, though a pupil of Zeno the Stoic, was close to Plato (Cicero, *Acad.*, II. xlii. 129).

2. The Platonic contention. Cf. Socrates in Aristotle, *Nicomachaean Ethics*, VII, i. 6–ii, 7 (a commonplace: cf. Cognatus' Adages, *Indocto nihil iniquius* and *Nil scientia potentius*); vulgarized by Erasmus' *Apophthegmata* (*Socrates*, XXXIII): 'He said knowledge is the only good, ignorance the only evil.' The intemperate, say, believe inordinate reactions to be ordinate. 'The *summum bonum* is therefore knowledge of what is to be sought or avoided.'

3. A distinguished scholar and tutor from Toulouse (1499–1546). Similar praise in Lambin's dedication to him of Lucretius *De nat. rerum*, V.

recommended it to him as a book which was very useful for the period in which he gave it to him: that was when the novelties of Luther were beginning to be esteemed, in many places shaking our old religion. He was well advised, clearly deducing that this new disease would soon degenerate into loathsome atheism. The mass of ordinary people[4] lack the faculty of judging things as they are, letting themselves be carried away by chance appearances. Once you have put into their hands the foolhardiness of despising and criticizing opinions which they used to hold in the highest awe (such as those which concern their salvation), and once you have thrown into the balance of doubt and uncertainty [C] any [A] articles of their religion, they soon cast all the rest of their beliefs into similar uncertainty. They had no more authority for them, no more foundation, than for those you have just undermined; and so, as though it were the yoke of a tyrant, they shake off all those other concepts which had been impressed upon them by the authority of Law and the awesomeness of ancient custom.

[B]   *Nam cupide conculcatur nimis ante metutum.*

[That which once was feared too greatly is now avidly trampled underfoot.][5]

[A] They then take it upon themselves to accept nothing on which they have not pronounced their own approval, subjecting it to their individual assent.

Now, my father, a few days before he died, happened to light upon this book beneath a pile of old papers; he ordered me to put it into French for him. It is good to translate authors like these, where there is little to express apart from the matter. Authors much devoted to grace and elegance of language are a dangerous[6] undertaking, [C] especially when you are turning them into a weaker language. [A] It was a strange and novel occupation for me, but, happening to be at leisure and never being able to refuse any command from the best father that ever was, I did what I could and finished it. He took particular delight in it and gave instructions to have it printed. They were carried out after his death.[7]

I found the concepts of Sebond to be beautiful, the structure of his book well executed and his project full of piety. Many people spend time reading

4. '88: ordinary people (*and virtually everybody is in that category*) lack . . .

5. Lucretius, V, 1140 (alluding to regicide).

6. '88: a *difficult* undertaking.

7. '88: death, *with the carelessness which you can see from the infinite number of misprints left in by the printer, who alone was responsible for its execution* . . . Montaigne struck out his first printer's liminary material for the second edition.

it – especially ladies, to whom we owe greater courtesy. I have often been able to help them by relieving this book of the weight of the two main objections made against it. (Sebond's aim is a bold and courageous one, since he undertakes to establish against the atheists and to show by human, natural reasons the truth of all the articles of the Christian religion.)

Frankly, I find him so firm and so successful in this, that I do not think it is possible to do better on this topic and I do not believe that anyone has done so well.

It seemed too rich and too fine a book for an author whose name is so obscure – all we know of him is that he was a Spaniard professing medicine in Toulouse some two hundred years ago; so I once asked Adrian Turnebus – who knew everything – what he made of it.[8] He replied that he thought it was a quintessence distilled from St Thomas Aquinas, only a wit like Thomas's, full of infinite learning and staggering subtlety, being capable of such concepts. Anyway, whoever it was who conceived and wrote this book (and it is not reasonable to deprive Sebond of his title without greater cause), he was a most talented man, having many fine accomplishments.

The first charge made against the book is that Christians do themselves wrong by wishing to support their belief with human reasons: belief is grasped only by faith and by private inspiration from God's grace.

A pious zeal may be seen behind this objection; so any assay at satisfying those who put it forward must be made with gentleness and respect. It is really a task for a man versed in Theology rather than for me, who know nothing about it. Nevertheless, this is my verdict: in a matter so holy, so sublime, so far surpassing Man's intellect as is that Truth by which it has pleased God in his goodness[9] to enlighten us, we can only grasp that Truth and lodge it within us if God favours us with the privilege of further help, beyond the natural order.

I do not believe, then, that purely human means have the capacity to do this; if they had, many choice and excellent souls in ancient times – souls abundantly furnished with natural faculties – would not have failed to reach such knowledge by discursive reasoning. Only faith can embrace, with a lively certainty, the high mysteries of our religion.[10]

But that is not to imply that it is other than a most fair and praiseworthy undertaking to devote to the service of our faith those natural, human tools

8. He is also highly praised by Montaigne in vol. I, chapter 25, 'On schoolmasters' learning', and vol. II, chapter 17, 'On Presumption'.

9. '88: his *sacrosanct* goodness . . .

10. A 'lively' faith shows itself in good works; Christian 'mysteries' are not accessible to unaided human reason: that is standard orthodox doctrine.

which God has granted us. It is not to be doubted that it is the most honourable use that we could ever put them to and that there is no task, no design, more worthy of a Christian than to aim, by assiduous reflection, at beautifying, developing and clarifying the truth of his beliefs. We are not content merely to serve God with our spirits and our souls: we owe him more than that, doing him reverence with our bodies; we honour him with our very members, our actions and with things external. In the same way we must accompany our faith with all the reason that lies within us – but always with the reservation that we never reckon that faith depends upon ourselves or that our efforts and our conjectures can ever themselves attain to a knowledge so supernatural, so divine.

If faith does not come and dwell within us as something infused, beyond the natural order; if she comes in, not just by reasoning but by any human means, then she is not there in her dignity and splendour. And yet I fear that we do only enjoy her presence in that way. If we held fast to God by means of a lively faith; if we held fast to God by God, not by ourselves; if our footing and our foundation were divine: then human events would not have the power to shake us which they do have; our fortress would not be for surrendering to so feeble a battery; the love of novelty, the constraint of Princes, the good luck of one party or rash and fortuitous changes in our own opinions, would have no power to shake our beliefs or modify them. We would not let our faith be troubled at the mercy of some new argument or by persuasion – not by all the rhetoric there ever was. We would withstand such billows with a firmness, unbending and unmoved:

> Illisos fluctus rupes ut vasta refundit,
> Et varias circum latrantes dissipat undas
> Mole sua.

[As a mighty rock, by its very mass, withstands the lashing waves, pouring them back and breaking up the waters raging round about it . . .][11]

If a ray of God's light touched us even slightly, it would be everywhere apparent: not only our words but our deeds would bear its lustre and its brightness. Everything emanating from us would be seen shining with that noble light. We ought to be ashamed: among the schools of human philosophy there never was an initiate who did not make his conduct and his life conform, at least in some respect, to their teachings, however difficult or strange: and

11. Anon. The poem (based on *Aeneid*, VII, 587 ff.) praises the staunchly Catholic Ronsard and accompanies his reply to Protestant critics, *Response aux injures et calomnies*, 1563.

yet so holy and heavenly an ordinance as ours only marks Christians on their tongues.

[B] Do you want to see that for yourself? Then compare our behaviour with a Moslem's or a pagan's: you always remain lower than they are. Yet, given the advantage of our own religion, our superiority ought to outshine them, far beyond any comparison. Men ought to say: 'Are they really so just, so loving, so good? Then these people must be Christians.'[12]   [C] All other manifestations are common to all religions: hope, trust, deliverances, ceremonies, penances and martyrdoms. The distinctive mark of the Truth we hold ought to be virtue, which is the most exacting mark of Truth, the closest one to heaven and the most worthy thing that Truth produces.

[B] That is why our good St Louis was right, when the Tartar king who was converted to Christianity planned to come to Lyons to kiss the Pope's feet and to study the holiness he hoped to find in our behaviour, to turn him away from it at once, fearing that our disordered way of life would sour his taste for so sacred a belief.[13]

The actual outcome, on the other hand, was different for that later convert who went to Rome for the same purpose: seeing the dissolute life of the prelates and people there at that time, he became even more firmly attached to our religion: he considered how much strength and holiness it must have to be able to maintain its dignity and splendour in the midst of corruption so great, in hands so vicious![14]

[A] The Word of God says that if we had one single drop of faith we would 'move mountains':[15] our actions, guided and accompanied by God, would not be simply human: they would partake of the miraculous, just as our belief does. [C] 'Brevis est institutio vitae honestae beataeque, si credas' [Laying the principles for an honourable and blessed life is soon done . . . . if you believe].[16]

Some people make the world believe that they hold beliefs they do not hold. A greater number make themselves believe it, having no idea what 'believing' really means, once you go deeply into the matter. [A] We find it strange when, in the wars now besetting our country, we see the outcome of events drifting and changing in a manner marked by nothing unusual or

12. Guillaume Postel, the French orientalist, highly praised the fervour of Moslem believers. He believed that, once converted, they would be the most exemplary of Christians.

13. Cf. Joinville, Histoire, XIX.

14. Boccaccio, Decameron, day I, tale 2.

15. Matthew 17:20.

16. Quintillian, XII, 11, 12 – enjoining men to will to achieve natural virtue.

beyond the natural order. That is because we bring to it nothing beyond ourselves. There is Justice on one of the sides, but only as a decoration and a cloak – often cited but never received, welcomed and truly wedded. Justice is lodged as in the mouth of a lawyer, not as in the heart and emotions of the man whose suit it is. God owes help – beyond the natural order – to our faith, to our religion: he does not owe it to our passions.[17] Men take the lead in them, making use of religion: things ought to be clean contrary.[18]

[C] Think whether we do not take religion into our own hands and twist it like wax into shapes quite opposed to a rule so unbending and direct. Has that ever been seen more clearly than in France today? Some approach it from this side, some from the other; some make it black, others make it white: all are alike in using religion for their violent and ambitious schemes, so like each other in managing their affairs with excess and injustice, that they make you doubt whether they really do hold different opinions over a matter on which depends the way we conduct and regulate our lives. Could you find behaviour more like, more closely identical even, coming from the same teaching in the same school? Just see the horrifying impudence with which we toss theological arguments to and fro and how irreligiously we cast them off or take them up again, whenever we happen to switch places in these civil tumults. Take that most formal proposition: Whether it be permitted for a Subject to rebel and to take up arms against his Ruler, in defence of his religion? First, remember which side, only last year, was mouthing the affirmative, making it the buttress of their faction, and what side was mouthing the negative, making their buttress out of that. Then listen from what quarter come voices defending which side now, and judge whether they are rattling their swords less for this side than they did for the other![19] We burn people at the stake for saying that Truth must bow to our necessities: and, in France, how much worse is what we do than what we say!

[A] Let us confess the truth: pick out, even from the lawful, moderate army,[20] those who are fighting simply out of zeal for their religious convictions; then add those who are concerned only to uphold the laws of their country and to serve their King: you would not have enough to form one full company of fighting men. How does it happen that so few can be found who

17. '88: to *men*. Men take . . .

18. J.-A. de Thou in his *Historia sui temporis* relates how Montaigne made similar remarks to him directly.

19. Many Catholics and Protestants switched positions as their rival candidates drew near to the throne. The Catholic Henry III, assassinated 2 August 1589, was succeeded by the Protestant Henry IV, who became a Catholic in 1593.

20. '88: from *our armies* those . . .

maintain a consistent will and action in our civil disturbances? How does it happen that you can see them sometimes merely ambling along, sometimes charging headlong – the very same men sometimes ruining our affairs by their violence and harshness and at other times by their lukewarmness, their softness and their sloth? It must be that they have been motivated by private concerns,   [C]   by ones due to chance;   [A]   as these change, so do they.

[C]   It is evident to me that we only willingly carry out those religious duties which flatter our passions. Christians excel at hating enemies. Our zeal works wonders when it strengthens our tendency towards hatred, enmity, ambition, avarice, evil-speaking . . . and rebellion. On the other hand, zeal never makes anyone go flying towards goodness, kindness or temperance, unless he is miraculously predisposed to them by some rare complexion. Our religion was made to root out vices: now it cloaks them, nurses them, stimulates them.

There is a saying: 'Do not try to palm off sheaves of straw on God.' If we believed in God – I do not mean by faith but merely with bare credence, indeed (and I say it to our great shame) if we believed him and knew him just as we believe historical events or one of our companions, then we would love him above all other things, on account of the infinite goodness and beauty shining within him: at the very least he would march equal in the ranks of our affections with riches, pleasure, glory and friends.[21]   [C]   The best among us does not fear to offend him as much as offending neighbour, kinsman, master. On this side there is the object of one of our vicious pleasures: on the other, the glorious state of immortality, equally known and equally convincing – is there anyone so simple-minded as to barter one for the other? And yet we often give it up altogether, out of pure contempt; for what attracts us to blasphemy except, perhaps, the taste of the offence itself?

Antithenes, the philosopher, was being initiated into the Orphic mysteries; the priest said that those who make their religious profession would receive after death joys, perfect and everlasting. He replied: 'Why do you not die yourself then?' Diogenes' retort was more brusque (that was his fashion) and rather off our subject: when the priest was preaching at him to join his order so as to obtain the blessings of the world to come, he replied: 'Are you asking me to believe that great men like Agesilaus and Epaminondas will be wretched, whilst a calf like you will be happy, just because you are a priest?'[22]

21. Historical faith (by which one believes historical facts) is a low form of faith, quite insufficient for salvation; Montaigne's contemporaries fail (he suggests) even to have that.

22. Diogenes Laertius, *Lives* (VI, 4 and 39), a major source of Montaigne's knowledge of scepticism.
   '95: like you *who does nothing worthwhile?* . . .

[A]  If we were to accept the great promises of everlasting blessedness as
having the same authority as a philosophical argument, no more, we would
not hold death in such horror as we do:

> [B]  *Non jam se moriens dissolvi conquereretur;*
> *Sed magis ire foras, vestemque relinquere, ut anguis,*
> *Gauderet, praelonga senex aut cornua cervus.*

[The dying man would not then complain that he is being 'loosened asunder', but
would, rather, rejoice to be 'going outside', like a snake casting off its skin, or an old
stag casting off his over-long antlers.][23]

[A]  'I wish to be loosened asunder', he would say, 'and to be with Jesus
Christ.' The force of Plato's dialogue on the immortality of the soul led some
of his disciples to kill themselves, the sooner to enjoy the hopes which he
gave them.[24]

All this is a clear sign that we accept our religion only as we would fashion
it, only from our own hands – no differently from the way other religions
gain acceptance. We happen to be born in a country where it is practised, or
else we have regard for its age or for the authority of the men who have upheld
it; perhaps we fear the threats which it attaches to the wicked or go along
with its promises. Such considerations as these must be deployed in defence
of our beliefs, but only as support-troops. Their bonds are human. Another
region, other witnesses, similar promises or similar menaces, would, in the
same way, stamp a contrary belief on us.   [B]  We are Christians by the
same title that we are Périgordians or Germans.

[A]  Plato said few men are so firm in their atheism that a pressing danger
does not bring them to acknowledge divine power;[25] such behaviour has
nothing to do with a true Christian; only mortal, human religions become
accepted by human procedures. What sort of faith must it be that is planted
by cowardice and established in us by feebleness of heart!   [C]  What an
agreeable faith, which believes what it believes, because it is not brave enough

23. Lucretius, III, 612 f. (Lambin, 1563, p. 230), alludes to the *De divino praemio*,
VII, of the Christian writer Lactantius for an answer to these words. Montaigne provides an answer in his own way.

24. Paul (Philippians 1:23) becomes an answer to Lucretius. For the highly orthodox association of Paul with Platonizing suicides, see my study, *Montaigne and Melancholy*, chapter 5, §1.

25. '88: pressing danger, *extreme pain or closeness of death* do not . . . Idea taken
possibly from Plato, *Laws*, X (cf. Montaigne in vol. I, chapter 56, 'On Prayers') and
Plato, tr. Ficino, *Republic*, I, 330, 532.

to disbelieve it! [A] How can vicious passions, such as inconstancy and sudden dismay, produce in our souls anything right?

[C] Plato says that people first decide, by reasoned judgement, that what is told about hell and future punishment is just fiction. But when they have the opportunity really to find out, by experience, when old age or illness brings them close to death, then the terror of it fills them with belief again, out of horror for what awaits them.

To impress such ideas upon people is to make them timorous of heart: that is why Plato in his *Laws* forbids any teaching of threats such as these or of any conviction that ill can come to Man from the gods. (When it does happen, it is for man's greater good or like a medical purgation.)[26]

They tell that Bion, infected by the atheistic teachings of Theodorus, used to mock religious men; but eventually, when death approached, he gave himself over to the most extreme superstitions, as though the gods took themselves off and brought themselves back according to the needs of Bion.[27]

Plato – and these examples – lead to the conclusion that either love or force can bring us back to a belief in God. Atheism, as a proposition, is a monstrous thing, stripped, as it were, of natural qualities. It is awkward and difficult to fix it firmly in the human spirit, however impudent or however unruly. We have seen plenty of people who are egged on by vanity and pride to conceive lofty opinions for setting the world to rights; to put themselves in countenance they affect to profess atheism: but even if they are mad enough to try and plant it in their consciousness, they are not strong enough to do so. Give them a good thrust through the breast with your sword and they never fail to raise clasped hands to heaven. And when fear or sickness has cooled down the licentious fever-heat of that transient humour, they never fail to come back to themselves again, letting themselves be reconciled to recognized standards and beliefs. Seriously digested doctrine is one thing: these surface impressions are quite another. They are born of a mind unhinged, in the spirit of debauchery; they drift rashly and erratically about in the fancies of men. What wretched, brainless men they are, trying to be worse than they can be!

That great soul [C] of Plato [A] – great, however, with merely human greatness – was led into a neighbouring mistake by the error of paganism and his ignorance of our holy Truth: he held that it is children and old men who are most susceptible to religion, as if religion were born of human

26. Plato, *Republic* (Ficino, III, 391; cf. II, 379).
27. Diogenes Laertius, *Lives*, Bion.

weakness and drew her credibility from it.[28]  [A]  The knot which ought to attach our judgement and our will and to clasp our souls firmly to our Creator should not be one tied together with human considerations and strengthened by emotions: it should be drawn tight in a clasp both divine and supernatural, and have only one form, one face, one lustre; namely, the authority of God and his grace.

But, once our hearts and souls are governed by Faith, it is reasonable that she should further her purposes by drawing upon all of our other parts, according to their several capacities. Moreover, it is simply not believable that there should be no prints whatsoever impressed upon the fabric of this world by the hand of the great Architect, or that there should not be at least some image within created things relating to the Workman who made them and fashioned them. He has left within these lofty works the impress of his Godhead: only our weakness stops us from discovering it. He tells us himself that he makes manifest his unseen workings through those things which are seen. Sebond toiled at this honourable endeavour, showing us that there is no piece within this world which belies its Maker. God's goodness would be put in the wrong if the universe were not compatible with our beliefs. All things, Heaven, Earth, the elements, our bodies and our souls are in one accord: we simply have to find how to use them. If we have the capacity to understand, they will teach us.  [B]  For this world is a most holy Temple into which Man has been brought in order to contemplate the Sun, the heavenly bodies, the waters and the dry land – objects not sculpted by mortal hands but made manifest to our senses by the Divine Mind in order to represent intelligibles.  [A]  'The invisible things of God', says St Paul, 'are clearly seen from the creation of the world, his Eternal Wisdom and his Godhead being perceived from the things he has made.'[29]

> *Atque adeo faciem coeli non invidet orbi*
> *Ipse Deus, vultusque suos corpusque recludit*
> *Semper volvendo; seque ipsum inculcat et offert,*
> *Ut bene cognosci possit, doceatque videndo*
> *Qualis eat, doceatque suas attendere leges.*

[God himself does not begrudge to the world the sight of the face of heaven, which, ever-rolling, unveils his countenance, his incorporate being inculcating and offering

28. Cf. Erasmus: *Praise of Folly,* LXVI.
29. Plutarch, tr. Amyot, *De la tranquillité de l'âme,* I, 76; Romans I:20; cf. Introduction, p. xvii.

himself to us, so that he may be known full well; he teaches the man who contemplates to recognize his state, teaches him, also, to wait upon his laws.][30]

Our human reasonings and concepts are like matter, heavy and barren: God's grace is their form, giving them shape and worth. The virtuous actions of Socrates and of Cato remain vain and useless, since they did not have, as their end or their aim, love of the true Creator of all things nor obedience to him: they did not know God; the same applies to our concepts and thoughts: they have a body of sorts, but it is a formless mass, unenlightened and without shape, unless accompanied by faith in God and by grace. When Faith tinges the themes of Sebond and throws her light upon them, she makes them firm and solid. They then have the capacity of serving as a finger-post, as an elementary guide setting an apprentice on the road leading to knowledge such as this; they fashion him somewhat into shape and make him capable of God's grace, which then furnishes out our belief and perfects it.

I know a man of authority, a cultured, educated man, who admitted to me that he had been led back from the errors of disbelief by means of the arguments of Sebond. Even if you were to strip them of their ornaments and of the help and approbation of Faith – even if you were to take them for purely human notions – you would find, when it comes to fighting those who have plunged down into the dreadful, horrible darkness of irreligion, that they still remain more solid and more firm than any others of the same kind which you can set up against them. We rightly can say to our opponents, '*Si melius quid habes, accerse, vel imperium fer*' [If you have anything better, produce it, or submit]:[31] let them allow the force of our proofs or else show us others, elsewhere, on another subject, as closely woven or of better stuff.

Without thinking I have already half-slipped into the second of the charges which I set out to counter on behalf of Sebond.

Some say that his arguments are weak and unsuited to what he wants to demonstrate; they set out to batter them down with ease. People like those need to be shaken rather more roughly, since they are more dangerous than the first and more malicious.   [C]   We are only too willing to couch other men's writings in senses which favour our settled opinions: an atheist prides himself on bringing all authors into accord with atheism, poisoning harmless

30. Manilius, IV, 907;

'88 (after quotation, referring to his translation of Sebond): *If my printer were so enamoured of those studied, borrowed prefatory-pieces with which (according to the humour of this age) there is no book from a good publishing-house but has its forehead garnished, he should make use of verses such as these, which are of a better and more ancient stock than the ones he has planted there.*

31. Horace, *Epistles*, V, 6.

matter with his own venom.[32] [A] Such people have some mental prepos-
session which makes Sebond's reasons seem insipid. Moreover it seems to
them that they have been allowed an easy game, with freedom to fight against
our religion with purely human weapons: they would never dare to attack
her in the full majesty of her imperious authority. The means I use and which
seem more fitted to abating such a frenzy is to trample down human pride
and arrogance, crushing them under our feet; I make men feel the emptiness,
the vanity, the nothingness of Man, wrenching from their grasp the sickly
arms of human reason, making them bow their heads and bite the dust
before the authority and awe of the Divine Majesty, to whom alone belong
knowledge and wisdom; who alone can esteem himself in any way, and from
whom we steal whatever worth or value we pride ourselves on: Οὐ γὰρ ἐᾷ
φρονεῖν ὁ Θεὸς μέγα ἄλλον ἢ ἑωυτόν [God permits no one to esteem himself
higher than He].[33]

[C] Let us smash down such presumption. It is the very foundation of
the tyrannous rule of the Evil Spirit: '*Deus superbis resistit; humilibus autem
dat gratiam*' [God resisteth the proud, and giveth grace to the humble]. 'There
is intelligence in all the gods,' says Plato, 'but very little of it in men.'[34]

[A] Yet it is a great source of consolation to a Christian man to see our
transitory mortal tools so properly matched to our holy and divine faith that
when we use them on subjects which, like them, are transitory and mortal,
it is precisely then that they are most closely and most powerfully matched.
Let us try and see, then, whether a man has in his power any reasons stronger
than those of Sebond – whether, indeed, it is in man to arrive at any certainty
by argument and reflection.

[C] St Augustine, pleading his case against presumptuous people, has
cause to criticize their injustice when they consider those parts of our faith
to be false which human reason is unable to establish. In order to show that
many things can exist or have had existence, even though their nature and
causes have no foundation which can be fixed by rational discourse, he
advances various indubitable, recognized experiences, for which Man admits

32. '88: malicious. *Anyone who is already imbued with a belief more readily accepts
arguments which support it than does a man who has drunk draughts from a contrary opinion,
as do these people here. Some mental predisposition makes Sebond's reasons* . . .

'95: opinions. *For an Atheist all writings lean towards atheism. He infects harmless
matter* . . .

33. Herodotus, VII, 10, *apud* John Stobaeus, *Apophthegmata*, 22. This was inscribed
by Montaigne on a beam in his library.

34. I Peter V:5. Cf. Augustine, *City of God*, XVII, 4; Plato, tr. Ficino, *Timaeus*,
1546, p. 715.

he can see no explanation. Augustine does this, as he does all things, after careful and intelligent search.[35] We must do even more, teaching such people the lesson that the weakness of their reason can be proved without our having to marshal rare examples; that reason is so inadequate, so blind, that there is no example so clear and easy as to be clear enough for her; that the easy and the hard are all one to her; that all subjects and Nature in general equally deny her any sway or jurisdiction.

[A]   What is Truth teaching us, when she preaches that we must fly from the wisdom of this world; when she so frequently urges that what seems wise to Man is but foolishness to God; that of all vain things, Man is the most vain; that a man who dares to presume that he knows anything, does not even know what knowledge is; that Man, who is nothing yet thinks he is something, misleads and deceives himself? These are verdicts of the Holy Ghost;[36] they express so clearly and so vividly what I myself wish to uphold that I would need no other proof to use against people who, with due submission and obedience, would surrender to his authority. But these people simply ask to be whipped, and will not let us fight their reason, save by reason alone.

So let us consider for a while Man in isolation – Man with no outside help, armed with no arms but his own and stripped of that grace and knowledge of God in which consist his dignity, his power and the very ground of his being.[37] Let us see how much constancy there is in all his fine panoply. Let Man make me understand, by the force of discursive reason, what are the grounds on which he has founded and erected all those advantages which he thinks he has over other creatures and who has convinced him that it is for his convenience, his service, that, for so many centuries, there has been established and maintained the awesome motion of the vault of heaven, the everlasting light of those tapers coursing so proudly overhead or the dread surging of the boundless sea? Is it possible to imagine anything more laughable than that this pitiful, wretched creature – who is not even master of himself, but exposed to shocks on every side – should call himself Master and Emperor of a universe, the smallest particle of which he has no means of knowing, let alone swaying! Man claims the privilege of being unique in that, within this created frame, he alone is able to recognize its structure and its beauty; he alone is able to render thanks to its Architect or to tot up the

35. *City of God*, XXI, 5.

36. Colossians 2:8; I Corinthians 3:19; I Corinthians 8:2; Galatians 6:3 (the last two inscribed in Montaigne's library). For Montaigne, the Bible is the Holy Ghost speaking through men.

37. From here to the last page, revealed wisdom is left aside. See Introduction, p.xxi.

profit or loss of the world . . . But who impressed his seal on such a privilege? If Man has been given so great and fair a commission, let him produce documents saying so. [C] Were they drawn up in favour of wise men only? (They apply to few enough!)[38] Are fools and knaves worthy of a favour so far exceeding the normal order – the worst thing in the world exalted above all others? Are we supposed to believe that fellow who wrote: '*Quorum igitur causa quis dixerit effectum esse mundum? Eorum scilicet animantium quae ratione utuntur. Hi sunt dii et homines, quibus profecto nihil est melius*' [Who will tell for whose sake this world has been brought about? Why, for the sake of beings having souls able to use reason, those most perfect of beings, gods and men].[39] Coupling gods and men together! We can never do enough to batter down such impudence.

[A] Poor little wretch! What is there in man worthy of such a privilege?

Consider the sun, moon and stars, with their lives free from corruption, their beauty, their grandeur, their motions ever proceeding by laws so just:

> *cum suspicimus magni caelestia mundi*
> *Templa super, stellisque micantibus Aethera fixum,*
> *Et venit in mentem Lunae Solisque viarum;*

[When we gaze upwards to the celestial temples of this great Universe, to the Aether with its fixed and twinkling stars, and when there comes to mind the courses of the Moon and of the Sun . . .][40]

then consider the dominion and power which those bodies have, not only over our lives and the settled detail of our fortunes –

> *Facta etenim et vitas hominum suspendit ab astris*

[For he made the deeds and lives of man to depend upon the Sun, the Moon and the Stars][41]

– but over our very inclinations, our discursive reasoning and our wills, which are all governed, driven and shaken at the mercy of their influences. Our reason tells us that and finds it to be so,

> *speculataque longe*
> *Deprendit tacitis dominantia legibus astra,*
> *Et totum alterna mundum ratione moveri,*
> *Fatorumque vices certis discernere signis.*

38. Cicero, *De nat. deorum*, I, ix, 23.
39. *Ibid.*, II, liii, 133 (where the idea is attributed to Balbus the Stoic).
40. Lucretius, V, 1203 f.
41. Manilius, III, 58 (Montaigne mistranscribed *Fata* (fate) as *facta* (deeds). *Fata* makes better sense); then, I, 60–63; I, 55 and IV, 93; IV, 79 and 118.

[it gazes in the distance, grasping that the heavenly bodies govern us by silent laws, that all the world is moved by periodic causes; and it discerns changing Fate in fixed and certain signs.]

Then see how not merely one man or one king is sent reeling by the slightest motion of the heavenly bodies, but whole monarchies, empires and all this lower world:

> *Quantaque quam parvi faciant discrimina motus:*
> *Tantum est hoc regnum, quod regibus imperat ipsis!*

[When such small motions produce such changes, how great must be the kingdom which rules over kings themselves!]

Then allow that our reason judges that our virtues and our vices, our competencies, our knowledge, and this very discourse we are making here and now about the power of the heavenly bodies, comes to us by their means and by their favour:

> *furit alter amore,*
> *Et pontum tranare potest et vertere Trojam;*
> *Alterius sors est scribendis legibus apta;*
> *Ecce patrem nati perimunt, natosque parentes;*
> *Mutuaque armati coeunt in vulnera fratres:*
> *Non nostrum hoc bellum est; coguntur tanta movere,*
> *Inque suas ferri poenas, lacerandaque membra;*
> *Hoc quoque fatale est, sic ipsum expendere fatum.*

[One man, mad with love, can cross the sea and topple Troy: another's lot is to be apt at prescribing laws. Look: children kill parents: parents, children; brothers bear arms and clash to wound each other. Such wars do not belong to men alone. Men are compelled to do such things, compelled to punish themselves, to tear their limbs apart. And when we ponder thus on Fate, that too is fated . . .]

If we are dependent upon the disposition of the heavens for such little rationality as we have, how can our reason make us equal to the Heavens? How can their essence, or the principles on which they are founded, be subjects of human knowledge? Everything that we can see in those bodies produces in us ecstatic wonder. [C] '*Quae molitio, quae ferramenta, qui vectes, quae machinae, qui ministri tanti operis fuerunt?*' [What engineering, what tools, what levers, what contrivances, what agents were used in such an enterprise?][42]

[A] Why do we deprive the heavenly bodies of souls, life or rationality? Have we, who have no dealings with them beyond pure obedience, been

---

42. Cicero, *De nat. deorum*, I, viii, 19.

able to recognize in them some kind of stupor, motionless and insensible? [C] Shall we say that we have seen no other creature but Man possessed of a rational soul? What do we mean? Have we ever seen anything like the Sun? And just because we have seen nothing like it, does it cease to be; or, since we have seen nothing like its movements, shall they, too, cease to be? If things we have not actually seen do not exist, then our knowledge is wondrously diminished! '*Quae sunt tantae animi angustiae*' [What narrow defiles has our mind].[43]

[A] What vain human dreams, to make the Moon into some celestial Earth, [C] dreaming up, like Anaxagoras, mountains and valleys for it, [A] planting human dwellings and habitations on it and, like Plato and Plutarch, settling colonies there for our convenience: and then to make our own Earth into a brightly shining star: [C] '*Inter caetera mortalitatis incommoda et hoc est, calligo mentium, nec tantum necessitas errandi sed errorum amor*' [Among the other disorders of our mortal condition there is that mental darkness which not only compels us to go wrong but makes us love to do so]. '*Corruptibile corpus aggravat animam, et deprimit terrena inhabitatio sensum multa cogitantem*' [For the corruptible body is a load upon the soul, and the earthly habitation presseth down the mind that museth on many things].[44]

[A] The natural, original distemper of Man is presumption. Man is the most blighted and frail of all creatures and, moreover, the most given to pride.[45] This creature knows and sees that he is lodged down here, among the mire and shit of the world, bound and nailed to the deadest, most stagnant part of the universe, in the lowest storey of the building, the farthest from the vault of heaven; his characteristics place him in the third and lowest category of animate creatures, yet, in thought, he sets himself above the circle of the Moon, bringing the very heavens under his feet. The vanity of this same thought makes him equal himself to God; attribute to himself God's mode of being; pick himself out and set himself apart from the mass of other creatures; and (although they are his fellows and his brothers) carve out for them such helpings of force or faculties as he thinks fit. How can he, from the power of his own understanding, know the hidden, inward motivations

---

43. *Ibid.*, I, xxxi, 87 and 88 (refuting Epicurus).

44. Plutarch, tr. Amyot, *De la face qui apparoist dedans le rond de la Lune*; Diogenes Laertius, II, viii, 100; Seneca, *De ira*, II, ix; Wisdom of Solomon 9:15, *apud* Augustine, *City of God*, XII, 15.

45. '88: moreover, *says Pliny*, the most given . . . (This quotation is used by Montaigne to conclude vol. II, chapter 14, 'How our Spirit Entangles Itself'; it was cited in Montaigne's library.)

of animate creatures? What comparison between us and them leads him to conclude that they have the attributes of senseless brutes?

[C]   When I play with my cat, how do I know that she is not passing time with me rather than I with her?[46]

In his description of the Golden Age under Saturn, Plato counted among one of the principal advantages which Man then had his ability to communicate with the beasts; enquiring and learning from them, Man knew what they were really like and how they differed from each other. By this means Man used to acquire a full understanding and discretion, leading his life far more happily than we ever can now. After that, do we need a better proof of the impudence of Man towards beast? Well, that great author then opined that Nature mainly gave the beasts their bodily forms to enable the men in his time to foretell the future![47]

[A]   Why should it be a defect in the beasts not in us which stops all communication between us? We can only guess whose fault it is that we cannot understand each other: for we do not understand them any more than they understand us. They may reckon us to be brute beasts for the same reason that we reckon them to be so. It is no great miracle if we cannot understand them: we cannot understand Basques or Troglodytes! –

[A]   Some have boasted, though, that they could understand the beasts: Apollonius of Thyana, [B] Melampus, Tiresias, Thales [A1] and others.   [B]   And since there are nations (so the cosmographers tell us) who acknowledge a dog as their king, they must interpret its bark and its movements as having some definite meaning.[48]   [A]   We ought to note the parity there is between us. We have some modest understanding of what they mean: they have the same of us, in about equal measure. They fawn on us, threaten us and entreat us – as we do them. Meanwhile we discover that they manifestly have converse between themselves, both whole and entire: they understand each other, not only within one species but across different species.

[B]   *Et mutae pecudes et denique secla ferarum*
*Dissimiles suerunt voces variasque cluere,*
*Cum metus aut dolor est, aut cum jam gaudia gliscunt.*

46. '95: her? *We entertain ourselves with mutual monkey-tricks. If I have times when I want to begin or to say no, so does she.*

47. Plato, tr. Ficino, *Politics*, p. 206; *Timaeus*, p. 274 (cf. Montaigne in vol. I, chapter 11, 'On Prognostications').

48. Benedetto Varchi, *L'Hercolano. Dialogo nel qual si ragiona . . . delle lingue*; Richerius Rhodiginus, *Antiquae Lectiones*, XVII, xiii (disapprovingly); Pliny, *Hist. nat.*, VI, xxxv, etc.

[And dumb cattle and, finally, the generations of wild beasts customarily make sounds having various meanings, when they feel fear or pain or when joy overflows.][49]

[A]   A horse knows there to be anger in a given bark of a dog; but that horse does not take fright when the same dog makes some other meaningful cry. Even in beasts who cannot utter meaningful sounds we can readily conclude that there is some other means of communication between them, from the way they work purposefully together;   [C]   their very movements serve as arguments and ideas.

> [B]   *Non alia longe ratione atque ipsa videtur*
> *Protrahere ad gestum pueros infantia linguae.*

[In a not dissimilar way, the very inability to speak leads infants to make gestures.][50]

[A]   And why not? Our deaf-mutes have discussions and arguments, telling each other stories by means of signs.[51] I have seen some who are so nimble and so practised at this that they truly lack nothing necessary for making themselves perfectly understood. After all, lovers quarrel, make it up again, beg favours, give thanks, arrange secret meetings and say everything, with their eyes.

> [A1]   *E'l silentio ancor suole*
> *Haver prieghi e parole.*

[Silence itself can talk and beg requests.][52]

[C]   And what about our hands? With them we request, promise, summon, dismiss, menace, pray, supplicate, refuse, question, show astonishment, count, confess, repent, fear, show shame, doubt, teach, command, incite, encourage, make oaths, bear witness, make accusations, condemn, give absolution, insult, despise, defy, provoke, flatter, applaud, bless, humiliate, mock, reconcile, advise, exalt, welcome, rejoice, lament; show sadness, grieve, despair; astonish, cry out, keep silent and what not else, with a variety and multiplicity rivalling the tongue.

What of the head? We summon, dismiss, admit, reject, deny, welcome, honour, venerate, disdain, request, refuse, rejoice, lament, fondle, tease, submit, brave, exhort, menace, affirm and inquire.

---

49. Lucretius, V, 1058.
50. *Ibid.*, V, 1029.
51. '88: by means of *gestures*. I have . . . (Cf. Rabelais, *Tiers Livre*, TLF, XIX–XX and notes).
52. Torquato Tasso, *Aminta*, II, 34.

And what of our eyebrows or our shoulders? None of their movements fail to talk a meaningful language which does not have to be learned, a language common to us all. This suggests (given the variety and different usage among spoken languages) that it is, rather, sign-language that should be judged the 'property' of Man.[53]

I shall leave aside what Necessity can suddenly teach men in individual cases of particular need, as well as finger-alphabets, grammars of gesture and those branches of learning conducted and expressed through them and, finally, those peoples who, according to Pliny, have no other tongue.[54]

[B]   An ambassador from the city of Abdera, after delivering a long address to King Agis of Sparta, asked him: 'Sire, what reply do you want me to bear back to our citizens?' – 'That I allowed you to say all you wanted, for as long as you wanted, without uttering a word.' Was that not an eloquent and most intelligible silence?[55]

[A]   After all, what aspects of our human competence cannot be found in the activities of animals? Is there any form of body politic more ordered, more varied in its allocation of tasks and duties or maintained with greater constancy than that of the bees? Can we conceive that an allocation of tasks and activities, so striking for its orderliness, should be conducted without reasoned discourse and foresight?

> *His quidam signis atque haec exempla sequuti,*
> *Esse apibus partem divinae mentis et haustus*
> *Aethereos dixere.*

[From such signs and examples men conclude that bees have been given some part of the divine Mind and have drunk Aethereal draughts.][56]

Take the swallows, when spring returns; we can see them ferreting through all the corners of our houses; from a thousand places they select one, finding it the most suitable place to make their nests: is that done without judgement or discernment? And then when they are making their nests (so beautifully and so wondrously woven together) can birds use a square rather than a circle, an obtuse angle rather than a right angle,

53. Quintillian, XI, iii, 66, 85–87; 68, 71–72; 78–86. Laughter and/or speech were normally considered the 'specific characteristic' (the 'property') of Man.

54. Pliny, VI, 30; cf. Rabelais, *Pantagruel*, TLF, XIII; *Tiers Livre*, XXX; J.-B. della Porta, *De furtivis litterarum notis*, 1563; etc.

55. Plutarch, tr. Amyot, *Les Dicts notables des Lacedemoniens*, I, 214 A.

56. Virgil, *Georgics*, IV, 219 f. For what follows, cf. Plutarch, tr. Amyot, *Quels sont les animaux les plus advisez ceulx de la terre ou ceulx des eaux?* 512 CD.

without knowing their properties or their effects? Do they bring water
and then clay without realizing that hardness can be softened by
dampening? They cover the floors of their palaces with moss or down;
do they do so without foreseeing that the tender limbs of their little
ones will lie more softly there and be more comfortable? Do they protect
themselves from the stormy winds and plant their dwellings to the east-
ward, without recognizing the varying qualities of those winds and considering that one is more healthy for them than another? Why does the
spider make her web denser in one place and slacker in another, using
this knot here and that knot there, if she cannot reflect, think or reach
conclusions?

We are perfectly able to realize how superior they are to us in most of their
works and how weak our artistic skills are when it comes to imitating them.
Our works are coarser, and yet we are aware of the faculties we use to construct them: our souls use all their powers when doing so. Why do we not
consider that the same applies to animals? Why do we attribute to some sort
of slavish natural inclination works that surpass all that we can do by nature
or by art?

In this, we thoughtlessly give them a very great superiority over us: we
make Nature take them by the hand and guide them with a mother's gentle
care in all the actions and advantages of their lives; we, on the other hand,
are abandoned by Nature to chance and to Fortune, obliged to seek, by art,
all things necessary for our conservation; meanwhile, Nature refuses us the
very means which would enable us to reach, by education or intelligent
application, the level reached by the natural industry of other creatures. In
this way we make their brutish stupor have every advantage over our divine
intelligence![57]

In truth, on this account, we would be right to treat Nature as a very unjust
stepmother. But it is not so. We do not live under so misshapen or so lawless
a constitution:[58] Nature clasps all her creatures in a universal embrace; there
is not one of them which she has not plainly furnished with all means necessary to the conservation of its being.

There are commonplace lamentations which I hear men make (as the
unruly liberty of their opinions raises them above the clouds and then tumbles
them down lower than the Antipodes): We are, they say, the only animal
abandoned naked on the naked earth; we are in bonds and fetters, having
nothing to arm or cover ourselves with but the pelts of other creatures; Nature

57. '88: over our *invention and our arts* . . .
58. '88 so *monstrous* a constitution . . .

has clad all others with shells, pods, husks, hair, wool, spikes, hide, down, feathers, scales, fleece or silk, according to the several necessities of their being; she has armed them with claws, teeth and horns for assault and defence; and, as is proper to them, has herself taught them to swim, to run, to fly or to sing. Man, on the other hand, without an apprenticeship, does not know how to walk, talk, eat or to do anything at all but wail:[59]

> [B]  *Tum porro puer, ut saevis projectus ab undis*
> *Navita, nudus humi jacet, infans, indigus omni*
> *Vitali auxilio, cum primum in luminis oras*
> *Nixibus ex alvo matris natura profudit;*
> *Vagituque locum lugubri complet, ut aequum est*
> *Cui tantum in vita restet transire malorum.*
> *At variae crescunt pecudes, armenta, feraeque,*
> *Nec crepitacula eis opus est, nec cuiquam adhibenda est*
> *Almae nutricis blanda atque infracta loquella;*
> *Nec varias quaerunt vestes pro tempore coeli;*
> *Denique non armis opus est, non moenibus altis,*
> *Queis sua tutentur, quando omnibus omnia large*
> *Tellus ipsa parit, naturaque daedala rerum.*

[Then the child, like a sailor cast up by raging seas, lies naked on the earth, unable to talk, bereft of everything that would help him to live, when Nature first tears him struggling from his mother's womb and casts him on the shore of light. He fills the place with his mournful cries – rightly, for one who still has to pass through so many evils. Yet all sorts of cattle, farm animals as well as wild beasts, thrive; they need no rattles nor the winsome baby language of the gentle nurse; they do not need clothing varying with the weather; and finally they need no weapons nor lofty walls to make them safe, since Earth herself and skilful Nature give all of them, amply, everything they need.][60]

[A]  Such plaints are false. There are more uniform relationships and greater fairness in the constitution of this world.[61] Our skin, like theirs, is adequately provided with means to resist intemperate weather with firmness: witness those many peoples who have yet to acquire a taste for clothing.  [B]  Our ancient Gauls wore hardly any clothes: nor do the Irish, our neighbours, under a sky so cold.

[A]  But we can judge that from ourselves; all parts of the body which we

59.  Commonplace deriving from Pliny, VII. Erasmus exploited it (Adage, *Dulce bellum inexpertis*); Rabelais satirized it (*Tiers Livre*, TLF, VIII).

60.  Lucretius, V. 223; cf. Lambin, 389.

61.  this world: *our feebleness at birth is found, more or less, at the birth of the other creatures*. Our skin . . .

are pleased to leave uncovered to air and wind prove able to endure it: face, feet, hands, legs, shoulders, head, as custom suggests. If there be a part of us so weak that it does seem that it has to fear the cold it is our belly, in which digestion takes place: yet our forefathers left it uncovered – and in our society ladies (however soft and delicate they are) occasionally go about with it bare down to the navel. Binding and swaddling up children is not necessary. The mothers of Sparta used to bring up their children with complete freedom of movement for their limbs, without binders or fastenings.[62] Infant cries are common to most other animals; nearly all can be seen wailing and whining long after they are born; such behaviour is quite appropriate to the helplessness that they feel. As for eating, it is natural to us and to them; it does not have to be learned.

[B] *Sentit enim vim quisque suam quam possit abuti.*

[For every creature feels the powers at its disposal.][63]

[A]  Does anyone doubt that a child, once able to feed himself, would know how to go in search of food? And Earth, with no farming and with none of our arts, produces quite enough for his needs and offers it to him – perhaps not at all seasons, but neither does she do that for the beasts: witness the stores we can see ants or others provide for the barren season of the year. Those peoples we have recently discovered, so abundantly furnished with food and natural drinks needing no care or toil, have taught us that there is other food beside bread and that Mother Nature can provide us plenteously, without ploughing, with all we need – indeed (as is likely) more straightforwardly and more richly than she does nowadays, when we have brought in our artificial skills.

> *Et tellus nitidas fruges vinetaque laeta*
> *Sponte sua primum mortalibus ipsa creavit;*
> *Ipsa dedit dulces foetus et pabula laeta,*
> *Quae nunc vix nostro grandescunt aucta labore,*
> *Conterimusque boves et vires agricolarum.*

[And Earth herself first willingly provided grain and cheerful vines; she gave sweet produce and good pastures, such as, with all our increased toil, we can but scarcely make to grow; we wear out oxen and the strength of farmers . . .][64]

62. Plutarch, tr. Amyot, *Lives*, Lycurgus, XIII.
63. Lucretius, V, 1032.
64. Lucretius, II, 1157.

The lawless flood of our greed outstrips everything we invent to try and slake it.

As for armaments, we have more natural ones than most other animals do, as well as a greater variety in our movements; we draw greater service from them, too – naturally, without being taught. Men trained to fight naked throw themselves into danger just as our men do. Although some beasts are better armed than we are, we are better armed than others. And we are given to covering the body with acquired means of protection because Nature teaches us to do so instinctively.

To see that this is true, note how the elephant sharpens to a point the teeth which it uses to fight with (for it has special teeth reserved for fighting, and never used for other tasks); when bulls come out to fight they throw up dust and scatter it round about; wild boars whet their tusks; and the ichneumon, before coming to grips with the crocodile, takes mud, kneaded and compressed, and smears it over itself as a crust to serve as body-armour. Why do we not say, therefore, that arming ourselves with sticks and iron bars is equally natural?[65]

As for the power of speech, it is certain that, if it is not natural, then it cannot be necessary. And yet I believe (though it would be difficult to assay it) that if a child, before learning to talk, were brought up in total solitude, then he would have some sort of speech to express his concepts; it is simply not believable that Nature has refused to us men a faculty granted to most other animals; we can see they have means of complaining, rejoicing, calling on each other for help or inviting each other to love; they do so by meaningful utterances: if that is not talking, what is it? [B] How could they fail to talk among themselves, since they talk to us and we to them? How many ways we have of speaking to our dogs and they of replying to us! We use different languages again, and make different cries, to call birds, pigs, bulls and horses; we change idiom according to each species.

> [A1]  *Così per entro loro schiera bruna*
> *S'ammusa l'una con l'altra formica*
> *Forse à spiar lor via, e lor fortuna.*

[As one ant from their dark battalion stops to talk to another, perhaps asking the way or how things are faring.]

And does not Lactantius appear to attribute not only speech to animals, but laughter too?

[A]  The different varieties of speech found among men of different

65. Plutarch, tr. Amyot, *Quels animaux?*, 512 CD.

countries can be paralleled in animals of the same species. On this subject
Aristotle cites the ways in which the call of the partridge varies from place to
place.

> [B]   *variaeque volucres*
> *Longe alias alio jaciunt in tempore voces,*
> *Et partim mutant cum tempestatibus una*
> *Raucisonos cantus.*

[At different times some birds utter highly different sounds, some even making their
songs more raucous with changes in the weather.]

[A]   But we do not know what language an isolated child would actually
speak and the guesses made about it all seem improbable.[66]

If anyone challenges my opinion, citing the fact that people who are born
deaf never learn to talk at all, I have an answer to that: it is not simply because
they are unable to receive instruction in speech through the ear but rather
because of the intimate relationship which exists between the faculty of hearing (the power they are deprived of) and the faculty of speech, which are by
their nature closely sutured together. Whenever we talk, we must first talk
as it were to ourselves: our speech first sounds in our own ears, then we utter
it into the ears of other people.

I have gone into all this to emphasize similarities with things human, so
bringing Man into conformity with the majority of creatures. We are neither
above them nor below them. 'Everything under the Sky', said the Wise Man,
'runs according to like laws and fortune.'[67]

> [B]   *Indupedita suis fatalibus omnia vinclis.*

[All things are enchained in the fetters of their destiny.]

[A]   Some difference there is: there are orders and degrees: but always
beneath the countenance of Nature who is one and the same.

> [B]   *res quaeque suo ritu procedit, et omnes*
> *Foedere naturae certo discrimina servant.*

66. Commonplace; for Herodotus, II, 2, Phrygian is Man's natural language. Principal sources: Aristotle, *Hist. animal.*, IV, ix; Varchi, *L'Hercolano* (citing Dante, *Purga-
torio*, XXXVI, 34) and L. Joubert, *Erreurs populaires au faict de la médecine*, 1578, *ad
fin.*, (Lucretius, V. 1077, cited directly). Same scepticism, Rabelais, *Tiers Livre*, XIX.
If Lactantius is right and if some animals can laugh, then laughter is not the 'property'
of Man.

67. Already cited by Montaigne in vol. I, chapter 36 ('On the Habit of Wearing
Clothing'); inscribed in Montaigne's library and attributed to 'Eccl. IX'.

[Each thing proceeds after its own manner, and all things maintain their distinctive qualities by the fixed compact of Nature.][68]

[A]   Man must be restrained, with his own rank, within the boundary walls of this polity: the wretch has no stomach for effectively clambering over them; he is trussed up and bound, subject to the same restraints as the other creatures of his natural order. His condition is a very modest one. As for his essential being, he has no true privilege or pre-eminence: what he thinks or fancies he has, has no savour, no body to it. Granted that, of all the animals, Man alone has freedom to think and such unruly ways of doing so that he can imagine things which are and things which are not, imagine his wishes, or the false and the true! but he has to pay a high price for this advantage – and he has little cause to boast about it, since it is the chief source of the woes which beset him: sin, sickness, irresolution, confusion and despair.

To get back to the subject, there is, I say, no rational likelihood that beasts are forced to do by natural inclination the selfsame things which we do by choice and ingenuity. From similar effects we should conclude that there are similar faculties. Consequently, we should admit that animals employ the same method and the same reasoning as ourselves when we do anything.[69] Why should we think that they have inner natural instincts different from anything we experience in ourselves? Added to which, it is more honourable that we be guided towards regular, obligatory behaviour by the natural and ineluctable properties of our being: that is more God-like than rash and fortuitous freedom; it is safer to leave the driver's reins in Nature's hands, not ours. Our empty arrogance makes us prefer to owe our adequacies to our selves rather than to the bounty of Nature; we prefer to lavish the natural goods on other animals, giving them up so as to flatter and honour ourselves with acquired properties. We do that, it seems to me, out of some simple-minded humour. Personally I value graces which are mine since I was born with them more than those which I have had to beg and borrow as an apprentice. It is not within our power to acquire a higher recommendation than to be favoured by God and Nature.

Consider the fox which Thracians employ when they want to cross the ice of a frozen river; with this end in view they let it loose. Were we to see it

68. Lucretius, V, 874; 921 (Lambin, pp. 430–34).

69. '95: similar faculties, *and from richer effects, richer faculties*. Consequently we should admit that the animals employ the same method *or some better one* and the same reasoning . . . (*Imagination* in Montaigne can include *thought*. Sebond, LXIII, champions a contention rejected here by Montaigne: it is not convincing to unaided human reason.)

stopping at the river's edge, bringing its ear close to the ice to judge from the noise how near to the surface the current is running; darting forward or pulling back according to its estimate of the thickness or thinness of the ice, would it not be right to conclude that the same reasoning passes through its head as would pass through ours and that it ratiocinates and draws consequences by its natural intelligence like this: 'That which makes a noise is moving; that which moves is not frozen; that which is not frozen is liquid; that which is liquid bends under weight'? Attributing all that exclusively to its keen sense of hearing, without any reasoning or drawing of consequences on the part of the fox, is unthinkable, a chimera. The same judgement should apply to all the ingenious ruses by which beasts protect themselves from our schemes against them.

Should we pride ourself on our ability to capture them and make them work for us? But that is no more than the advantage we have over each other: our slaves are in the same condition. [B] Were not the *Climacides* Syrian slave-women who went down on all fours to serve as steps or ladders for the ladies to climb up into their coaches? [A] Even the majority of free men and women, for very slight advantages, place themselves in the power of others. [C] Thracian wives and concubines beg to be selected for slaughter over the dead husband's tomb. [A] Have tyrants ever failed to find men sworn and devoted to them – even though some require them to follow them in death as in life? [B] Whole armies have been bound to their captains that way.

The form of oath used in that rough school which trained gladiators to fight to the finish included the vows: 'We swear to let ourselves be fettered, burned, beaten or killed by the sword, suffering all that true gladiators suffer at the hands of their Master'; they most scrupulously bound themselves, body and soul, to his service:

> *Ure meum, si vis, flamma caput, et pete ferro*
> *Corpus, et intorto verbere terga seca.*

[Burn my head, if you will, with fire, plunge your iron sword through my body or lash my back with your twisted thongs.]

It was a real, binding undertaking. And yet, one year, ten thousand men were found to enter that school and perish there.

[C] When the Scythians buried their king, over his body they strangled his favourite concubine, his cup-bearer, his ostler, his chamberlain, the guard to his bedchamber and his cook. And on the anniversary of his death they would take fifty pages mounted on fifty horses and kill them, impaling them from behind, from spine to throat, and leaving them dead on parade about his tomb.[70]

[A]   The men who serve us do so more cheaply than our falcons, our horses or our hounds; and they are less carefully looked after –   [C]   what menial tasks will we not bow to for the convenience of those animals! The most abject slaves, it seems to me, will not willingly do for their masters what princes are proud to do for such creatures. When Diogenes saw his parents striving to purchase his freedom he exclaimed: 'They must be fools: my Master looks after me and feeds me; he is my servant!'[71] So too those who keep animals can be said to serve them, not be served by them.

[A]   There is as well a nobility in animals such that, from want of courage, no lion has ever been enslaved to another lion; no horse to another horse. We go out to hunt animals: lions and tigers go out to hunt men; each beast practises a similar sport against another: hounds against hares; pike against tenches; swallows against grasshoppers; sparhawks against blackbirds and skylarks:

> [B]   *serpente ciconia pullos*
> *Nutrit, et inventa per devia rura lacerta,*
> *Et leporem aut capream famulae Jovis, et generosae*
> *In saltu venantur aves.*

[The stork feeds her young on snakes and on lizards found in trackless country places; eagles, those noble birds, servants of Jupiter, hunt hares and roes in the forests.][72]

We share the fruits of the chase with our hounds and our hawks, as well as its skill and hardships. In Thrace, above Amphipolis, huntsmen and wild falcons each share a half of the booty, very exactly, just as the fisherman by the marshes of the Sea of Azov sets aside, in good faith, half of his catch for the wolves: if not, they go and tear his nets.

[A]   We have a kind of hunting conducted more with cunning than with force, as when we use gin-traps, hooks and lines. Similar things are found among beasts. Aristotle relates that the cuttle-fish casts a line of gut from its neck, pays it out and lets it float. When it wants to, it draws it in. It spots some little fish approaching, remains hiding in the sand or mud and allows

70. Plutarch, *Quels animaux?*, 513 G; *Comment on pourra discerner le flatteur d'avec l'ami*, 41A; Herodotus, IV, 71–72; Petronius, *Satyricon*, and Tibullus, I, ix, 21, cited by Justus Lipsius, *Saturnalia*, II, 5.

71. Diogenes Laertius, *Lives*, Diogenes. The following pages are largely based on Plutarch, *Quels animaux?* and *Que les brutes usent de la raison*, with additions from Pliny, X, 43, and Plutarch's *Life of Sylla*, etc. Cf. n. 94, below.

72. Juvenal, *Satires*, XIV, 74; 81.

it to nibble at the end of the gut and gradually draws it in until that little fish is so close it can pounce on it.

As for force, no animal in the world is liable to so many shocks as Man. No need for a whale, an elephant, a crocodile or animals like that, any one of which can destroy a great number of men. Lice were enough to make Sylla's dictatorship vacant; and the heart and life-blood of a great and victorious Emperor serve as breakfast for some tiny worm.

Why do we say, in the case of Man, that distinguishing plants which are useful for life or for medicines from those which are not (recognizing, say, the virtues of rhubarb or polypody) is a sign that he has scientific knowledge based on skill and reason? Yet the goats of Candia can be seen picking out dittany from a million other plants when they are wounded by spears; if a tortoise swallows a viper it at once goes in search of origanum as a purge; the dragon wipes its eyes clear and bright with fennel; storks give themselves salt-water enemas; elephants can remove darts and javelins thrown in battle from their own bodies, from those of their fellows and even from those of their masters (witness the elephant of that King Porus who was killed by Alexander); they do so with more skill than we ever could while causing so little pain. Why do we not call it knowledge and discretion in their case? To lower them in esteem we allege that Nature alone is their Schoolmaster; but that is not to deprive them of knowledge or wisdom: it is to attribute them to them more surely than to ourselves, out of respect for so certain a Teacher.

In all other cases Chrysippus was as scornful a judge of the properties of animals as any philosopher there ever was, yet he watched the actions of a dog which came upon three crossroads – it was either looking for its master or chasing some game fleeing before it; it tried first one road then a second; then, having made sure that neither of them bore any trace of what it was looking for, it charged down the third road without hesitation. Chrysippus was forced to admit that that dog at least reasoned this way: 'I have tracked my master as far as these crossroads; he must have gone down one of these three paths; not this one; not that one; so, inevitably, he must have gone down this other one.' Convinced by this reasoned conclusion, it did not sniff at the third path; it made no further investigations but let itself be swayed by the power of reason. Here was pure dialectic: the dog made use of disjunctive and copulative propositions and adequately enumerated the parts. Does it matter whether he learned all this from himself or from the *Dialectica* of George of Trebizond?

Yet beasts, like us, are not incapable of instruction. Blackbirds, ravens, magpies and parrots can be taught to speak:[73] we recognize in them a capacity

73. Persius, *Choliambics*, which often appear as a preface or postscript to the *Satires*.

for making their voice and their breath subtle and pliant enough for us to mould and restrict them to a definite number of letters and syllables. That capacity witnesses to an inward power of reasoning which makes them teachable – and willing to learn. We have all had our fill I expect of the sort of monkey-tricks which minstrels teach their dogs to do: those dances in which they never miss a note they hear or those varied jumps and movements which they perform on command. But I am much more moved to wonder by the action of the guide-dogs used by the blind in town and country, common enough as they are. I have watched those dogs stop at certain doors where people regularly give alms, and seen how, even when there is room enough to squeeze through themselves, they still avoid encounters with carts and coaches; I have seen one, following the town trench but abandoning a level, even path for a worse one, in order to keep its master away from the ditch. How was that dog brought to realize that it was its duty to neglect its own interests and to serve its master? How does it know that a path might be wide enough for itself but not wide enough for a blind man? Could all that be grasped without thought and reasoning?

I should not overlook what Plutarch tells us about a dog he saw with the elder Vespasian, the Emperor, in the theatre of Marcellus in Rome. This dog served a juggler who was putting on a play with several scenes and several parts. The dog had his own part: it had to pretend, among other things, to swallow some poison and to lie dead for a while. First it swallowed the supposedly poisoned bread; then it began to shake and tremble as though it were dizzy; finally, it lay down and stiffened as though it were dead. It let itself be pulled about and dragged from one place to another, as the plot required. Then, when it knew the time was right, it began to stir very gently, as though awakening from a deep sleep and raised its head, looking from side to side in a way which made the audience thunderstruck.

Oxen were used to water the Royal Gardens of Susa: they had to draw up the water by turning large wheels with buckets attached – you can see plenty of them in Languedoc. Each one had been ordered to do one hundred turns of the wheel a day. They grew so used to this number that nothing would force them to do one more; when their alloted task had been done they stopped dead. Yet we have reached adolescence before we can count up to a hundred; and we have just discovered peoples with no knowledge of numbers at all.

You need still greater powers of reason to teach others than to be taught yourself. Democritus thought, and proved, that we had been taught most of our arts by animals: the spider taught us to weave and to sew and the swallow to build; the swan and nightingale taught us music and many other animals taught us by imitation the practice of medicine. Moreover, Aristotle maintains that nightingales teach their young to sing, spending time and trouble doing so: that explains why the song of nightingales brought up in cages, with no freedom to be schooled by their parents, loses much of its charm. [B] From that we may conclude that any improvement is due to learning and study.

Even nightingales born free do not all sing one and the same song: each one sings according to its capacity to learn. They make jealous classmates, squabbling and vying with each other so heartily that the vanquished sometimes drops down dead, not from lack of song but lack of breath. The youngest birds ruminate thoughtfully and then begin to imitate snatches of song; the pupils listen to the lessons of their tutors and then give an account of themselves, taking it in turns to stop their singing. You can hear their faults being corrected; some of the criticisms of their tutors are perceptible even to us.

Arrius[74] said that he once saw an elephant with cymbals hanging from each thigh and a third on its trunk; the other elephants danced round in a ring, rising and falling to the cadences of this musical instrument, which was harmonious and pleasant to listen to.    [A]   In the great spectacles of Rome it was quite usual to see elephants trained to execute dance steps to the sound of the human voice; such performances comported several intricate movements, interlacings, changes of step and cadenzas, all very hard to learn. Some were seen revising their lessons in private, practising and studying so as to avoid being beaten or scolded by their masters.

But strange indeed is the account of a female magpie vouched for by Plutarch, no less. It lived in a barber's shop in Rome and was wonderfully clever at imitating any sounds it heard. It happened one day that some musicians stopped quite a while in front of the shop, blasting away on their trumpets. Immediately the magpie fell pensive, mute and melancholic, remaining so all the following day. Everyone marvelled, thinking that the blare of the trumpets had frightened and confused it, making it lose both hearing and song at the same time. But they eventually found that it had been deeply meditating and had withdrawn into itself; it had been inwardly practising, preparing its voice to imitate the noise of those trumpeters. The first sound it did make was a perfect imitation of their changes, repetitions and stops; after this new apprenticeship it quit with disdain all that it was able to do before.

74. Or rather, Flavius Arrianus, tr. Vuitart, *Les faicts d'Alexandre*, 1581, XIV.

I do not want to leave out another example of a dog, also seen by Plutarch. (I realize I am digressing, showing no sense of order, but I can no more observe order when arranging these examples than I can in the rest of my work.) Plutarch was on board ship when he saw a dog which wanted to lap up some oil in the bottom of a jar; it could not get its tongue right down into the vessel because the neck was too narrow, so it went in search of pebbles which it dropped into the jar until the oil rose near to the top where it could get at it. What is that if not the actions of a very subtle intelligence? It is said that Barbary ravens do the same when the water they want to drink is too low to get at.

The above action is somewhat akin to what is related by Juba (a king in elephant country): hunters cunningly prepare deep pits hidden beneath a cover of undergrowth; when an elephant is trapped in one, its fellows promptly bring a great many sticks and stones to help it clamber out.

But so many of their actions bring elephants close to human capacities that if I wanted to relate in detail everything that experience has shown us about them, I would easily win one of my regular arguments: that there is a greater difference between one man and another than between some men and some beasts.

An elephant-driver in a private household in Syria used to steal half the allotted rations at every feed. One day the master himself wanted to attend to things; he tipped into the elephant's manger the right measure of barley, as prescribed. The elephant glared at its driver and, with its trunk, set half the ration aside, to reveal the wrong done to it. Another elephant, whose driver used to adulterate its feed with stones, went up to the pot where he was stewing meat for his own dinner and filled it with ashes. Those are special cases, but we all know from eyewitnesses that the strongest elements in the armies based in the Levant were elephants; their effectiveness surpassed what we can obtain nowadays from our artillery, which more or less replaces elephants in line of battle (as can be easily judged by those who know their ancient history).

[B]  *siquidem Tirio servire solebant*
*Annibali, et nostris ducibus, regique Molosso,*
*Horum majores, et dorso ferre cohortes,*
*Partem aliquam belli et euntem in praelia turmam.*

[Their sires served Hannibal of Carthage, as well as our generals and the Molossian King, bearing on their backs into the fray cohorts and squadrons, and taking part in the battle themselves.][75]

75. Juvenal, XII, 107.

[A]  To make over to them like this the vanguard of their army soldiers must
have seriously relied on the trustworthiness of these beasts and on their
powers of reason; because of their size and bulk the slightest stoppage on
their part or else the slightest panic making them head back towards their
own side would be enough to undo everything. There are fewer examples of
their turning and charging their own troops than of us men charging back on
each other in rout. They were entrusted not with one simple manoeuvre but
with several different roles in combat.

[B]  The Spaniards, likewise, employed dogs in their recent conquest of
the American Indies; they paid them like soldiers and gave them a share in
the booty. Those animals displayed eagerness and fierceness but no less skill
and judgement, whether in pursuing victory or in knowing when to stop, in
charging or withdrawing as appropriate, and in telling friend from foe.[76]

[A]  Much more than everyday things, far-off things move us to wonder;
they impress us more; otherwise I would not have spent so much time over
this long catalogue; for, in my opinion, anyone who took careful note of the
everyday animals we see living among us would find them doing things
just as astonishing as the examples we gather from far-off times and
places.[77]  [C]  Nature is One and constant in her course. Anybody who
could adequately understand her present state could draw reliable conclusions about all the future and all the past.

[A]  I once saw men brought to us from distant lands overseas. We could
understand nothing of their language; their manners and even their features
and clothing were far different from ours. Which of us did not take them for
brutes and savages? Which of us did not attribute their silence to dullness
and brutish ignorance? After all, they knew no French, were unaware of our
hand-kissings and our low and complex bows, our bearing and our behaviour
– such things must, of course, serve as a pattern for the whole human race . . .

Everything which seems strange we condemn, as well as everything we do
not understand; that applies to our judgements on animals. Many of their
characteristics are related to ours; that enables us to draw conjectures from
comparisons. But they also have qualities peculiar to themselves: what can
we know about that? Horses, dogs, cattle, sheep, birds and most other animals living among men recognize our voices and are prepared to obey them.
Why, Crassus even had a lamprey which came to him when he called it, and
there are eels in the fountain of Arethusa which do the same.  [B]  I have seen

76. Lopez de Gomara, tr. Fumée, *Hist. générale des Indes*, 1584, II, 9. Cf. G.
Bouchet, *Sérées*, I, 7.

77. '88: places. *We live, both they and ourselves, under the same roof and breathe the same
air. There is, save for more or less, a perpetual similarity between us.* I once saw . . .

stews in plenty where the fish, on hearing a particular cry from those who
tend them, all rush to be fed.

[A]   *nomen habent, et ad magistri*
      *Vocem quisque sui venit citatus.*

[They have a name and each comes to its master when he calls them.][78]

Such evidence we can judge.

We can also go on to say that elephants have some notion of religion since,
after ablutions and purifications, they can be seen waving their trunks like
arms upraised, while gazing intently at the rising sun; for long periods at
fixed times in the day (by instinct, not from teaching or precept) they stand
rooted in meditation and contemplation; there may be no obvious similarities
in other animals, but that does not allow us to make judgements about their
total lack of religion. When matters are hidden from us, we cannot in any
way conceive them.

We can partly do so in the case of an activity noticed by Cleanthes the
philosopher, because it resembles our own. He saw, he said, ants leave their
own ant-hill for another one, bearing the body of a dead ant. Several others
came out to meet them, as if to parley. They remained together for some
time; then the second group of ants went back to consult, it was thought,
their fellow citizens. They made two or three such journeys, because of hard
bargaining. In the end, the newcomers brought a worm out from their heap,
apparently as a ransom for the dead ant. The first lot loaded it on their
shoulders and carried it back, leaving the body of the dead ant with the
others.

That is the interpretation given by Cleanthes; it witnesses to the fact that
voiceless creatures are not deprived of mutual contact and communication;
if we cannot share in it, that is because of a defect in us; we would be very
stupid indeed to have any meddlesome opinions on the matter.

Animals do many actions which surpass our understanding; far from being
able to imitate them we cannot even conceive them in our thoughts. Many
hold that in that last great sea-fight which Antony lost against Augustus, the
flag-galley was stopped dead in its course by the fish which is called Remora
('Hindrance') since it has the property of hindering any ship it clings to.
When the Emperor Caligula was sailing along the coast of Romania with a
large fleet, his galley alone was pulled up short by this very fish. Attached as
it was to the bottom of his vessel, he caused it to be seized, angry that so
small a creature – it is a shellfish – could just cling by its mouth to his galley

78. Cf. vol. I, chapter 31, 'On Cannibals' (*ad fin.*); Martial, *Epigrams*, IV, xxix, 6.

and outdo the combined might of the sea, the winds and all his oarsmen.
Understandably, he was even more amazed to learn that, once it was brought
aboard ship, it no longer had the power it had had in the water.

A citizen of Cyzicum once acquired a reputation as a good mathematical
astrologer from noticing the practice of the hedgehog: its den is open in
various places to various winds; it can foretell from which direction the wind
will blow and plugs up the hole on the windward side. Observing that, he
supplied the town with reliable forecasts about the direction of the winds.

The chameleon takes on the colour of its surroundings, but the octopus
assumes whatever colour it likes to suit the occasion, hiding, say, from something fearful or lurking for its prey. The chameleon changes passively, the
octopus actively. We change hue as well, from fear, anger, shame and other
emotions which affect the colour of our faces. That happens to us, as to the
chameleon, passively. Jaundice, not our will, has the power to turn us yellow.

Such characteristics in other animals which we realize to surpass our own
show that they have, to an outstanding degree, a faculty which we classify as
'occult'. Similarly, animals probably have many other characteristics and
powers   [C]   which are in no way apparent to us.

[A]   Of all the omens of former times, the most ancient and the most
certain were those drawn from the flight of birds. We have nothing corresponding to that, nothing as wonderful. The beatings of the birds' wings,
from which consequences were drawn about the future, show rule and order:
only some very special means could produce so noble an activity: to attribute
so great an effect entirely to some ordinance of Nature, without any understanding, agreement and thought on the part of the creatures which perform
it, is to be taken in by words; such an opinion is evidently false. Here is proof
of that: the torpedo is a fish with the property of benumbing the limbs of
anyone who directly touches it; in addition it can even send a numbing torpor
into the hands of anyone touching it or handling it indirectly through a net
or something similar. They even say that, if you pour water on to it, you can
feel this effect working upwards, numbing your sense of touch through the
water. This force is worth marvelling at, but is not without its usefulness to
the torpedo; that fish knows it has it and uses it to trap its prey when hunting;
it snuggles down into the mud: other fish gliding overhead, struck by its cold
torpor, are benumbed and fall into its power.

Cranes, swallows and other birds of passage which change dwellings with
the seasons, clearly show that they are aware of their ability to foretell and
put it to good use.

Hunters assure us that the way to choose from a litter the puppy which
will turn out best is simply to make the bitch choose it herself: take the

puppies out of their kennel and the first one she brings back will always prove
the best; or else make a show of putting a ring of fire around their kennel;
then take the first puppy she dashes in to rescue. From that it is obvious
that either bitches have powers of foresight which we lack or else that
they have a capacity for judging their young which is more lively than our
own.[79]

Beasts are born, reproduce, feed, move, live and die in ways so closely
related to our own that, if we seek to lower their motivations or to raise our
own status above theirs, that cannot arise from any reasoned argument on
our part. Doctors recommend us to live and behave as animals do – and
ordinary people have ever said:

> *Tenez chauts les pieds et la teste;*
> *Au demeurant, vivez en beste.*

> [Keep feet and head warm:
> Then live like the beasts.]

Sexual generation is the principal natural action. Our human members are
rather more conveniently arranged for that purpose; and yet we are told that
if we want to be really effective we should adopt the position and posture of
the animals:

> *more ferarum*
> *Quadrupedumque magis ritu, plerumque putantur*
> *Concipere uxores; quia sic loca sumere possunt,*
> *Pectoribus positis, sublatis semina lumbis.*

[Most think that wives conceive more readily in the posture of wild animals and four-
footed beasts; that is because the semen can find its way better when the breasts are
low down and the loins up-raised.]

[A1] All those immodest and shameless movements that women have
invented out of their own heads are condemned as positively harmful; women
are advised to return to the more modest and poised comportment of animals
of their sex.

> *Nam mulier prohibet se concipere atque repugnat,*
> *Clunibus ipsa viri Venerem si laeta retractet,*
> *Atque exossato ciet omni pectore fluctus.*
> *Ejicit enim sulci recta regione viaque*
> *Vomerem, atque locis avertit seminis ictum.*

79. '88: own, *for in our own children it is certain that until they are nearly grown up, we
can find nothing to go on but their physical form.*

[For the woman hinders or averts conception when passion leads her to withdraw Venus and her buttocks from the man, diverting the flow entirely over her yielding belly; she makes the plough-share leap out of its furrow and broadcasts the seed where it does not belong.][80]

[A] If justice consists in rendering everyone his due, then animals who serve, love and protect those that treat them well and who attack strangers and those that do them harm show some resemblance to aspects of our own justice; as they also do by maintaining strict fair-shares for their young.

As for loving affection, theirs is incomparably more lively and consistent than men's. King Lisimachus had a dog called Hircanus. When its master died it remained stubbornly by his bed, refusing to eat or drink; when the day came to cremate the body, it ran dashing into the fire and was burned to death. The dog of a man called Pyrrhus did the same: from the moment he died it would not budge off its master's bed, and when they bore the body away, it let itself be carried off too, finally throwing itself into the pyre as they were burning its master's corpse.

There are also inclinations where our affection arises not from reasoned counsel but by that random chance sometimes called *sympathy*. Animals are capable of it too. We can see horses grown so attracted to each other that we can hardly get them to live or travel apart. We can see them attracted to a particular kind of coat among their fellow horses, as we are to particular faces; whenever they come across it they straightway approach it with pleasure and display their affection, whereas they dislike or hate a different kind of coat.

Animals, like us, have a choice of partners and select their females. Nor are they free from our jealousies and great irreconcilable hatreds.

Desires are either natural and necessary, like eating and drinking; natural and not necessary, such as mating with a female; or else neither natural nor necessary, like virtually all human ones, which are entirely superfluous and artificial. Nature needs wonderfully little to be satisfied and leaves little indeed for us to desire. The activities of our kitchens are not Nature's ordinance. Stoics say that a man could feed himself on one olive a day. The choiceness of our wines owes nothing to Nature's teachings, any more than do the refinements we load on to our sexual appetites:

80. Lucretius, IV, 1261 f.; 1266 f. (cited with approval by Tiraquellus, *De Legibus Connubialibus*, who is similarly disapproving of women's provocatory movements: see his Law XV, *in toto*).

*neque illa*
*Magno prognatum deposcit consule cunnum.*

[That does not demand a cunt descended from some great consul.][81]

False opinions and ignorance of the good have poured so many strange desires into us that they have chased away almost all the natural ones, no more nor less than if a multitude of strangers in a city drove out all the citizens who were born there, snuffed out their ancient power and authority, seized the town and entirely usurped it.

Animals obey the rules of Nature better than we do and remain more moderately within her prescribed limits – though not so punctiliously as to be without something akin to our debaucheries. Just as there have been mad desires driving humans to fall in love with beasts, so beasts have fallen in love with us, admitting monstrous passions across species: witness the elephant who was the rival of Aristophanes the Grammarian for the affection of a young Alexandrian flower-girl and which was every bit as dutiful in its passion as he was: when walking through the fruit market it took fruit in its trunk and brought it to her. It never took its eyes off her except when it had to and sometimes slipped its trunk into her bosom through her neckband and stroked her breasts. We are also told of a dragon who fell in love with a maiden; of a goose enamoured of a boy in the town of Asopus, and of a ram who sighed for Glaucia the minstrel-girl – and baboons falling madly in love with women are an everyday occurrence. You can also see some male animals falling for males of their own kind.

Oppianus[82] and others relate some examples to show that beasts in their couplings respect the laws of kinship, but experience frequently shows us the contrary:

*nec habetur turpe juvencae*
*Ferre patrem tergo; fit equo sua filia conjux;*
*Quasque creavit init pecudes caper; ipsaque cujus*
*Semine concepta est, ex illo concipit ales.*

[The heifer feels no shame if covered by the sire nor does the mare; the billy-goat goes on to the nanny-goats he has fathered, and birds conceive from the semen that begot them.][83]

Has there ever been a more express case of subtle malice than that of the

81. Horace, *Satire* I, 2, 69.
82. Oppianus was translated into Latin by both Adrian Turnebus and Jean Bodin, scholars admired by Montaigne.
83. Ovid, *Metam.*, X, 325.

mule of Thales the philosopher? Laden with salt, it chanced to stumble when fording a river, so wetting the sacks; noticing that the salt dissolved and lightened its load, it never failed, whenever it could, to plunge fully loaded into a stream. Eventually its master discovered its trick and ordered it to be laden with wool. Finding its expectations deceived, it gave up that trick.

Some animals so naturally mirror the face of human avarice that you can see them stealing anything they can and hiding it carefully, even though they never have any use for it.

As for household management beasts surpass us in the foresight necessary to gather and store for the future, and also possess many of the kinds of knowledge required to do so. When ants notice their grain or seeds going mouldy and smelling badly, they stop them from spoiling or going rotten by spreading them on the ground outside their storehouses, airing, drying and freshening them up. But the measures and precautions they take to gnaw out their grains of corn surpass any imaginable human foresight. Corn does not always stay dry and wholesome but gets soft, flabby and milky, as a step towards germinating and sprouting anew; to stop it turning to seed-corn and losing its nature and properties as grain in store for future use, ants gnaw off the end which does the sprouting.

As for war – the most grandiose and glorious of human activities – I would like to know whether we want to use it to prove our superiority or, on the contrary, to prove our weakness and imperfection. We know how to defeat and kill each other, to undermine and destroy our own species: not much there, it seems, to make them want to learn from us.

> [B]   *quando leoni*
> *Fortior eripuit vitam Leo? quo nemore unquam*
> *Expiravit aper majoris dentibus apri?*

[When has a stronger lion ever torn life from a weaker lion? In what woodlands has a wild boar ever died at the teeth of a stronger?][84]

[A]   They are not universally free from this, though – witness the furious encounter of bees and the enterprises of their monarchs in the opposing armies:

> *saepe duobus*
> *Regibus incessit magno discordia motu,*
> *Continuoque animos vulgi et trepidantia bello*
> *Corda licet longe praesciscere.*

84. Juvenal, *Satires*, XV, 160.

[Often there arises great strife between two King bees; great movements are afoot; you may imagine the passion and the warlike frenzy which animates the populace.][85]

I can never read that inspired account without thinking that I am reading a description of human vanity and ineptitude.

The deeds of those warriors which ravish us with their horror and their terror; those tempestuous sounds and cries:

> [B]   *Fulgur ibi ad coelum se tollit, totaque circum*
> *Aere renidescit tellus, subterque virum vi*
> *Excitur pedibus sonitus, clamoreque montes*
> *Icti rejectant voces ad sidera mundi;*

[There, armour glitters up to heaven and all the surrounding fields shimmer with bronze; the earth shakes beneath the soldiers' tread; the mountains re-echo to the stars above, the clamour striking against them;][86]

[A]   that dread array of thousands upon thousands of soldiers bearing arms; such bravery, ardour, courage: be pleased to consider the pretexts, many and vain, which set them in motion and the pretexts, many and frivolous, which make them cease.

> *Paridis propter narratur amorem*
> *Graecia Barbariae diro collisa duello.*

[They narrate how Greece, for the love of Paris, made fatal war against the Barbarians.][87]

It was because of the lechery of Paris that all Asia was ruined and destroyed: one man's desires, the annoyance and pleasure of one man, one single family quarrel – causes which ought not to suffice to set two fishwives clawing at each other's throats – were the soul, the motive-force, of that great discord.

Do we want to trust the word of those who were the main authors and prime movers of wars like these? Then let us listen to Augustus, the greatest, most victorious and most powerful Emperor there ever has been, sporting and jesting (most amusingly and wittily) about several battles risked on land and sea, the life and limb of the five hundred thousand men who followed his star, and the might and treasure of both parts of the Roman world, exhausted in the service of his adventures:

> *Quod futuit Glaphyran Antonius, hanc mihi poenam*
> *Fulvia constituit, se quoque uti futuam.*

85. Virgil, *Georgics*, IV, 67. For the Ancients, Queen bees were Kings.
86. Lucretius, II, 325 (Lambin, p. 127).
87. Horace, *Epistle* I, 2, 6.

*Fulviam ego ut futuam? Quid, si me Manius oret*
*Paedicem, faciam? Non puto, si sapiam.*
*Aut futue, aut pugnemus, ait. Quid, si mihi vita*
*Charior est ipsa mentula? Signa canant!*

[Because Antony fucked Glaphyra, Fulvia decided I had to fuck her – as revenge. Me, fuck Fulvia! Supposing Manius begged me to bugger him? Not if I can help it! 'Fuck or we fight,' she said. What if my cock is dearer than life to me? . . . Sound the war trumpets!]

(I quote my Latin with freedom of conscience! You, my Patroness, have given me leave.)[88]

Now this mighty Body, War, with so many facets and movements, which seems to threaten both earth and heaven –

[B]   *Quam multi Lybico volvuntur marmore fluctus,*
*Saevus ubi Orion hybernis conditur undis,*
*Vel cum sole novo densae torrentur aristae,*
*Aut Hermi campo, aut Lyciae flaventibus arvis,*
*Scuta sonant, pulsuque pedum tremit excita tellus.*

[As the waves innumerable which roll in the Libyan sea, when fierce Orion plunges into the billows as winter returns; or, as when the summer sun bakes the thick shooting corn on the plains of Hermus or the golden fields of Lycia: so clash the shields, and the stricken land trembles beneath their feet] –

[A]   this mad Monster with all its many arms and legs, is only Man: weak, miserable, wretched Man. An ant-hill disturbed and hot with rage!

*It nigrum campis agmen.*

[The black battalion advances in the plain.][89]

A contrary wind, the croak of a flight of ravens, a stumbling horse, an eagle chancing by, a dream, a word, a sign, a morning mist, all suffice to cast him down and bring him to the ground. Let a ray of sunlight dazzle him in the face, and there he lies, limp and faint. Let a speck of dust blow into his eyes (as our poet Virgil writes of the bees), and all our ensigns, all our legions, even with Pompey the Great himself at the head of them, are broken and shattered . . . (I believe it was Pompey who was defeated by Sertorius in

88. Verses attributed to Augustus, in Martial, *Epigrams*, XI, 20. The patroness may be Margaret of France, the future wife of Henry of Navarre.
89. Virgil, *Aeneid*, VII, 718 f., IV, 404; here cited with Seneca in mind (Preface to *Quaestiones Naturales*).

Spain with such fine arms as these,   [B]   which also served a turn for others
– for Eumenes against Antigonus, and for Surena against Crassus:

[A]   *Hi motus animorum atque haec certamina tanta*
      *Pulveris exigui jactu compressa quiescent.*

[These passionate commotions and these great battles are calmed down with a handful
of dust.][90]

[C]   Send out a detachment made up of a couple of bees: they will be strong
and brave enough to topple the Monster of war. We still recall how the
Portuguese were investing the town of Tamly in their territory of Xiatime
when the inhabitants, who had hives in plenty, carried a great many of them
to their walls and smoked the bees out so vigorously that their enemies were
unable to sustain their stinging attacks and were all put to rout. They owed
the freedom of their town and their victory to such novel reinforcements –
and with so happy an outcome that not one bee was reported missing.[91]

[A]   The souls of Emperors and of cobblers are cast in the same mould.
We consider the importance of the actions of Princes and their weight and
then persuade ourselves that they are produced by causes equally weighty,
equally important. In that we deceive ourselves. They are tossed to and fro
by the same principles as we are. The reasons that make us take issue with a
neighbour lead Princes to start a war; the same reason which makes us flog
a lackey makes kings lay waste a province.   [B]   They can do more but
can wish as lightly.   [A1]   The same desires trouble a fleshworm and an
elephant.

[A]   As for faithfulness, there is no animal in the world whose treachery
can compete with Man's. Our history books tell of certain dogs which vigorously reacted to the murders of their masters. King Pyrrhus once came across
a dog guarding the body of its dead master; when he was told the dog had
done this duty for three days, he ordered the corpse to be buried and took
the dog away with him. Later, when he was making a general review of his
troops the dog recognized the murderers of its master and ran at them barking
loudly and angrily. This was the first piece of evidence leading to its master's
murder being avenged; justice was soon done in the courts. The dog of Hesiod
the Wise did the same, leading to the sons of Ganistor (a man from Naupactus)
being convicted of the murder of its master.

Another dog was guarding a temple in Athens when it spotted a thief
sacrilegiously making off with the finest jewels. It began barking at him as

90. Plutarch, *Lives*, Sertorius (but it was not Pompey); Virgil, *Georgics*, IV, 86.
91. S. Goulard, *Histoire du Portugal*, 1581 (1587), VIII, 19, 244v°.

loud as it could, but the temple sextons never woke up; so the dog started to trail the thief and, when day broke, hung behind a little without losing him from sight. When the thief offered it food, it refused to take anything from him, whilst accepting it from others who passed by, treating them all to a good wagging of its tail. When the thief stopped to sleep, so did the dog, in the same place. News of this dog reached the sextons of that church; they set out to find it; by making enquiries about the colour of its coat, they eventually caught up with it at Cromyon. The thief was there too; they brought him back to Athens, where he was punished. In recognition of its good sense of duty, the judges awarded the dog a fixed measure of wheat out of public funds to pay for its keep and ordered the priests to look after it. This happened in Plutarch's own time and he himself asserts that the account was very thoroughly vouched for.

As for gratitude – and it seems to me that we could well bring this word back into repute – one example will suffice. Apion relates it as something he had seen himself. He tells how, one day, the people of Rome were given the pleasure of watching several strange animals fight – mainly, in fact, unusually big lions; one of these drew the eyes of the entire audience by its wild bearing, the strength and size of its limbs and its proud and terrifying roar. Amongst the slaves presented to the populace to fight with these beasts was Androdus, a slave from Dacia, belonging to a Roman lord of consular rank. This lion, seeing him from afar, first pulled up short, as though struck with wonder; it then came gently towards him; its manner was soft and peaceful, as if it expected to recognize an acquaintance. Then, having made certain of what it was looking for, it began to wag its tail as dogs do when fondly greeting their masters; it kissed and licked the hands and thighs of that poor wretch, who was beside himself, ecstatic with fear. The gracious behaviour of the lion brought Androdus back to himself so that he fixed his gaze on it, staring at it and then recognizing it. It was a rare pleasure to see the happy greetings and blandishments they lavished on each other. The populace raised shouts of joy; the Emperor sent for the slave to learn how this strange event had come about. He gave him an account, novel and wonderful: 'My Master', he said, 'was a proconsul in Africa; he treated me so cruelly and so harshly, flogging me every day, that I was forced to steal myself from him and run away. I found the quickest way to hide myself safely from a person having such great Provincial authority was to make for that country's uninhabited sandy deserts, fully resolved, if there was no means of keeping myself in food, to kill myself. The midday sun was so fierce and the heat so intolerable that when I stumbled on a hidden cave, difficult of access, I plunged into it. Soon afterwards this lion came in, its paw all wounded and bloody; it was groaning and whining with pain. I was very frightened when it arrived but, when it saw me hiding in a corner of its lair, it came gently up to me and showed me its wounded paw, as though asking for help. I removed a great splinter of wood; when I had made it a little more used to me, I squeezed out the filthy pus that had collected in the wound, wiped it and made it as clean as I could. The lion, aware that things were better and that the pain had been relieved, began to rest, falling asleep with its paw in my hands. After that we lived together in that cave for three whole years; we ate the same food since the lion brought me choice morsels of the animals it had killed in the hunt; I had no fire but I fed myself by cooking the meat in the heat of the sun. In the end I grew disgusted with this savage, brutish life and so, when the lion had gone out one day on its usual quest for food, I slipped away. Three days later I was surprised by soldiers who brought me from Africa to Rome and handed me over to my master. He promptly condemned me to die by being exposed to the beasts in the arena. I realize now that the lion was also captured soon afterwards and that it wanted to repay me for my kindness in curing its wound.'

That is the account which Androdus told to the Emperor and which he also spread from mouth to mouth. Androdus was given his freedom by general acclaim and relieved of his sentence; by order of the people he was made a gift of the lion.

Ever since, says Apion, we can see Androdus leading the lion about on a short leash, going from tavern to tavern in Rome collecting money, while the lion lets itself be strewn with flowers. All who meet them say: 'There goes the Lion, host to the Man: there goes the Man, doctor to the Lion.'[92]

[B] We often shed tears at the loss of animals which we love: they do the same when they lose us:

> *Post, bellator equus, positis insignibus, Aethon*
> *It lachrymans, guttisque humectat grandibus ora.*

[Then comes Aethon, the war-horse, stripped of its insignia, weeping and drenching its face in mighty tears.][93]

Some peoples hold their wives in common while in others each man has a wife of his own; can we not see the same among the beasts? Do they not have marriages better kept than our own?

92. Aulus Gellius, *Attic Nights*, V, 15, etc. This tale of 'Androdus' and the lion is related in Ravisius Textor's *Officina*, which is a probable source of some of Montaigne's animal lore throughout the *Apology*.

93. Virgil, *Aeneid*, XI, 89.

[A]   As touching the confederations and alliances which animals make to
league themselves together for mutual succour, oxen, pigs and other animals
can be seen rushing in to help when one of their number is being attacked
and rallying round in its defence. If a scar-fish swallows a fisherman's hook,
its fellows swarm around and bite through the line; if one of them happens
to get caught in a wicker trap, the others dangle their tails down into it from
outside while it holds on grimly with its teeth. In this way they drag it right
out. When a barbel-fish is hooked, the others stiffen the spine which projects
from their backs; it is notched like a saw; they rub it against the line and saw
it through.

As for the special duties we render to each other in the service of life, there
are several similar examples amongst the animals. The whale, it is said, never
travels without a tiny fish like a sea-gudgeon swimming ahead of it (for this
reason it is called a 'guide-fish'). The whale follows it everywhere, allowing
itself to be directed and steered as easily as a rudder turns a boat. Everything
else – beast or ship – which falls into the swirling chaos of that creature's
mouth is straightway lost and swallowed up: yet that little fish can retire there
and sleep in its mouth in complete safety. While it is asleep, the whale never
budges, but as soon as it swims out, the whale constantly follows it; if it
should chance to lose its guide-fish it flounders about all over the place, often
dashing itself to pieces against the rocks like a rudderless ship. Plutarch
testifies to having seen this happen on the island of Anticyra.

There is a similar companionship between the tiny wren and the crocodile:
the wren stands guard over that big creature; when the crocodile's enemy,
the ichneuman, closes in for a fight, this little bird is afraid that its companion
may be caught napping, so it pecks it awake and sings to warn it of danger.
The wren lives on the leftovers of that monstrous crocodile, which welcomes
it into its jaws and lets it pick at the meat stuck between its teeth. If it wants
to shut its mouth it warns the wren to fly out by gradually closing its jaws a
little, without squashing it or harming it in any way.

The shellfish called a nacre lives in similar company with the pinnothere, a
kind of small crab which serves it as tout and doorkeeper; squatting by the
orifice which the crab always keeps half-open, it waits until some little fish
worth catching swims into it. The crab then slips into the nacre, pinching its
living flesh to make it close its shell. Having imprisoned the fish they both set
about eating it.

Three parts of Mathematics are particularly well known to tunny-fish: the
way they live shows that.

First, Astrology; it is they who teach it to men: wherever they may be
when surprised by the winter solstice, there they remain until the following

equinox (which explains why even Aristotle readily allows them a knowledge of that science).

Next Geometry and Arithmetic: tunny-fish always form up in the shape of a cube, equally square on all sides. Drawing themselves up into a solid battalion, a corps enclosed and protected all round by six faces of equal size, they swim about in this order, square before, square behind – so that if you count one line of them you have the count of the whole school, since the same figure applies to their depth, breadth and length.

As for greatness of spirit, it would be hard to express it more clearly than that great dog which was sent to King Alexander from India. It was first presented with a stag, next with a boar, then with a bear: it did not deign to come out and fight them, but as soon as it saw a lion it leaped to its feet, clearly showing that it thought such an animal was indeed worthy of the privilege of fighting against it.

[B] Touching repentance and the acknowledging of error, they tell of an elephant which killed its master in a fit of anger; its grief was so intense that it refused to eat and starved itself to death.

[A] As for clemency, they tell of a tiger – the most inhuman of all beasts – which was given a goat to eat. It fasted for two days before being even tempted to harm it; by the third day, it considered the goat as a familiar guest, so, rather than attack it, it broke out of its cage and sought food elsewhere.

As for rights bred of familiarity and friendly converse, it is quite normal to train cats, dogs and hares to live tamely together.

But surpassing all human imagination is what experience has taught travellers by sea – especially those in the sea of Sicily – about the halcyons. Has Nature ever honoured any creature as she has honoured these kingfishers in their procreation, lying-in and birth? The poets feign that one single island, Delos, was a floating land before being anchored so that Latona might give birth upon it. But God himself has wished the entire sea to be settled, smooth and calm, free from wave and wind and rain, on those halcyon days when these creatures produce their young. (This befalls, precisely, about the shortest day of the year, the solstice: this privilege of theirs gives us seven days and nights at the very heart of the winter, when, without danger, we can sail the seas.) Each female knows no male but its own; it helps it all its life and never forsakes it. If the male is weak or crippled the female carries it everywhere on her back, serving it till death.

But no ingenuity has ever fathomed the miraculous artifice by which the halcyons build their nest for their young nor divined its fabric. Plutarch saw several of them and handled them. He thinks they may be composed of the

bones of certain fish, joined, bound and interwoven together, some length-
wise, some crosswise; bent and rounded struts are then added, eventually
forming a coracle ready to float upon the water. The female halcyon then
brings them where they can be lapped around by the waves of the sea. The salt
water gently beats upon them, showing her where ill-fitting joints need
daubing and where she needs to strengthen the sections where her construction is coming loose or pulling apart at the beating of the sea. On the other
hand this battering by the waves binds all the good joints up tight and knits
them so close that they can only with difficulty be smashed, broken or even
damaged by blows with stone or iron. Most wonderful of all are the shape and
proportions of the concave hold, for it is shaped and proportioned to admit
only one creature snugly: the one who made it. To everything else it is closed,
barred and impenetrable. Nothing can get in, not even sea water.

That is a fine description of this construction, taken from a fine book. Yet
even that, it seems to me, fails to enlighten us adequately about the difficulty
of such architecture. What silly vanity leads us to take products we can
neither imitate nor understand, range them beneath us and treat them with
disdain.[94]

Let us go further into such equalities and correspondences between us and
the beasts. The human soul takes pride in its privilege of bringing all its
conceptions into harmony with its own condition: everything it conceives is
stripped of its mortal and physical qualities; it compels everything which it
judges worthy of notice to divest itself completely of such of its own conditions as are corruptible – of all physical accidents such as depth, length,
breadth, weight, colour, smell, roughness, smoothness, hardness, softness; it
casts them aside like old garments; it clothes everything in its own condition,
spiritual and immortal: the Rome or the Paris which exists in my soul – the
Paris imagined in thought – is conceived in my imagination without size,
without place, without stone, without plaster, without wood. Well, that selfsame privilege seems evidently shared with the beasts; for, asleep on its litter,
a war-horse accustomed to trumpet, harquebus and combat can be seen
twitching and trembling as though in the thick of battle: clearly its mind
is conceiving a drum without drum-beats, an army without arms, without
physical body.

> *Quippe videbis equos fortes, cum membra jacebunt*
> *In somnis, sudare tamen, spirareque saepe,*
> *Et quasi de palma summas contendere vires.*

94. The long series of borrowings from Plutarch on animals ends here (cf. n. 71,
above). The paragraphs which follow are indebted to Sebond, chapters 217 and 293.

[You can, indeed, see vigorous racehorses, resting their limbs in sleep, yet often sweating and panting as though disputing the prize with all their might.]

The greyhound imagines a hare in a dream: we can see it panting after it in its sleep as it stretches out its tail, twitches its thighs and exactly imitates its movements in the chase: that hare has no coat and no bones.

> Venantumque canes in molli saepe quiete
> Jactant crura tamen subito, vocesque repente
> Mittunt, et crebras reducunt naribus auras,
> Ut vestigia si teneant inventa ferarum.
> Expergefactique sequuntur inania saepe
> Cervorum simulachra, fugae quasi dedita cernant:
> Donec discussis redeant erroribus ad se.

[Often hunting dogs lying quietly asleep, suddenly paw about, bark out loud and sharply draw their breath as if they were on the track of their prey. Even after they have started out of their sleep they still pursue that empty ghost of a stag as though they could see it fleeing before them, until the error fades and they come back to themselves.]

Guard dogs can be found growling in their sleep, then yapping and finally waking with a start as though they saw some stranger coming: that stranger which their souls can see is a spiritual man, not perceptible to the senses, without dimensions, without colour and without being.

> consueta domi catulorum blanda propago
> Degere, saepe levem ex oculis volucremque soporem
> Discutere, et corpus de terra corripere instant,
> Proinde quasi ignotas facies atque ora tueantur.

[The dog, that fawning creature at home in our houses, often quivers its eyelids in winged sleep and starts to its feet as if it saw the faces and features of strangers.]⁹⁵

As for physical beauty, before I can go any further I need to know if we can agree over its description. It seems we have little knowledge of natural beauty or of beauty in general, since we humans give so many diverse forms to our own beauty;  [C]  if it had been prescribed by Nature, we would all hold common views about it, just as we all agree that fire is hot. We give human beauty any form we fancy:

[B]   Turpis Romano Belgicus ore color.

[On the face of a Roman a Belgian's colour is ugly.]⁹⁶

95. Lucretius, IV, 988 f., 992 f., 999 f. (Lambin, p. 345).
96. Propertius, II, 18, 26.

[A]  For a painter in the Indies beauty is black and sunburnt, with thick swollen lips and broad flat noses;   [B]  there, they load the cartilege between the nostrils with great rings of gold, so that it hangs right down to the lips; the lower lip is similarly weighed down to the chin with great hoops studded with precious jewels; for them it is elegant to lay their teeth bare  [C]  exposing the gum below their roots.    [B]  In Peru, big ears are beautiful: they stretch them as far as they can, artificially.   [C]  A man still alive today says that he saw in the East a country where this custom of stretching ears and loading them with jewels is held in such esteem that he was often able to thrust his arm, clothes and all, through the holes women pierced in their lobes.    [B]  Elsewhere there are whole nations who carefully blacken their teeth and loathe seeing white ones. Elsewhere they dye them red.  [C]  Not only in the Basque country do they prefer beautiful women to have shaven heads; the same applies elsewhere – even, according to Pliny, in certain icy lands.    [B]  The women of Mexico count low foreheads as a sign of beauty: so, while they pluck hair from the rest of their body, there they encourage it to grow thick and propagate it artificially. They hold large breasts in such high esteem that they affect giving suck to their children over their shoulders.[97]

[A]  We would fashion ugliness that way.

Italians make beauty fat and heavy; Spaniards gaunt and skinny; some of us French make it fair, others dark; some soft and delicate; others strong and robust; some desire grace and delicacy; others proud bearing and majesty.    [C]  Similarly, while Plato considered the sphere to be the perfection of beauty[98] the Epicureans preferred the pyramid or the square, finding it hard to swallow a god who was shaped like a ball!

[A]  Anyway, Nature has no more given man privileges in beauty than in any other of her common laws. If we judge ourselves fairly we will find some animals less favoured than we are, others (more numerous) which are more so:   [C]  'a multis animalibus decore vincimur' [we are surpassed in beauty by many of the beasts][99] – especially among our fellow-citizens, the denizens of dry land. As for the creatures of the sea, we can leave their beauty of form aside, since it has no point of comparison with ours; we are thoroughly beaten by them in colour, brightness, sheen and the general disposition of our

97. Lopez de Gomara, II: XX, 73; LXXXIV, 170 f.; IV: III, 276; Pliny, Hist. Nat. VI, xiii; Gasparo Balbi, Viaggio dell'Indie Orientali, 1590, 76; Pliny, Hist. Nat. VI, xiii.

98. Cf. Cicero, De nat. deorum, I. x. 24.

99. Seneca, Ep. moral. 124, 22 (reading multis for mutis).

members; beaten by the birds of the air, too, in all qualities. And  [A]  then there is that privilege the poets stress – the fact that we hold ourselves erect, gazing up to heaven, from whence we came:

> Pronaque cum spectent animalia caetera terram,
> Os homini sublime dedit, coelumque videre
> Jussit, et erectos ad sydera tollere vultus.

[The other animals look downwards to the ground; God gave Man a face held high and ordered him to look towards heaven and raise his eyes towards the sun, moon and stars.][100]

That privilege is well and truly poetic! Some quite small animals gaze up to heaven all the time; camels and ostriches seem to me to have necks straighter than ours and more erect.  [C]  And which are these animals which are supposed not to have faces in front and on top, not to look straight ahead as we do nor, in their normal posture, to see as much of heaven and earth as we do? What characteristics of man's body as described by Plato and Cicero do not equally apply to a thousand other animals![101]  [A]  The animals most like us are the worst and the ugliest of the bunch: the one with an outward appearance and face closest to ours is the baboon;

> [C]  Simia quam similis, turpissima bestia, nobis!

[That vilest of beast, the monkey – how like us!][102]

[A]  the one with inwards and vital organs closest to ours is the pig.[103]

When I think of the human animal, stark naked, with all its blemishes, natural weaknesses and flaws, I find that we have more cause to cover ourselves up than any other animal. (That even applies to the female sex which seems to have a greater share of beauty.) We could be excused for having borrowed from those which Nature has favoured more than us, decking ourselves in their beauty,[104] hiding ourselves in their coats: wool, feathers, hide or silk.

100. Ovid, *Metam.*, I, 84; it was often (as by Sebond) taken very seriously (cf. J. du Bellay, *Regrets*, TLF, Sonnet 53, notes), but it does not commend itself to unaided, or unilluminated, human reason.

101. Cicero, *De nat. deorum*, II, liv, 133 ff. (A long praise of the Immortals' care in shaping Man. It is indebted to Plato's *Timaeus*.)

102. Ennius, *apud* Cicero, *ibid.*, I, xxxv, 97.

103. '88: vital, *noble organs closest to ours is, according to the doctors*, the pig . . .

104. '88: beauty. *And since Man did not have the wherewithal to present himself naked to the sight of the world, he was right to hide himself behind the coats of others*: wool, feathers, hide or silk, *and other borrowed commodities* . . .

We may note *en passant* that we are the only animals whose physical defects are offensive to our fellows; we are also the only ones to hide from others of our species when answering the calls of Nature. Also worth considering is the fact that those who know prescribe for lovesickness a good look at the totally naked body which is so much desired. To cool amorous passion, all you need to do is to be free to look at the one you love!

> *Ille quod obscoenas in aperto corpore partes*
> *Viderat, in cursu qui fuit, haesit amor.*

[It has been known for a man to see his mistress's private parts and to find his ardour pulled up short.][105]

It is true that this prescription may result from a cool and delicate humour in Man; nevertheless it is a striking sign of our weakness that it is enough for us to frequent and know each other for us to feel disgust. [B] Ladies are circumspect and keep us out of their dressing-rooms before they have put on their paint and decked themselves out for public show: that is not so much modesty as skill and foresight.

> [A1]    *Nec veneres nostras hoc fallit: quo magis ipsae*
> *Omnia summopere hos vitae post scenia celant,*
> *Quos retinere volunt adstrictoque esse in amore.*

[Fair women know this: they are all the more careful to hide the changing-rooms of their lives from those lovers they wish to hold and bind to them.][106]

[A] Yet we like all the parts of some animals, finding them so pleasing to our tastes that from their very droppings, discharges and excreta we make dainty things to eat as well as ornaments and perfumes.

Such arguments only apply to the common order of men; they are not sacrilegious enough to want to include those beauties, supernatural and beyond the common order, which can sometimes be seen shining among us like stars beneath a bodily and earthly veil.

Now even that share in Nature's favour which we do concede to the animals is much to their advantage. To ourselves we attribute goods which are purely imaginary and fantastical; future, absent goods, which it exceeds our human capacity, of itself, to vouch for; or else they are goods which our unruly opinions attribute to ourselves quite wrongly, such as knowledge, rationality or pre-eminence. We abandon to animals a share in solid, palpable goods which really do exist: peace, repose, security, innocence, health . . . Health!

105. Ovid, *Remedia amoris*, 429.
106. Lucretius, IV, 1182 (Lambin, p. 359 f.).

the fairest and finest gift that Nature can bestow. That is why even Stoic
Philosophy dares to assert that Heraclitus (who had dropsy) and Pherecydes
(who had been infected by lice) would have been right, if they could, to barter
their wisdom against a cure. By weighing and comparing wisdom against
health they make it even more splendid than in another of their assertions.
Supposing Circe (they say) had presented Ulysses with two different potions,
one to make a madman wise, the other a wise man mad: rather than allow
her to transform him from human to beast, he ought to have accepted the
one that would make him mad. Wisdom herself, they say, would have
argued like this: 'Leave me, forsake me, rather than lodge me in the
bodily shape of an ass.' What? Will philosophers forsake Wisdom, great
and divine, to cleave to the veil of this earthy body?[107] So we do not, after
all, excel over beasts by wit and our power of reason but merely by our
physical beauty, our beautiful colour, the beautiful way our members are
arranged! For things like that we must forsake our intellect, our moral
wisdom and what not!

Well, that is a frank and artless admission and I accept it. At least
philosophers have admitted that all those qualities they make such a fuss
about are fantastic and vain: even if beasts had all the virtue, knowledge,
wisdom and contentment of the Stoic  [C]  they would still be beasts,
[A]  in no way to be compared to any man, however wretched, wicked or
daft!  [C]  In fine, nothing is worth anything if it does not look like us.
Even God has to become like us, to be appreciated – I shall go into that
later.[108] It is clear from this that  [A]  we do not place ourselves above
other animals and reject their condition and companionship by right reason
but out of stubbornness and insane arrogance.

To get back to the subject: we have been allotted inconstancy, hesitation,
doubt, pain, superstition, worries about what will happen (even after we
are dead), ambition, greed, jealousy, envy, unruly, insane and untameable
appetites, war, lies, disloyalty, backbiting and curiosity. We take pride in
our fair, discursive reason and our capacity to judge and to know, but we
have bought them at a price which is strangely excessive if it includes those
passions without number which prey upon us.  [B]  Unless, that is, we
choose, like Socrates, to pride ourselves on the one noteworthy prerogative
we do have over the beasts: Nature lays down limits and seasons to their
lusts, but gives us a full rein – anytime, any place.

107. Plutarch, tr. Amyot, *Des conceptions communes contre les Stoïques*, 577 AB; cf.
Erasmus, *Praise of Folly*, XXXV and XI.
'88:to the *mask* of . . .
108. Cf. p. 82.f.
'88: daft. *All our perfection, then, consists in being men.* We do not . . .

[C] *Ut vinum aegrotis, quia prodest raro, nocet saepissime, melius est non adhibere omnino, quam, spe dubiae salutis, in apertam perniciem incurrere: sic haud scio an melius fuerit humano generi motum istum celerem cogitationis, acumen, solertiam, quam rationem vocamus, quoniam pestifera sint multis, admodum paucis salutaria, non dari omnino, quam tam munifice et tam large dari.* [Wine is often bad and rarely good for the sick, so it is better to let them have none at all than to run known risks for a doubtful remedy. So too with that mental agility, shrewdness and ingenuity which we call *reason*: it is baleful to many and good for only a few. It would have been better for Man not to have been given it at all than to have been given it with such great munificence.][109]

[A] What good did their great erudition do for Varro and Aristotle? Did it free them from human ills? Did it relieve them of misfortunes such as befall a common porter? Could logic console them for the gout – and did they feel it any the less because they knew how that humour lodged in their joints? Did it help them to come to terms with death, knowing that whole tribes take delight in it? Did they not mind being cuckolded, since they knew that in some place or other men have wives in common? Not at all. Varro among the Romans and Aristotle among the Greeks were ranked first for knowledge at a time when learning was flourishing and at its best. Yet nobody says that their lives were particularly outstanding. There are, in fact, notorious stains on the life of the Greek one, which he cannot easily escape.[110]  [B] Have we discovered that health and pleasure taste better if you know astrology or grammar –

*Illiterati num minus nervi rigent?*

[Men who cannot read do not find it harder to get an erection, do they?]

– or that shame and poverty become more bearable?

*Scilicet et morbis et debilitate carebis,*
*Et luctum et curam effugies, et tempora vitae*
*Longa tibi post haec fato meliore dabuntur.*

[You will doubtless be free from ills and weakness and be free from grief and care, and a long life will be granted you, one with a better destiny.][111]

I have seen in my time hundreds of craftsmen and ploughmen wiser and happier than University Rectors – and whom I would rather be like. Among

109. Socrates: Xenophon, *Memorabilia*, I, iv. 12; Cicero, *De nat. deorum*, III, xxvii, 69.

110. Epicureans, especially, accused Aristotle of disloyalty and of a misspent youth.

111. Horace, *Epodes*, VIII, 17; Juvenal, XIV, 156.

the necessities of life learning seems to me to rank with fame, noble blood and dignity[112]  [C] or, at most, with beauty, riches  [A]  and such other qualities which do indeed contribute a great deal to life, but from a distance and somewhat more in the mind than in nature.

[C]  We hardly need more duties, laws and rules of conduct in human society than cranes or ants do in theirs: they have no learning, yet live their lives quite ordinately. If Man were wise he would gauge the true worth of anything by its usefulness and appropriateness to his life.

If anyone were to tot up our deeds and our actions he would find more outstanding men among the ignorant than among the wise – outstanding in virtues of every kind. Old Rome seems to me to have borne many men of greater worth, both in peace and war, than the later, cultured Rome which brought about its own downfall. Even if everything else were identical, at very least valour and uprightness would still tilt the balance towards Old Rome, for they make uniquely good bedfellows with simplicity.

But I will let this subject drop; it would draw me further on than I want to go. I will merely add this: only humility and submissiveness[113] can produce a good man. We must not let everyone work out for himself what his duties are. Duty must be laid down for him, not chosen by him from his own reasoning; otherwise, out of the weakness and infinite variety of our reasons and opinions, we will – as Epicurus said – end up forging duties for ourselves which will have us eating each other. The first commandment which God ever gave to Man was the law of pure obedience. It was a bare and simple order, leaving Man no room for knowing or arguing  [C]  – since the principal duty of a reasonable soul which acknowledges a Superior and a Benefactor in heaven is to obey him. All other virtues are born of submission and obedience, just as all other sins are born of pride.  [B]  The first temptation came to humankind from the opposite extreme: the Devil first poured his poison into our ears with promises about knowledge and understanding: '*Eritis sicut dii, scientes bonum et malum*' [Ye shall be as Gods, knowing good and evil].  [C]  In Homer, when the Sirens wished to deceive Ulysses, draw him into their dangerous snares and so destroy him, they offered him the gift of knowledge.[114]

[A]  There is a plague on Man: his opinion that he knows something. That is why ignorance is so strongly advocated by our religion as a quality appropriate to belief and obedience.  [C]  '*Cavete ne quis vos decipiat per*

112. [B]: for: '*Among . . . dignity*', this sentence reads: *Learning is even less necessary in the service of life than glory and such other qualities.*

113. '88: only *obedience* can . . .

114. References to the Fall in Genesis, including III:5, and to Homer *apud* Cicero, *De fin.*, V, xviii, 49.

*philosophiam et inanes seductiones secundum elementa mundi'* [Beware lest any man cheat you through philosophy and vain deceptions, according to the rudiments of the world].[115]

[A]   All the philosophers of all the sects are in general accord over one thing: that the sovereign good consists in peace of mind and body.   [B]   But where are we to find it?

> [A]   *Ad summum sapiens uno minor est Jove: dives,*
> *Liber, honoratus, pulcher, rex denique regum:*
> *Praecipue sanus, nisi cum pituita molesta est.*

[To sum up then: the wise man has only one superior – Jupiter – and is rich, free, honourable, beautiful, the king of kings in fact . . . especially when well and not troubled by snot!]

It does seem true that Nature allotted us one thing only to console us for our pitiful, wretched condition: arrogance. Epictetus agrees, saying that Man has nothing properly his own except his opinions. For our portion we have been allotted wind and smoke.[116]

[B]   Philosophy asserts that gods enjoy health as it really is, though they can understand illness; Man, on the contrary, enjoys his goods only in fantasy, but knows ills as they really are.[117]   [A]   We have done right to emphasize our imaginative powers: all our goods exist only in a dream.

Man is a wretched creature, subject to calamities;[118] but just listen to him bragging: 'There is no occupation', says Cicero, 'so sweet as scholarship; scholarship is the means of making known to us, while still in this world, the infinity of matter, the immense grandeur of Nature, the heavens, the lands and the seas. Scholarship has taught us piety, moderation, greatness of heart; it snatches our souls from darkness and shows them all things, the high and the low, the first, the last and everything between; scholarship furnishes us with the means of living well and happily; it teaches us how to spend our lives without discontent and without vexation.' . . .[119] Is this fellow describing the properties of almighty and everlasting God! In practice, thousands of little

115. '88: he knows something. That is why *simplicity and ignorance are* so strongly advocated by our religion as *elements properly conducive to subjection*, belief and obedience. All the philosophers . . . (Colossians 2:8. Cf. Augustine, *City of God*, VIII, ix, a key text for Christian folly, the praise of which is soon to be taken up by Montaigne.)
116. Horace, *Epistles*, I, i. 106; John Stobaeus, *Apophthegmata*, Sermo 21.
117. Plutarch, *Contre les Stoïques*, 578 G.
118. Plutarch, *Que les bestes brutes usent de raison*, 270 F.
119. Cicero: *Tusc. disput.*, V, xxxvi.

women in their villages have lived lives more gentle, more equable, more constant than his.

[A1]   *Deus ille fuit, Deus, inclute Memmi,*
      *Qui princeps vitae rationem invenit eam, quae*
      *Nunc appellatur sapientia, quique per artem*
      *Fluctibus e tantis vitam tantisque tenebris*
      *In tam tranquillo et tam clara luce locavit.*

[It was a god, noble Memmius, yes, a god who first discovered that rule of life which we now call Wisdom and who, through his skill, brought our lives out from storm and darkness and fixed them in such tranquillity and light.]

Beautiful, magnificent words, those! Yet, despite the god who taught him such divine wisdom, a minor accident reduced the wits of the fellow who wrote them to a state worse than that of the meanest shepherd![120]

[A]   Of similar impudence are   [C]   that promise of Democritus in his preface: 'I am going to write about Everything'; the stupid title Aristotle bestows on us men: 'Mortal Gods';[121] and   [A]   Chrysippus' judgement that Dion was as virtuous as God. And even Seneca, my favourite, asserts that, by God's gift he is living: but living well he owes to himself   [C]   – which conforms to what that other fellow said: '*In virtute vere gloriamur; quod non contingeret, si id donum a deo, non a nobis haberemus*' [We rightly glory in our virtue; that would not arise if it were a gift of God and not of ourselves]. This is in Seneca, too: 'The wise man has fortitude similar to God's, but since he has it within human weakness, he surpasses God.'[122]

[A]   There is nothing more common than rash quips like these. We are so much more jealous of our own interests than of those of our Creator that not one of us is more shocked when he sees himself made equal to God than reduced to the ranks of the other animals. We must trample down this stupid vanity, violently and boldly shaking the absurd foundations on which we base such false opinions. So long as Man thinks he has means and powers deriving from himself he will never acknowledge what he owes to his Master. All his geese will be swans, as the saying goes. So we must strip him down

120. Lucretius, V, 8; Montaigne discusses his madness in vol. II, chapter 2, 'On drunkenness': 'That great poet Lucretius vainly philosophizes and braces himself: there he was, driven out of his senses by a love potion.'

121. Cicero, *Acad.: Lucullus*, II, xxiii, 73; *De finibus*, II, xiii, 40: 'As Aristotle says: Man is born for thought and action: he is, as it were, a mortal god.'

122. Plutarch, *Contre les Stoïques*, 583 E; cited with Seneca in La Primaudaye, *Académie françoyse*, 1581, p. 5; Cicero, *De nat. deorum*, III, xxxvi, 87; Seneca, *Epist. moral.*, LIII, 11–12.

to his shirt-tails. Let us look at some notable examples of what his philosophy actually produces.

Possidonius was beset with an illness so painful that it made him twist his arms and grind his teeth; he thought he could cock a snook at Pain by crying out at her: 'It's no good; whatever you do I will never admit that you are evil.' He boasts that he will at least contain his speech within the rules of his sect, yet he feels exactly the same pain as my footman.¹²³ [C] 'Re succumbere non oportebat verbis gloriantem' [If you boast in words you should not surrender in fact].

Arcesilus was suffering from gout. Carneades came to see him and was just going sadly away when he called him back; he pointed from his feet to his heart and said, 'Nothing has passed from here to there.' There is a little more elegance in that: he admits to pain and would gladly be rid of it; it is an evil, all right, but his heart is neither cast down nor weakened by it. That other fellow clings to his position, which is, I fear, more a matter of words than of reality. When Dionysius of Heraclea was nearly driven out of his mind by stabbing pains in his eyes, he was forced to give up such Stoical assertions.¹²⁴

[A] But supposing knowledge actually could produce the effects claimed for it, actually could blunt and reduce the pangs of the misfortunes which beset us: even then, what does it really achieve over and beyond what ignorance does – more purely and more evidently? When Pyrrho, the philosopher, was exposed to the hazards of a mighty tempest, he could set no better example before his companions than the indifference of a pig on board ship with them: it gazed at the storm quite free from fear. When Philosophy has run out of precepts she sends us back to athletes and mule-drivers. Such men are usually less apprehensive of death, pain and other misfortunes. They also show more steadfastness than scholarship affords to any man not already predisposed to it by birth and by a duly cultivated natural talent.¹²⁵ What is it if not ignorance which allows our surgeons to make incisions in the tender limbs of children more easily than in our own? [C] (The same applies to horses.) [A] How many men have been made ill by the sheer force of imagination? Is it not normal to see men bled, purged and swallowing medicines to cure ills which they feel only in their minds? When we run out of genuine ills, Learning will lend us some of her own: this or that colour are symptoms of a catarrh you *will* have; this heat-wave threatens you with some turbulent fever; this break in the line of life on your left hand warns you of

123. '88: footman. *It is all wind and words.* But supposing . . .
124. Cicero, *Tusc. disput.*, II, xiii; *De fin.*, V, xxxi, 94.
125. '88: natural talent. *Knowledge sharpens our feelings for ills rather than lightening them.* What . . .

some grave and imminent illness . . . Finally Learning openly makes assaults against health itself: that youthful vigour and liveliness of yours cannot remain stable for long! Better bleed away some of their force in case it turns against you . . .

Compare the life of a man enslaved by such fantasies with the life of a ploughman who, free from learning and prognostics, merely follows his natural appetites and judges things as they feel at present. He only feels ill when he really is ill; the other fellow often has stone in the mind before stone in the kidney. As though it were not time enough to suffer pain when it really comes along, our thoughts must run ahead and meet it.

What I say about medicine applies to erudition in general – hence that ancient philosophical opinion that sovereign good lies in recognizing the weakness of our powers of judgement. My ignorance can supply as good a cause to hope as to fear; for me, the only rule of health lies in the example of other people and how I see them fare in similar circumstances; but since I can find all sorts of examples, I dwell on the comparisons which are most favourable to me! Health, full, free and entire, I welcome with open arms. I whet my appetites so that I can truly enjoy it, all the more so since health is not usual to me any more, but quite rare. Far be it from me to trouble the sweet repose of health with bitterness arising from a new regime based on restraint. The very beasts can show us that illness can be brought on by mental agitations.

[C] The natives of Brazil are said to die only of old age; they attribute that to the serenity and tranquillity of the air: I would attribute it to the serenity and tranquillity of their souls; they are not burdened with intense emotions and unpleasant tasks and thoughts: they pass their lives in striking simplicity and ignorance. They have no literature, no laws, no kings and no religion of any kind.[126]

[A] Experience shows that gross, uncouth men make more desirable and vigorous sexual partners; lying with a mule-driver is often more welcome than lying with a gentleman. How can we explain that except by assuming that emotions within the gentleman's soul undermine the strength of his body, break it down and exhaust it,   [A1]   just as they exhaust and harm the soul itself? Is it not true that the soul can be most readily thrown into mania and driven mad by its own quickness, sharpness and nimbleness – in short by the qualities which constitute its strength?   [B]   Does not the most subtle wisdom produce the most subtle madness? As great enmities are born of great friendships and fatal illnesses are born of radiant health, so too the most exquisite and delirious of manias are produced by the choicest and the

126. S. Goulard, Hist. du Portugal, II, xv, 46v°.

most lively of the emotions which disturb the soul. It needs only a half turn
of the peg to pass from one to the other. [A1] When men are demented
their very actions show how appropriate madness is to the workings of our
souls at their most vigorous. Is there anyone who does not know how imper-
ceptible are the divisions separating madness from the spiritual alacrity of a
soul set free or from actions arising from supreme and extraordinary virtue?
Plato says that melancholics are the most teachable and the most sublime;
yet none have a greater propensity towards madness. Spirits without number
are undermined by their own force and subtlety. There is an Italian poet,
fashioned in the atmosphere of the pure poetry of Antiquity, who showed
more judgement and genius than any other Italian for many a long year; yet
his agile and lively mind has overthrown him; the light has made him blind;
his reason's grasp was so precise and so intense that it has left him quite
irrational; his quest for knowledge, eager and exacting, has led to his becoming like a dumb beast; his rare aptitude for the activities of the soul has left
him with no activity . . . and with no soul. Ought he to be grateful to so
murderous a mental agility? It was not so much compassion that I felt as
anger when I saw him in so wretched a state, surviving himself, neglecting
himself (and his works, which were published, unlicked and uncorrected; he
had sight of this but no understanding).[127]

Do you want a man who is sane, moderate, firmly based and reliable? Then
array him in darkness, sluggishness and heaviness. [C] To teach us to be
wise, make us stupid like beasts; to guide us you must blind us.

[A] If you say that the convenience of having our senses chilled and
blunted when tasting evil pains must entail the consequential inconvenience
of rendering us less keenly appreciative of the joys of good pleasures, I agree.
But the wretchedness of our human condition means we have less to relish
than to banish: the most extreme pleasures touch us less than the lightest of
pains: [C] *'Segnius homines bona quam mala sentiunt'* [Men feel pleasure
more dully than pain]. We are far less aware of perfect health than of the
slightest illness:

*pungit*
*In cute vix summa violatum plagula corpus,*
*Quando valere nihil quemquam movet. Hoc juvat unum,*
*Quod me non torquet latus aut pes: caetera quisquam*
*Vix queat aut sanum sese, aut sentire valentem.*

[A man feels the slightest prick which scarcely breaks his skin; yet he remains unmoved

127. Aristotle, *Problems*, 30–1. (For Tasso's madness, see *Montaigne and Melancholy*, p. 371.)

by excellent health. Personally I feel delight in simply being free from pain in foot or side, while another scarcely realizes he is well and remains unaware of his good health.]

For us, being well means not being ill. So that philosophical school which sets the highest value on pleasure reduces it to the mere absence of pain. To be free from ill is the greatest good that Man can hope for.   [C]   As Ennius puts it,

*Nimium boni est, cui nihil est mali*

[Ample good consists in being free from ill].[128]

[A]   Even that tickling excitement which seems to exalt us above mere good health and freedom from pain, that kind of shifting delight, active, inexplicably biting and sharp, which accompanies certain pleasures, eventually aims at a total absence of pain. The appetite which enraptures us when we lie with women merely aims at banishing the pain brought on by the frenzy of our inflamed desires; all it seeks is rest and repose, free from the fever of passion.

The same applies to all other appetites. I maintain, therefore, that if ignorant simplicity can bring us to an absence of pain, then it brings us to a state which, given the human condition, is very blessedness.

[C]   Yet we should not think of a simplicity so leaden as to be unable to taste anything. Crantor was right to attack 'freedom from pain' as conceived by Epicurus, insofar as it was built upon foundations so deep that pain could not even draw near to it or arise within it. I have no words of praise for a 'freedom from pain' which is neither possible nor desirable. I am pleased enough not to be ill but, if I am ill, I want to know; if you cut me open or cauterize me, I want to feel it. Truly, anyone who could uproot all knowledge of pain would equally eradicate all knowledge of pleasure and finally destroy Man: '*Istud nihil dolere, non sine magna mercede contingit immanitatis in animo, stuporis in corpore*' [That 'freedom from pain' has a high price: cruelty in the soul, insensate dullness in the body]. For Man, ill can be good at times; it is not always right to flee pain, not always right to chase after pleasure.

[A]   It greatly advances the honour of Ignorance that Learning has to throw us into her arms when powerless to stiffen our backs against the weight of our ills; she has to make terms, slipping the reins and giving us leave to seek refuge in the lap of Ignorance, finding under her protection a shelter from the blows and outrages of Fortune.

Learning instructs us to   [C]   withdraw our thoughts from the ills which beset us now and to occupy them by recalling the good times we have

128. Livy, XXX, xxi; La Boëtie (ed. Bonnefon, 1892, p. 234); Ennius, *apud* Cicero, *De fin.*, II, xiii, 41.

known; [A] to make use of the memory of past joys in order to console ourselves for present sorrows, or to call in the help of vanished happiness to set against the things which oppress us now – [C] 'Levationes aegritudinum in avocatione a cogitanda molestia et revocatione ad contemplandas voluptates ponit' [He found a way to lessen sorrows by summoning thoughts away from troubles and calling them back to gaze on pleasure] – [A] when Learning runs out of force, she turns to cunning; when strength of arm and body fails, she resorts to conjuring tricks and nimble footwork; if that is not what is meant, what does it mean? When any reasonable man, let alone a philosopher, feels in reality a blazing thirst brought on by a burning fever, can you buy him off with memories of the delights of Greek wine? [B] That would only make a bad bargain worse.

> *Che ricordarsi il ben doppia la noia.*

> [Recalling pleasure doubles pain.]

[A] Of a similar nature is that other counsel which Philosophy gives us: to keep only past pleasures in mind and to wipe off the sorrows we have known – as if we had the art of forgetfulness in our power. [C] Anyway, such advice makes us worse:

> *Suavis est laborum praeteritorum memoria.*

> [Sweet is the memory of toils now past.]

[A] Philosophy ought to arm me with weapons to fight against Fortune; she should stiffen my resolve to trample human adversities underfoot; how has she grown so weak as to have me bolting into burrows with such cowardly and stupid evasions? Memory reproduces what she wants, not what we choose. Indeed there is nothing which stamps anything so vividly on our memory as the desire not to remember it: the best way to impress anything on our souls and to make them stand guard over it, is to beg them to forget it.

– [C] The following is false: 'Est situm in nobis, ut et adversa quasi perpetua oblivione obruamus, et secunda jucunde et suaviter meminerimus' [There is within us a capacity for consigning misfortunes to total oblivion, while remembering favourable things with joy and delight].

The following is true: 'Memini etiam quae nolo, oblivisci non possum quae volo' [I remember things I do not want to remember and I cannot forget things I want to forget].[129] –

---

129. Cicero, *Tusc. disput.*, III, vi; xv; xvi; *De fin.*, II, xxx–xxxii (citing Euripides, *Andromeda*, 133); I, xvii, 57. The Italian verse remains unidentified.

[A]   Whose advice have I just cited? Why, that of the man   [C]   *'qui se unus sapientem profiteri sit ausus'* [who, alone, dared to say he was wise];

> [A]   *Qui genus humanum ingenio superavit, et omnes*
> *Praestrinxit stellas, exortus uti aetherius sol.*

[who soared above human kind by his genius and who, like the Sun rising in heaven, obscured all the stars.]

Emptying and stripping memory is, surely, the true and proper road to ignorance.   [C]   *'Iners malorum remedium ignorantia est'* [Ignorance is an artless remedy for our ills].[130]

[A]   We find several similar precepts permitting us, when strong and lively Reason cannot suffice, to borrow the trivial pretences of the vulgar, provided that they make us happy or provide consolation. Those who cannot cure a wound are pleased with palliatives which deaden it. If philosophers could only find a way of adding order and constancy to a life which was maintained in joy and tranquillity by weakness and sickness of judgement, they would be prepared to accept it. I do not think they will deny me that.

> *Potare et spargere flores*
> *Incipiam, patiarque vel inconsultus haberi!*

[I may appear silly, but I am going to start drinking and strewing flowers about!][131]

You would find several philosophers agreeing with Lycas: he was a man of very orderly habits, living quietly and peaceably at home; he failed in none of the duties he owed to family and strangers; he guarded himself effectively from harm; however, some defect in his senses led him to imprint a mad fantasy on his brain: he always thought he was in the theatre watching games, plays and the finest comedies in the world. Being cured of this corrupt humour, he nearly took his doctors to court to make them restore those sweet fantasies[132] to him:

130. Epicurus (in Cicero, *De fin.*, II, iii, 7 and in Lucretius, III, 1043-44); Seneca (the dramatist) *Oedipus*, III, 17.

131. Horace, *Epist.* I, v, 14.

132. '88: *vain* fantasies. (What follows is virtually all from Erasmus' adage, *In nihil sapiendo jucundissima vita* (including references to Horace, *Epist.*, II, ii, 138; Sophocles, *Ajax*, 554; Ecclesiastes I:18). Also, Erasmus, *Praise of Folly*, XXXVII.)

*pol! me occidistis, amici,*
*Non servastis, ait, cui sic extorta voluptas,*
*Et demptus per vim mentis gratissimus error.*

['You have killed me, my friends, not cured me,' he said. 'You have wrenched my pleasure from me and taken away by force that most delightful wandering of my mind.']

Thrasilaus, son of Pythodorus, had a similar mad fantasy; he came to believe that all the ships sailing out of the port of Piraeus or coming in to dock there were working for him alone. When good fortune attended their voyages he rejoiced in it and welcomed them with delight. His brother Crito brought him to his senses, but he sorely missed his former condition, which had been full of happiness, not burdened by troubles.

A line of Ancient Greek poetry says 'There is great convenience in not being too wise': Ἐν τῷ φρονεῖν γὰρ μηδέν ἥδιστος βίος. So does Ecclesiastes: 'In much wisdom there is much sadness, and he that acquireth knowledge acquireth worry and travail.'

Philosophy in general agrees[133] that there is an ultimate remedy to be prescribed for every kind of trouble: namely, ending our life if we find it intolerable. [C] *'Placet? Pare. Non placet? Quacunque vis, exi.'* [All right? Then put up with it. Not all right? Then out you go, any way you like.] – *'Pungit dolor? Vel fodiat sane. Si nudus es, da jugulum; sin tectus armis Vulcaniis, id est fortitudine, resiste.'* [Does it hurt? Is it excruciating? If you are defenceless, get your throat cut; if you are armed with the arms of Vulcan (that is, fortitude) then fight it!] As the Greeks said at their banquets: 'Let him drink or be off!' (*'Aut bibat, aut abeat!'*) – That is particularly apt if you pronounce Cicero's language like a Gascon, changing your 'B's to 'V's: *Aut vivat* – 'Let him *live* . . .'

[A]  *Vivere si recte nescis, decede peritis;*
*Lusisti satis, edisti satis atque bibisti;*
*Tempus abire tibi est, ne potum largius aequo*
*Rideat et pulset lasciva decentius aetas.*

[If you do not know how to live as you should, give way to those who do. You have played enough in bed; you have eaten enough, drunk enough: it is time to be off, lest

133. '88 onwards: *All* Philosophy *agrees* . . . (The remedies of Philosophy are not of course those of revealed religion (which supersedes them when there is a clash). But Christianity welcomes Philosophy. For the usual view, see Melanchthon, *On the First Book of the Ethics of Aristotle*, 'On the distinction between Philosophy and the Christian Religion', *Opera*, 1541, IV, 127.)

you start to drink too much and find that pretty girls rightly laugh at you and push you away.]

But what does this consensus amount to, if not to a confession of powerlessness on the part of Philosophy? She sends us for protection not merely to ignorance but to insensibility, to a total lack of sensation, to non-being.

> *Democritum postquam matura vetustas*
> *Admonuit memorem motus languescere mentis,*
> *Sponte sua leto caput obvius obtulit ipse.*

[When mature old age warned Democritus that he was losing his memory and his mental faculties, he spontaneously offered his head to Destiny.]

As Antisthenes said: We need a store of intelligence, to understand; failing that, a hangman's rope. In this connection Chrysippus used to quote from Tyrtaeus the poet: '*Draw near to virtue . . . or to death.*' [C] Crates used to say that love was cured by time or hunger; those who like neither can use the rope. [B] Sextius – the one whom Seneca and Plutarch talk so highly of – gave up everything and threw himself into the study of philosophy; he found his progress too long and too slow, so he decided to drown himself in the sea. In default of learning, he ran to death.

Philosophy lays down the law on this subject in these words: If some great evil should chance upon you – one you cannot remedy – then a haven is always near: swim out of your body as from a leaky boat; only a fool is bound to his body, not by love of life but by fear of death.[134]

[A] Just as life is made more pleasant by simplicity, it is also made better and more innocent (as I was about to say earlier on). According to St Paul, it is the simple and the ignorant who rise up and take hold of heaven, whereas we, with all our learning, plunge down into the bottomless pit of hell.[135] I will not linger here over two Roman Emperors, Valentian – a sworn enemy of knowledge and scholarship – and Licinius, who called them a poison and a plague within the body politic;[136] nor over Mahomet who, [C] I am told, [A] forbade his followers to study. What we must do is to attach great weight to the authoritative example of a great man, Lycurgus, as well as to

134. Seneca, *Epist. moral.* LXX, 15–16 (adapted); Cicero, *Tusc. disput.*, V, xli; Horace, *Epist.*, II, ii, 213; Lucretius, III, 1039 (Lambin, pp. 266–67); Plutarch, *Contre les Stoïques*, 564 CD; Diogenes Laertius, *Lives*, Crates; Plutarch, tr. Amyot, *Comment l'on pourra apparcevoir si l'on amende et profite en l'exercice de la vertu*, 114 EF; for Seneca's praise of Quintus Sextius the Elder, cf. Seneca, *Epist. moral.*, XCVIII, 13.

135. H. C. Agrippa, *De Vanitate omnium scientiarum et de excellentia verbi Dei*, 1537, 1. St Paul is loosely paraphrased here, not quoted, on Christian Folly.

136. *Idem* (where *Valentian* also appears for *Valentinian*).

the respect we owe to Sparta, a venerable, great and awe-inspiring form of
government, where letters were not taught or practised but where virtue
and happiness long flourished. Those who come back from the New World
discovered by the Spaniards in the time of our fathers can testify how those
peoples, without magistrates or laws, live lives more ordinate and more just
than any we find in our own countries, where there are more laws and legal
officials than there are deeds or inhabitants.

> Di cittatorie piene e di libelli,
> D'esamine e di carte, di procure,
> Hanno le mani e il seno, e gran fastelli
> Di chiose, di consigli e di letture:
> Per cui le faculta de poverelli
> Non sono mai ne le citta sicure;
> Hanno dietro e dinanzi, e d'ambi ilati,
> Notai procuratori e advocati.

[Their hands and their law-bags are full of summonses, libels, inquests, documents
and powers-of-attorney; they have great folders full of glosses, counsels' opinions and
statements. For all that, the poor are never safe in their cities but are surrounded, in
front, behind and on both sides, by procurators and lawyers.][137]

A later Roman senator meant much the same when he said that the breath of
their forebears stank of garlic but inwardly they smelt of the musk of a good
conscience; men of his time, on the contrary, were doused in perfume yet
inwardly stank of every sort of vice.[138] In other words he agrees with me:
they had ample learning and ability but were very short of integrity. Lack of
refinement, ignorance, simplicity and roughness go easily with innocence,
whereas curiosity, subtlety and knowledge have falsehood in their train; the
main qualities which conserve human society are humility, fear and goodness:
they require a soul which is empty, teachable and not thinking much of
itself.[139]

   In Man curiosity is an innate evil, dating from his origins: Christians know
that particularly well. The original Fall occurred when Man was anxious
to increase his wisdom and knowledge: that path led headlong to eternal
damnation. Pride undoes man; it corrupts him; pride makes him leave the
trodden paths, welcome novelty and prefer to be the leader of a lost band
wandering along the road to perdition; prefer to be a master of error and lies
than a pupil in the school of Truth, guided by others and led by the hand

137. Ariosto, *Orlando furioso*, XIV, §84.
138. Varro *apud* Nonius Marcellus, *Opera*, 201, 6.
139. '88: not thinking *anything* of itself.

along the straight and beaten path. That is perhaps what was meant by that old Greek saying, that Superstition follows Pride and obeys it as a father: ἡ δεισιδαιμονία κατάπερ πατρὶ τῷ τυφῷ πείτεται.[140]

[C] 'Oh Pride! How thou dost trammel us!' When Socrates was told that the god of Wisdom had called him wise, he was thunderstruck; he ransacked his mind and shook himself out but could find nothing to base this divine judgement upon. He knew other men who were as just, temperate, valiant and wise as he was: others he knew to be more eloquent, more handsome, more useful to their country. He finally concluded that, if he was different from others and wiser, it was only because he did not think he was; that his God thought any human who believed himself to be knowledgeable and wise was a singularly stupid animal; that his best teaching taught ignorance and his best wisdom was simplicity.[141]

[A] The Word of God proclaims that those of us who think well of ourselves are to be pitied: Dust and ashes (it says to them) what have ye to boast about? And elsewhere: God maketh man like unto a shadow: who will judge him when the light departeth and the shadow vanisheth?[142]

In truth we are but nothing.

It is so far beyond our power to comprehend the majesty of God that the very works of our Creator which best carry his mark are the ones we least understand. To come across something unbelievable is, for Christians, an opportunity to exercise belief; it is all the more reasonable precisely because it runs counter to human reason. [B] If it were reasonable, it would not be a miracle: if it followed a pattern, it would not be unique. [C] 'Melius scitur deus nesciendo' [God is best known by not knowing], said St Augustine. And Tacitus says, 'Sanctius est ac reverentius de actis deorum credere quam scire' [It is more holy and pious to believe what the gods have done than to understand them].[143] Plato reckons that there is an element of vicious impiety in inquiring too curiously about God and the world or about first causes. As for Cicero, he says: 'Atque illum quidem parentem hujus universitatis invenire difficile; et, quum jam inveneris, indicare in vulgus, nefas' [It is hard to discover

---

140. Genesis; then Socrates *apud* John Stobaeus, *Apophthegmata*, Sermo XXII (a saying inscribed in Montaigne's library).

141. Plato, *Apology for Socrates*, 6.

142. Sayings inscribed on Montaigne's library; the first from Ecclesiasticus 10:9; the second, ascribed to 'Eccl. 7', may perhaps be a paraphrase of Ecclesiastes 7:1 (Vulgate) or a loose rendering of the Septuagint.

143. Augustine, *De ordine*, II, xvi, and Tacitus, *De Moribus Germanum*, XXXIV, both cited in Justus Lipsius, *Politicorum sive Civilis Doctrinae*, 1584, I, ii.

the Begetter of this universe; and when you do discover him, it is impious to disclose him to the populace].[144]

[A] We confidently use words like might, truth, justice. They are words signifying something great. But what that 'something' is we cannot see or conceive. [B] We say that God 'fears', that God 'is angry', that God 'loves':

*Immortalia mortali sermone notantes.*

[Denoting immortal things in mortal speech.][145]

But they are disturbances and emotions which in any form known to us find no place in God. Nor can we imagine them in forms known to him. [A] God alone can know himself; God alone can interpret his works. [C] And he uses improper, human, words to do so, stooping down to the earth where we lie sprawling.

Take Prudence; that consists in a choice between good and evil; how can that apply to God? No evil can touch him. Or take Reason and Intelligence, by which we seek to attain clarity amidst obscurity; there is nothing obscure to God. Or Justice, which distributes to each his due and which was begotten for the good of society and communities of men; how can that exist in God? And what about Temperance? It moderates bodily pleasures which have no place in the Godhead. Nor is Fortitude in the face of pain, toil or danger one of God's qualities: those three things are unknown to him. That explains why Aristotle held that God is equally as free from virtue as from vice. '*Neque gratia neque ira teneri potest, quod quae talia essent, imbecilla essent omnia*' [He can experience neither gratitude nor anger; such things are found only in the weak].[146]

[A] Whatever share in the knowledge of Truth we may have obtained, it has not been acquired by our own powers. God has clearly shown us that: it was out of the common people that he chose simple and ignorant apostles to bear witness of his wondrous secrets; the Christian faith is not something obtained by us: it is, purely and simply, a gift depending on the generosity of Another. Our religion did not come to us through reasoned arguments or from our own intelligence: it came to us from outside authority, by commandments. That being so, weakness of judgement helps us more than strength; blindness, more than clarity of vision. We become learned in God's wisdom

144. Plato, *Laws*, VII (Ficino, 1546, p. 837); tr. Cicero, *Timaeus*, II (*in Fragmentis*).
145. Lucretius, V, 121 (Lambin, pp. 383–84).
146. Cicero, *De nat. deorum*, III, xv, 38, with quotation from I, xvii, 45. (Aristotle, *Nicomachaean Ethics*, VII, i. 1–2 may be in mind also.)

more by ignorance than by knowledge. It is not surprising that our earth-based, natural means cannot conceive knowledge which is heaven-based and supernatural; let us merely bring our submissiveness and obedience: 'For it is written: I will destroy the wisdom of the wise and bring to nothing the prudence of the prudent. Where is the wise? Where is the scribe? Where is the disputer of this world? Hath God not made the wisdom of this world like unto the foolishness as of beasts? For seeing that the world, through wisdom, knew not God, it pleased God through the vanity of preaching to save them that believe.'[147]

But is it within the capacity of Man to find what he is looking for? Has that quest for truth which has kept Man busy for so many centuries actually enriched him with some new power or solid truth? Now, at last, it is time to look into that question.

I think Man will confess, if he speaks honestly, that all he has gained from so long a chase is knowledge of his own weakness.[148] By long study we have confirmed and verified that ignorance does lie naturally within us. The truly wise are like ears of corn: they shoot up and up holding their heads proudly erect – so long as they are empty; but when, in their maturity, they are full of swelling grain, their foreheads droop down and they show humility. So, too, with men who have assayed everything, sounded everything; within those piles of knowledge and the profusion of so many diverse things, they have found nothing solid, nothing firm, only vanity. They then renounce arrogance and recognize their natural condition.[149]

[C]   For that is what Velleius reproached Cotta and Cicero with: they had learned from Philo that they had learned nothing.[150]

When one of the Seven Sages of Greece, Pherecides, lay dying, he wrote to Thales saying, 'I have commanded my family, once they have buried me, to send you all my papers; if you and the other Sages are satisfied with them, publish them; if not, suppress them: they contain no certainties which satisfy me. I make no claim to know what truth is nor to have attained truth. Rather than lay subjects bare, I lay them open.'[151]

[A]   The wisest man that ever was, when asked what he knew, replied

147. I Corinthians, 1:19–21, a key text for Christian Folly (cf. Erasmus, *Praise of Folly*, LXV).

148. '88: his own *vileness and his* weakness . . .

149. Plutarch, *Comment l'on peut apparcevoir si l'on amende et profite en l'exercice de la vertu*: 116 EF.

150. Cicero, *De nat. deorum*, I, vii, 17.

151. Diogenes Laertius, *Lives*, Pherecides, I, 122.

that the one thing he did know was that he knew nothing.[152] They say that the largest bit of what we do know is smaller than the tiniest bit of what we do not know; he showed that to be true. In other words, the very things we think we know form part of our ignorance, and a small part at that.    [C]    We know things in a dream, says Plato; we do not know them as they truly are.[153]

'*Omnes pene veteres nihil cognosci, nihil percipi, nihil sciri posse dixerunt; angustos sensus, imbecillos animos, brevia curricula vitae*' [Virtually all the Ancients say that nothing can be understood, nothing can be perceived, nothing can be known; our senses are too restricted, our minds are too weak, the course of our life is too short].[154]

[A]    Cicero himself, who owed such worth as he had to his learning, was said by Valerius to have begun to think less of literary culture in his old age.[155]    [C]    And even while he was still writing he felt bound to no sect; he followed the teachings of this school or that as seemed to him most probable, remaining always within that Doubt taught by the Academy: '*Dicendum est, sed ita ut nihil affirmem: quaeram omnia, dubitans plerumque et mihi diffidens*' [I have to write, but in such a way as to vouch for nothing; I shall always be seeking, mostly doubting, rarely trusting myself].[156]

[A]    It would be too easy a game if I limited myself to the ordinary run of men considered *en masse*; I would be justified in doing so by Man's curious convention that votes are not to be weighed but counted. But let us leave aside the ordinary people,

> *Qui vigilans stertit,*
> *Mortua cui vita est prope jam vivo atque videnti;*

[Who snore whilst they are awake and whose lives are dead even while they live and keep their eyes open;][157]

they have no self-awareness; they never judge themselves and let most of their natural faculties stand idle. I want to take Man in his highest state. Let us consider only that tiny number of outstanding, handpicked men who are born with a fine natural endowment peculiar to themselves and who then

---

152. Socrates; cf. Plato, *Apology for Socrates*, Lucretius, ed. Lambin, 309, etc.
    '88: ever was (*and who had no other just cause to be called wise apart from this saying*), when . . .
153. Plato, *Politicus*, 19, 277.
154. Cicero, *Academica*, I, xii, 44.
155. According to H. C. Agrippa, *De Vanitate omnium scientiarum*, I.
156. Cicero, *De divinatione*, II, iii, 8.
157. Lucretius, III, 1048; 1046 (Lambin pp. 266–68).

take care to strengthen and sharpen it by skill and study; by such means they raise it to the highest point [C] of wisdom [A] that it can attain to. They mould their souls in ways which keep them open on every side to every tendency; they assist their souls with the help of every appropriate outside support; they adorn them and enrich them with every advantage which they can discover both within and beyond this world. The highest possible form of human nature finds its home in such men. These are men who have given laws and constitutions to the world; it is their arts and sciences which have taught the world; so, too, the example of their astounding moral integrity. I will take account of the testimony and experience only of men such as these. Let us see how far they got and what they concluded. They form a fellowship such that any ills and defects found in them can confidently be accepted by the world as inherent ones.

Whoever sets out to find something eventually reaches the point where he can say that he has found it, or that it cannot be found, or that he is still looking for it. The whole of Philosophy can be divided into these three categories; her aim is to seek true, certain knowledge.

Peripatetics, Epicureans, Stoics[158] and others think they have discovered it. They founded the accepted disciplines and expounded their knowledge as certainties.

Clitomachus, Carneades and the Academics despaired of their quest; they conclude that Truth cannot be grasped by human means. Their conclusion is one of weakness, of human ignorance. This school has had the greatest number of adherents and some of the noblest.[159]

As for Pyrrho and the other Sceptics or Ephectics, [C] (whose teachings many of the Ancients derived from Homer, the Seven Sages, Archilochus and Euripides, and associated with Zeno, Democritus and Xeno- phanes,) [A] they say they are still looking for Truth. They hold that the philosophers who think they have found it are infinitely wrong. They go on to add that the second category – those who are quite sure that human strength is incapable of reaching truth – are overbold and vain. To determine the limits of our powers and to know and judge the difficulty of anything whatsoever constitutes great, even the highest, knowledge. They doubt whether Man is capable of it.

*Nil sciri quisquis putat, id quoque nescit*
*An scire possit quo se nil scire fatetur.*

158. '88: knowledge. *Aristotle, Epicurus*, Stoics . . .

159. Sextus Empiricus, *Hypotyposes*, I, i, 1; xix, xxii, xxiii. With the opening words of this book Montaigne begins his first major borrowing from one of the main sources of scepticism.

[Any man who thinks that 'nothing can be known', does not know whether he can know even that thing by which he asserts that he knows nothing.][160]

Ignorance which is aware of itself, judges itself, condemns itself, is not complete ignorance: complete ignorance does not even know itself. Consequently the professed aim of Pyrrhonians is to shake all convictions, to hold nothing as certain, to vouch for nothing. Of the three functions attributed to the soul (cogitation, appetite and assent) the Sceptics admit the first two but keep their assent in a state of ambiguity, inclining neither way, giving not even the slightest approbation to one side or the other.

[C] It was by gesture that Zeno illustrated his conception of the three functions of the soul: a hand stretched out open meant probability; half-closed, with the fingers bent over, meant assent; clenched, it meant understanding; with the other hand pressing it tighter still, it meant knowledge.[161]

[A] Now the Pyrrhonians make their faculty of judgement so unbending and upright that it registers everything but bestows its assent on nothing. This leads to their well-known *ataraxia*: that is a calm, stable rule of life, free from all the disturbances (caused by the impress of opinions, or of such knowledge of reality as we think we have) which give birth to fear, avarice, envy, immoderate desires, ambition, pride, superstition, love of novelty, rebellion, disobedience, obstinacy and the greater part of our bodily ills. In this way, they even free themselves from passionate sectarianism, for their disputes are mild affairs and they are never afraid of the other side having its say. When they assert that heavy things tend to fall downwards, they would be most upset if you believed them. They want you to contradict them in order to achieve their end: doubt and suspense of judgement. They only put forward propositions of their own in order to oppose the ones they think we believe in. Accept theirs, and they will gladly maintain the opposite. It is all the same to them: they take no sides. If you maintain that snow is black, they will argue that it is, on the contrary, white. If you say that it is neither, their task is to say that it is both. If you conclude that you definitely know nothing, they will maintain that you do know something. Yes, and if you present your doubt as axiomatic, they will challenge you on that too, arguing that you are not in doubt, or that you cannot decide for certain and prove that you are in doubt. This is doubt taken to its limits; it shakes its own foundations; such

160. Lucretius, IV, 469–70 (Lambin, p. 308). With these words begin Lucretius' dense criticism of scepticism. Montaigne borrows much from him and the commentary of Lambin.

161. Cicero, *Acad.: Lucullus*, II, xlvii, 144–45.

extremes of doubt separate them completely from many other theories including those which in many ways do indeed teach doubt and ignorance.[162]

[B]   If some Dogmatists call green what others call yellow, why, they ask, cannot they doubt both of them? Can there be any proposition capable of acceptance or rejection which it is not right to consider ambiguous?

Other people are prejudiced by the customs of their country, by the education given them by their parents or by chance encounter: normally, before the age of discretion, they are taken by storm and, without judgement or choice, accept this or that opinion of the Stoic or Epicurean sects. There they stay, mortgaged, enslaved, caught on a hook which they cannot get off – [C] '*ad quamcumque disciplinam velut tempestate delati, ad eam tanquam ad saxum adhaerescunt*' [they cling to any old teaching, like sailors washed up on a rock]. But why should people like these not also be allowed their freedom, making up their own minds without bonds and slavery?   [C]   '*Hoc liberiores et solutiores quod integra illis est judicandi potestas*' [They are all the more independent and free in that they enjoy the full power of judgement].[163] There is some advantage, surely, in being detached from the reins of the Necessity which curb others.   [B]   Is it not better to remain in doubt, than to get entangled in the many errors produced by human fantasy? Is it not better to postpone one's adherence indefinitely than to intervene in factions, both quarrelling and seditious?

[C]   'What ought I to choose?' – 'Anything you wish, so long as you choose something.' A daft enough reply! Yet it seems to be the one reached by every kind of dogmatism which refuses us the right not to know what we do not know.

[B]   Try siding with the school enjoying majority support: but it will never be safe enough: to defend it you will have to attack opponents by the hundreds. Is it not better to keep out of the fray altogether? You allow yourself to espouse, like honour and dear life, Aristotle's beliefs about the eternity of the soul; to do that you must reject and contradict Plato. In that case, why should others be forbidden simply to go on doubting?[164]

[C]   Panaetius was legally permitted to suspend judgement about dreams, oracles, prophecies and divination by entrails; yet his school, the Stoics, never doubted them. Why cannot a wise man dare to doubt anything and everything, if Panaetius could dare to doubt doctrines which were taught by

---

162. Sextus Empiricus, *Hypotyposes*, I, XII, 30; XIII, 33; cf. Rabelais, *Tiers Livre*, TLF, XXXVI.

163. Cicero, *Acad.: Lucullus*, II, iii, 8–9, the source of both quotations.

164. For Plato, *Forms* are created: for Aristotle, they exist from all eternity.

his own masters and founded on the common consent of the school he adhered to and whose doctrines he claimed to profess?

[B] If it is a child who makes the judgement, he does not know enough about the subject: if it is a learned man, then he has made up his mind already! – Pyrrhonians have given themselves a wonderful strategic advantage by shrugging off the burden of self-defence. It does not matter who attacks them, as long as somebody does. Anything serves their purpose: if they win, your argument is defective; if you do, theirs is. If they lose, they show the truth of Ignorance; if you lose, you do. If they can prove that nothing is known: fine. If they do not succeed in proving it, that is fine too.   [C]  'Ut quum in eadem re paria contrariis in partibus momenta inveniuntur, facilius ab utraque parte assertio sustineatur' [So that by finding equally good cases, for and against, on the very same subject, it is easier to suspend one's judgement about either side].¹⁶⁵

They make it their pride to be far more ready to find everything false than anything true and to show that things are not, rather than that they are. They prefer to proclaim what they do not believe, rather than what they do.  [A]  Their typical phrases include: 'I have settled nothing'; 'It is no more this than that'; 'Not one rather than the other'; 'I do not understand'; 'Both sides seem equally likely'; 'It is equally right to speak for and against either side'.   [C] To them, nothing seems true which cannot also seem false. They have sworn loyalty to the word ἐπέχω: 'I am in suspense'; I will not budge.¹⁶⁶

These sayings, and others like them, form refrains which lead to a pure, whole, complete suspension of their judgement, which is kept permanently in abeyance. They use their reason for inquiry and debate but never to make choices or decisions. If you can picture an endless confession of ignorance, or a power of judgement which never, never inclines to one side or the other, then you can conceive what Pyrrhonism is.

I have tried to explain this notion as clearly as I can, because many find it hard to grasp, and its very authors present it somewhat diversely and rather obscurely.

Where morals are concerned, they conform to the common mould. They find it appropriate to yield to natural inclinations, to the thrust and constraints of their emotions, to established laws and customs and to the traditional

165. Cicero, Acad.: Lucullus, II, xxxiii, 107, and I, xii, 45–46.

166. These and similar aphorisms from Sextus Empiricus were inscribed in Montaigne's library; Hypotyposes, I, 6, 21, 23, 26 and 27.

arts.[167]  [C] *'Non enim nos Deus ista scire, sed tantummodo uti voluit'* [For
God did not want us to know such things: merely to make use of
them].  [A]  They let their everyday activities be guided by such considerations, neither assenting nor adhering to anything. That is why I cannot
square with these conceptions what is told about Pyrrho himself. They[168]
describe him as emotionless and virtually senseless, adopting a wild way of
life, cut off from society, allowing himself to be bumped into by wagons,
standing on the edge of precipices and refusing to conform to the law. That
goes well beyond his teaching. He[169] was not fashioning a log or a stone but
a living, arguing, thinking man, enjoying natural pleasures and comforts of
every sort and making full use of all his parts, bodily as well as spiritual –
[C]  in, of course, a right and proper way.  [A]  Those false, imaginary and
fantastic privileges usurped by Man, by which he claims to profess, arrange
and establish the truth, were renounced and abandoned by Pyrrho, in good
faith.

–    [C]  Yet there is not one single school of philosophy which is not
forced to allow its Sage (if he wishes to live) to accept a great many things
which he cannot understand, perceive or give his assent to. Say he boards a
ship. He carries out his design, not knowing whether it will serve his purpose;
he assumes the vessel to be seaworthy, the pilot to be experienced and the
weather to be favourable. Such attendant details are, of course, merely probable: he is obliged to let himself be guided by appearances, unless they are
expressly contradicted. He has a body. He has a soul. He feels the impulsions
of his senses and the promptings of his spirit. He cannot find within himself
any sign specifically suggesting that it be appropriate for him to make an act
of judgement: he realizes he must not bind his consent to anything, since
something false may have every appearance of particular truth. Despite all
this, he never fails to do his duty in this life, fully and fittingly.

How many disciplines are there which actually profess to be based on
conjecture rather than on knowledge, and which, being unable to distinguish
truth from falsehood, merely follow what seems likely? Pyrrhonians say that
truth and falsehood exist: within us we have means of looking for them, but
not of making any lasting judgement: we have no touchstone.

We would be better off if we dropped our enquiries and let ourselves be
moulded by the natural order of the world. A soul safe from prejudice has

167. Sextus Empiricus, *Hypotyposes*, I, xi, 23–24, followed by quotation from
Cicero, *De divinat.*, I, xviii, 35.

168. '88: himself. *Laertius in the Life of Pyrrho says (and both Lucianus and Aulus
Gellius incline the same way) describe him . . .* (Laertius' *Life* was printed in Montaigne's copy of Sextus.)

169. Major borrowings follow from Cicero, *Acad.: Lucullus*, II, xxxi, 99–101.

made a wondrous advance towards peace of mind. People who judge their
judges and keep accounts of what they do fail to show due submissiveness.
Among people who are amenable to the legitimate teachings of religion and
politics, there are more simple and uninquisitive minds than minds which
keep a schoolmasterly eye on causes human and divine. –

[A] No system discovered by Man has greater usefulness nor a greater
appearance of truth [than Pyrrhonism] which shows us Man naked, empty,
aware of his natural weakness, fit to accept outside help from on high: Man,
stripped of all human learning and so all the more able to lodge the divine
within him, annihilating[170] his intellect to make room for faith;   [C]  he is
no scoffer,   [A]  he holds no doctrine contrary to established custom; he is
humble, obedient, teachable, keen to learn – and as a sworn enemy of heresy
he is freed from the vain and irreligious opinions introduced by erroneous
sects.   [B]  He is a blank writing-tablet, made ready for the finger of God
to carve such letters on him as he pleases. The more we refer ourselves to
God, commit ourselves to him and reject ourselves, the greater we are worth.
Ecclesiastes says: 'Accept all things in good part, just as they seem, just as
they taste, day by day. The rest is beyond thy knowledge':[171]   [C]  'Dominus
novit cogitationes hominum, quoniam vanae sunt' [The Lord knoweth the
thoughts of men, that they are vanity].

[A]  And so two out of the three generic schools of Philosophy make an
express profession of doubt and ignorance; it is easy to discover that most
who belonged to the third school, the Dogmatists, put on an assured face
merely because it looks better. They did not really think that they had established any certainties, but wanted to show us how far they had advanced in
their hunt for Truth,   [C]  'quam docti fingunt, magis quam norunt' [which
the learned feign rather than know]. When Timaeus had to reveal to Socrates
what he knew about the Gods, the world and mankind, he determined to
speak of such things as one man to another: it would be enough if the reasons
he gave had as much probability as anyone else's, since precise reasons were
neither in his grasp nor in the grasp of any mortal man.[172]

One of the followers of his school imitated him in these words: 'Ut potero,

170. '88: greater probability nor a greater appearance . . .
    '88: the divine instruction and belief, annihilating . . .

171. This 'quotation' from Ecclesiastes figures in Latin in Montaigne's library as
'Fruere jucunde praesentibus, caetera extra te'. (Its actual source is unknown.) Then, [C],
Psalm 94 (93): 11.

172. Plato, Timaeus, 29 (Ficino, p. 705). The Latin quotation is from Livy, Hist.,
xxvi, 22, 14. A marginal note authorized by Marie de Gournay reads, 'Perhaps Seneca in
Epistles' – a wrong guess.

*explicabo: nec tamen, ut Pythius Apollo, certa ut sint et fixa, quae dixero; sed, ut homunculus, probabilia conjectura sequens'* [I will unravel things as best I may. What I shall say is neither fixed nor certain: I am no Pythian Apollo; I am a little man seeking the probable through conjecture]. Yet he was merely treating a common, not supernatural theme: contempt for death! In another place he translates Timaeus directly from Plato: *'Si forte, de deorum natura ortuque mundi disserentes, minus id quod habemus animo consequimur, haud erit mirum. Aequum est enim meminisse et me qui disseram, hominem esse, et vos qui judicetis; ut, si probabilia dicentur, nihil ultra requiratis'* [If we are unable to achieve what we have in mind to do when we set out to treat the nature of the Gods and the origin of the world, that will not be surprising. It is right to remember that both I who am speaking and you who are judging are men. If what I say is probable, you can demand nothing more].[173]

[A] Aristotle regularly piles up many different opinions and beliefs, so as to evaluate his own against them. He shows how much farther he has gone and how much nearer he has approached to probability – Truth not being something we should accept on authority or from the testimony of others. [C] (That is why Epicurus scrupulously avoided citing such evidence in his writings.) [A] Aristotle is the Prince of the Dogmatists; and yet it is from him we learn that greater knowledge leads to further doubt. You can often find him hiding behind a deliberate obscurity,[174] so deep and impenetrable that you cannot make out what he meant. In practice it is Pyrrhonism cloaked in affirmation.

[C] Just listen to this assertion of Cicero, explaining to us another's notion by his own: *'Qui requirunt quid de quaque re ipsi sentiamus, curiosius id faciunt quam necesse est. Haec in philosophia ratio contra omnia disserendi nullamque rem aperte judicandi, profecta a Socrate, repetita ab Arcesila, confirmata a Carneade, usque ad nostram viget aetatem. Hi sumus qui omnibus veris falsa quaedam adjuncta esse dicamus, tanta similitudine ut in iis nulla insit certe judicandi et assentiendi nota.'* [Those who want to know what my personal opinions are on each of these subjects are more inquisitive than they ought to be. Up to now it has been a principle of philosophy to argue against anything but to decide nothing. This principle was established by Socrates; Arcesilus repeated it; Carneades strengthened it further. I am one of those who hold that there is, in all truths, an admixture of falsehood so like Truth that

---

173. Cicero: *Tusc. disput.* I, ix.; *Timaeus*, III (*in Fragmentis*).
174. '88: obscurity, (*as for example on the subject of the immortality of the soul*) so deep . . .

there is no way of deciding or determining anything whatever with complete
certainty.][175]

[B]  Not only Aristotle but most philosophers aim at being hard to understand; why? – if not to emphasize the vanity of their subject-matter and to give
our minds something to do! Philosophy is a hollow bone with no flesh on it: are
they providing us with a place to feed in, where we can chew on it?[176]

[C]  Clitomachus maintained that he could not tell from Carneades' books
what his opinions were.[177]   [B]   That is why Epicurus avoided perspicuity
in his writings and why Heraclitus was surnamed Σκοτεινὸς, 'Dark'. Difficulty is a coin   [C]   which the learned conjure with, so as not to reveal the
vanity of their studies and   [B]   which human stupidity is keen to accept
in payment.

> *Clarus, ob obscuram linguam, magis inter inanes,*
> *Omnia enim stolidi magis admirantur amantque*
> *Inversis quae sub verbis latitantia cernunt.*

[Clear was his fame, especially among the empty-headed, simply because his language
lacked clarity: for stupid people are filled with awe and wonder when they find ideas
wrapped up in words turned inside out.][178]

[C]  Cicero reproached some of his friends with being accustomed to give
more time than they were worth to such subjects as astrology, law, dialectic
and geometry: it kept them away from the more useful and honourable of
life's duties. The Cyrenaic philosophers held physics and dialectic in equal
contempt. At the very beginning of his books on the *Republic* Zeno pronounced all liberal disciplines to be useless.   [A]   Chrysippus said that what
Plato and Aristotle wrote about logic must have been written for sport or as
an exercise; he could not believe that they had anything serious to say on so
empty a subject.   [C]   Plutarch makes a similar remark about metaphysics.[179]   [A]   Epicurus would have spoken similarly about rhetoric,
grammar,   [C]   poetry, mathematics and all subjects of study other than
physics –   [A]   and Socrates, about every one of them, with the sole exception of the study of how we should behave in this life.   [C]   Whatever

175.  Cicero, *De nat. deorum*, I, v, 10 (adapted).

176.  Plato called a dog 'philosophical' since it strives to get at the marrow of a bare
bone (*Republic*, III, 375E; cf. Rabelais, *Gargantua*, TLF, p. 13).

177.  Cicero, *Acad.: Lucullus*, II, xlv, 139.

178.  Lucretius, I, 639–42, incorporating matter in Lambin, p. 63 (Vitruvius,
Cicero, etc.).

179.  Cicero, *De officiis*, I, vi, 19: Diogenes Laertius, *Lives*: Aristippus, II, 91; Zeno,
VII, 32; Plutarch, tr. Amyot, *Life of Alexander*.

question Socrates was asked, he first made the speaker give a detailed account of his way of life, both present and past; he made that the basis of his inquiries and judgements, believing as he did that any other approach was secondary to that and superfluous.

'*Parum mihi placeant eae literae quae ad virtutem doctoribus nihil profuerunt*' [I take no pleasure in the kind of writings which do not increase the virtue of those who teach them].[180]

[A] Learning[181] itself has despised most disciplines, but men have thought it not inappropriate to train and entertain their minds even by studying subjects where nothing solid is to be gained. Moreover, some have classified Plato as a Dogmatist; some, as a Doubter; others as both, depending on the subject.

[C] Socrates, who takes the lead in the *Dialogues*, always asks questions designed to provoke discussion: he is never satisfied and never reaches any conclusion. He says that the only thing he knew how to do was to make objections.

All schools of philosophy derive their foundations from Homer, but it was a matter of indifference to him what direction we then took; to show that, he gave equally good foundations to all of them. They say that ten distinct schools sprang from Plato. And indeed, as I see it, if his teachings are not faltering and unaffirmative, then I do not know whose are![182]

Socrates said that midwives were *Sage-women* who stop producing children of their own once they help others to do so; when, therefore, the gods conferred the title *Sage* on him, he too gave up his capacity for producing brain-children of his own by acts of manly love, in order to encourage and help other men to deliver theirs: he opened the genitals of their minds, lubricated the passages and made it easier for their child to issue forth; he then made an appreciation of that child, washed it, nursed it, strengthened it, swaddled it up and circumcised it. He used and exercised his own ingenuity: the others faced the perils and the risks.[183]

[A] What I said just now is true of other philosophers in the third category, [B] as the Ancients already noted in the writings of Anaxagoras, Democritus, Parmenides, Zenophanes and others: [A] their substance induces doubt; their purpose is inquiry rather than instruction, even though,

180. Sallust *apud* Justus Lipsius, *Politicorum*, 1584, I, 10.

181. '88: Learning *and philosophy have* despised . . . (Sextus Empiricus, *Hypotyposes*, I, XXXI, 221.)

182. Cf. Seneca, *Epist.*, LXXXVIII; Diogenes Laertius, *Lives*, Socrates (*ad fin.*).
'95: *circumscribed* for *circumcised*.

183. Plato, *Theaetetus*, 150-51.

in their works, they do at times interlard[184]  [C]  their style with Dogmatic
cadences. Is that not equally true of both Seneca and Plutarch? Go into it
closely and you see they are constantly talking from different points of view.
As for those jurisconsults whose task it is to harmonize the various legal
authorities, they first ought to harmonize each authority with himself.

Plato seems to me to have quite knowingly chosen to treat philosophy in
the form of dialogues: he was better able to expound the diversity and variety
of his concepts by putting them appropriately into the mouths of divers
speakers. Variety of treatment is as good as consistency. Better in fact: it
means being more copious and more useful.

Let us take one example from our own society. The highest degree of
dogmatic and conclusive speaking is reached in parliamentary rescripts. Of
the judicial decrees which French Parliaments hand down to the people, the
ones which are most exemplary (and the most proper to encourage the respect
which is rightly due to such high office, mainly on account of the ability of
those who exercise it) do not draw their beauty from their decisions as such.
Decisions are everyday affairs, common to all judges. Their beauty lies in the
disquisitions and that pursuit of varied and opposing arguments which legal
matters can so well accommodate.

When philosophers find fault with each other, their widest field of action
lies in the internal contradictions and inconsistencies which entangle them
all – either deliberately (so as to show the vacillations of the human mind
over any subject whatever) or else quite unintentionally, because all matters
are shifting and elusive.

[A]  What else can that refrain mean: 'In slippery, shifting places, let
us suspend our judgement'? For, as Euripides said, 'The works of God,
in divers ways, perplex us,'[185]  [B]  which is similar to the words which
Empedocles strewed throughout his books when he was shaken as by
divine mania and compelling truth: 'No, no! We feel nothing: we know
nothing! All things are hidden from us: we can determine the nature of
nothing whatsoever,'  [C]  words which conform to that holy saying:
'*Cogitationes mortalium timidae et incertae adinventiones nostrae et providentiae*'

184. '88 (in place of [C]): they do interlard them *often with traits, dogmatist in form.
In whom can one see that more clearly than in our Plutarch? How differently he treats the
same subjects! How many times does he present us with two or three incompatible causes and
divers reasons for the same subject, without selecting the one we ought to follow?* What else
can that refrain mean . . .

185. Cited from Plutarch, tr. Amyot, *Des oracles qui ont cessé*, 348B: '*Les oeuvres de
Dieu en diverses/Façons nous donnent des traverses.*'

[For the thoughts of mortal men are timorous, and our devices and fore-sight prone to fail].[186]

[A]   We ought not to find it strange that people who despair of the kill should not renounce the pleasure of the hunt: study is, in itself, a delightful occupation, so delightful that, among the forbidden pleasures which need to be held on a tight rein, the Stoics include pleasure arising from exercising the mind.[187]   [C]   They find intemperance in knowing too much.

[A]   Democritus ate some figs which tasted of honey. He at once began to rack his brains to try and explain this unusual sweetness. He was about to abandon his dinner and set out to trace and examine the place where the figs had been picked, when his servant-girl heard the cause of the commotion and began to laugh; she told him to stop worrying about all that, since she had put the figs in a jar which had previously held honey. He flew into a rage with her because she had deprived him of the chance of finding things out for himself and had robbed his curiosity of something to work on: 'Go away,' he said, 'you have offended me. I shall continue to look for the cause as though it were to be found in Nature.'   [C]   And he did manage to find some sort of 'true' explanation for a false and imaginary fact!

[A]   This story about a great and famous philosopher clearly illustrates that passion for study which keeps us occupied, hunting after things we can never hope to catch. Plutarch relates a similar anecdote about a man who did not want anyone to enlighten him on a subject of doubt, so as not to lose the pleasure of the search – like that other man, who would not allow his doctor to cure a thirst brought on by fever, so as not to lose the pleasure of quenching it!   [C]   *'Satius est supervacua discere quam nihil'* [Better to learn something useless than nothing at all].[188] It is the same with food of all kinds. Sometimes we eat just for pleasure: there are things we eat which are neither nutritious nor sustaining. So too for the pabulum which our spirits draw from erudition: it may be neither nutritious nor sustaining, but it gives great pleasure.

[B]   This is how they put it: contemplating Nature supplies good food to the spirit: it replenishes it, helps it to soar aloft, makes it despise low and earthly things by comparing them with heavenly things. It is delightful merely to study great and abstruse subjects: that remains true even of the

186. Cicero, *Acad.: Lucullus*, II, V, 14; Wisdom of Solomon 9:14. Cf. Augustine, *City of God*, XII, 16.

187. '88: mind; *and desire moderation.* Democritus . . . (Seneca, *Epist.*, LXXXVIII, 36.)

188. Plutarch, tr. Amyot; *Propos de Table*, 368 G–H.; King Philopappus (Plutarch, *loc. cit.*); Seneca, *Epist.*, LXXXVIII, 45.

man who acquires nothing from study except a sense of awe and a fear of making judgements on such matters.[189]

That, in a few words, is what they profess.

An express image of the vanity of such sickly curiosity can be better seen from another example, which philosophers are always honouring themselves by quoting. Eudoxus prayed to the gods, hoping to be allowed to have just one sight of the sun from close at hand, so as to apprehend its shape, grandeur and beauty. Even if it meant being burned alive, he would pay the price. He wanted to learn, at the cost of his life, something he would lose as soon as he had acquired it. For such a brief and fleeting glimpse of knowledge he was prepared to surrender all the knowledge he already had or could later have acquired.[190]

[A]   I cannot really convince myself that Epicurus, Plato and Pythagoras genuinely wanted us to accept their Atoms, Ideas and Numbers as valid currency. They were too wise to base the articles of their belief on foundations so shaky and so challengeable. Each of these great figures strove to bring some image of light into the dark ignorance of this world; they applied their minds to concepts which had at least some subtle and pleasing appearance of truth,   [C]   their only proviso being that they could stand up to hostile objections: '*unicuique ista pro ingenio finguntur, non ex scientiae vi*' [such theories are fictions, produced not from solid knowledge but from their individual wits].[191]

[A]   One of the Ancients was reproved for not judging philosophy to be of much account yet continuing to profess it; 'That is what being a philosopher means,' he replied.[192] Such men wanted to weigh everything in their mental balances; there is curiosity in all of us: this, they found, was a proper way to keep it occupied. Part of what they wrote was simply designed to meet the social needs of the general public – their accounts of their religion, for example.[193] With that end in view it was reasonable not to strip popularly held opinions of their living feathers. They had no wish to spawn ideas which would disturb the people's obedience to the laws and customs of their land.

[C]   When treating religious mystery Plato plays a very open game. Writ-

189. Cicero, *Acad.: Lucullus*, II, xli, 127.

190. Plutarch, tr. Amyot: *Que l'on ne sçauroit vivre selon la doctrine d'Epicurus*, 282H–283A.

191. Marcus Annaeus Seneca, *Suasoriae*, IV.

192. Diogenes, cf. Diogenes Laertius *apud* Guy de Brués, *Dialogues, contre les nouveaux Academiciens, que tout ne consiste point en opinion*, 1557, p. 46.

193. '88: public, their *account of religions*, for example: *for it is not forbidden for us to draw advantage even from a lie, if needs be*. With that . . .

ing in his own name he lays down nothing as certain, but, whenever he acts as Law-giver, he adopts an assertive professorial style. Even then, he is bold enough to work in a few of his most fantastic notions (which were as useful for convincing the people as they were ridiculous for convincing himself), well aware how receptive our minds are to any impressions, especially to the wildest and most extraordinary ones. That explains why, in the *Laws*, Plato is careful to allow no poetry to be recited in public unless its fables and fictions serve some moral end: it is so easy to impress fancies on the human mind that it is not right to feed minds on useless, harmful lies, when you can feed them on profitable ones. In the *Republic* he says quite bluntly that you must often deceive the people for their own good.[194]

You soon discover that some schools of philosophy were chiefly concerned to pursue truth, and others – gaining credit thereby – moral usefulness. Our human condition is pitiable: often, the things which strike our imagination as the most true are ones which appear least useful for the purposes of life. Even the most audacious of the schools, the Epicureans, the Pyrrhonians and the New Academy, are constrained in the end to bow to the laws of society.

[A]   There are other subjects which philosophers toss to and fro in their sieves, trying to dredge them (whether they deserve it or not) into some appearance of likelihood. Having discovered nothing so profound as really to be worth talking about, they are obliged to forge some weak and insane conjectures of their own, treating them not as bases for truth but for studious exercises.   [C] '*Non tam id sensisse quod dicerent, quam exercere ingenia materiae difficultate videntur voluisse*' [They do not seem to believe what they say, but, rather, to exercise their wits on difficult material].[195]

[A]   If you will not take it that way, how else can we explain the obvious inconstancy, diversity and vanity of the opinions produced by such excellent and, indeed, awesome, minds? What can be more vain, for example, than trying to make guesses about God from human analogies and conjectures which reduce him and the universe to our own scale and our own laws, taking that tiny corner of intellect with which it pleases God to endow the natural Man and then employing it at the expense of his Godhead? And since we cannot stretch our gaze as far as the seat of his Glory, are we to drag him down to our corruption and our wretchedness?

Of all the ancient opinions of men touching religion, it seems to me that the most excusable and verisimilitudinous was the one which recognized God as some incomprehensible Power, the Origin and Preserver of all things, of

194.  Diogenes Laertius, *Lives*, Plato, II, lxxx; Plato, *Republic*, II (end), III (beginning); *ibid.*, V, p. 459, tr. Ficino, p. 591.

195.  Quintilian, II, 17, 4.

all goodness and of all perfection, who took and accepted in good part, the
honour and reverence which human beings rendered him, under any guise,
under any name and in any way whatsoever.

[C]  *Jupiter omnipotens rerum, regumque deumque*
     *Progenitor genitrixque.*

[Almighty Jupiter, Father and Mother of the world, of rulers and of gods.][196]

Such devotion has always been regarded by Heaven with favour.

All forms of government have profited from their allegiance to it; under it,
men and impious deeds have met their just deserts; even pagan histories
acknowledge the dignity, order and justice of the portents and oracles mani-
fested in their fabulous religions for the benefit and instruction of men. With
such temporal benefits as these God in his mercy may perhaps have deigned
to protect those tender principles of rough-and-ready knowledge of Himself
which Natural Reason affords us, amid the false imaginings of our dreams.
But there are religions Man has forged entirely on his own: they are not only
false but impious and harmful.

[A]  Of all the religions which St Paul found honoured in Athens, the
most excusable, he thought, was the one dedicated to a hidden, 'unknown
God'.[197]

[C]  Pythagoras closely adumbrated truth when he concluded that any
conception we have of that First Cause, of that Being of beings, must be free
of limits, restrictions or definitions; it was in fact the utmost striving of our
intellect towards perfection, each of us enlarging the concept according to
his capacity.

But if Numa really did attempt to make his people's worship conform to
this model, tying them to an entirely cerebral religion with no object set up
before their eyes and no material elements mixed in with it, then his undertaking could serve no purpose.[198] The human mind cannot stand such wander-
ings through an infinity of shapeless thoughts: they must be brought together
into some definite concept modelled on man. The very majesty of God allows
itself to be, in some sense, circumscribed for us within physical limits: God's

196. Valerius Soranus *apud* Augustine, *City of God*, VII, 11.
  '88 (in place of [C]): *For the deities to which men have wished to give a form of their
own invention, are harmful, full of errors and impiety. That is why of* all the religions . . .
  197. Paul's sermon in Acts 17:23: 'I found also an altar with this inscription "TO
AN UNKNOWN GOD".' By adding *hidden* Montaigne links this text to God as *Deus
absconditus* (Introduction, p. xx). Even good natural religion requires grace if it is to
take root and grow.
  198. Plutarch, tr. Amyot, *Life of Numa*.

sacraments are supernatural and celestial, yet they bear signs of our own
condition, which is earthy; and we express our adoration in words and duties
perceptible to the senses. After all, it is Man who does the believing and the
praying.

I shall leave aside other arguments marshalled on this topic; consider the
sight of our crucifixes and the piteous chastisement which they portray; the
ornaments and moving ceremonial in our churches; the voices so aptly fitted
to the reverent awe of our thoughts, and all the stirring of our emotions: you
will have a hard time making me believe that such things do not set whole
nations' souls ablaze with a passion for religion, with very useful results.

[A]   Of all the deities to which bodies have been ascribed (as necessity
required during that universal blindness), I think[199] I would have most willingly gone along with those who worshipped the Sun:

> *la lumiere commune,*
> *L'œil du monde; et si Dieu au chef porte des yeux,*
> *Les rayons du Soleil sont ses yeux radieux,*
> *Qui donnent vie à tous, nous maintiennent et gardent,*
> *Et les faicts des humains en ce monde regardent:*
> *Ce beau, ce grand soleil qui nous faict les saisons,*
> *Selon qu'il entre ou sort de ses douze maisons;*
> *Qui remplit l'univers de ses vertus connues;*
> *Qui, d'un traict de ses yeux, nous dissipe les nues:*
> *L'esprit, l'ame du monde, ardant et flamboyant,*
> *En la course d'un jour tout le Ciel tournoyant;*
> *Plein d'immense grandeur, rond, vagabond et ferme;*
> *Lequel tient dessoubs luy tout le monde pour terme;*
> *En repos sans repos; oysif, et sans sejour;*
> *Fils aisné de nature et le pere du jour.*

[. . . the Common Light, the Eye of the World; if God himself has eyes they are radiant
ones made of the Sun's rays which give life to all, protect and guard us men, gazing
down upon our actions in this world; this fair, this mighty Sun who makes the seasons
change according to his journey through his dozen Mansions; who floods the earth
with his acknowledged power; who, with a flicker of his eye disperses clouds; the Spirit
and Soul of the World, ardent and aflame, encompassing the world in the course of
one single day; full of immense grandeur, round, wandering and firm; who holds
beneath him the boundaries of the world; resting, unresting; idle, never staying; the
eldest Son of Nature and the Father of Light.][200]

Even leaving its grandeur and beauty aside, the Sun is the most distant

199. '88: required, *because of the people's conception*), I think . . .
200. Ronsard, *Remonstrance au peuple de France*, 64f.

part of the universe which Man can descry, and hence so little known that
those who fell into reverent ecstasies before it were excusable.

[C] Thales[201] was the first to inquire into such matters: he thought God
was a Spirit who made all things out of water; Anaximander said that the
gods are born and die with the seasons and that there are worlds infinite in
number; Anaximenes said God was Air, immense, extensive, ever moving;
Anaxagoras was the first to hold that the delineation and fashioning of all
things was directed by the might and reason of an infinite Spirit; Alcmaeon
attributed Godhead to the Sun, the Moon, the stars and to the soul; Pythagoras made God into a Spirit diffused throughout all nature and from whom
our souls are detached; for Parmenides God was a circle of light surrounding
the heavens and sustaining the world with its heat; Empedocles made gods
from the four natural elements of which all things are compounded; Protagoras would not say whether the gods existed or not or what they are if they
do; Democritus sometimes asserted that the constellations and their circular
paths were gods, sometimes that God was that Nature whose impulse first
made them move; then he said our knowledge and our intellect were God;
Plato's beliefs are diffuse and many-sided: in the *Timaeus* he says that the
Father of the world cannot be named; in the *Laws* he forbids all inquiry into
the proper being of God: elsewhere, in these very same books, he makes
the world, the sky, the heavenly bodies, the earth and our souls into gods,
recognizing as well all the gods accepted by ancient custom in every country.
Xenophon records a similar confusion in the teachings of Socrates: sometimes
he has Socrates maintaining that no inquiry should be made into the properties of God; at other times he has him deciding that the Sun is God, that the
soul is God, that there is only one God and then that there are many. The
nephew of Plato, Speusippus, holds God to be a certain animate Power
governing all things; Aristotle sometimes says that God is Mind and sometimes the World; at times he gives the world a different Master and sometimes
makes a god from the heat of the sky. Zenocrates has eight gods: five are
named after the planets; the sixth has all the fixed stars as his members, the
seventh and eighth being the Sun and Moon. Heraclides of Pontus meanders
along beneath these various notions and ends up with a God deprived of all
sensation; he has him changing from one form to another and finally asserts
that he is heaven and earth. Theophrastus is similarly undecided, wandering
about between his many concepts, attributing the government of the world
sometimes to Intelligence, sometimes to the sky and sometimes to the stars;

201. There follows a massive borrowing, condensed, from Cicero, *De nat. deorum*,
I, X, 25–xii, 30 (with some errors), with additions from *ibid.*, I, viii, 18 f.; xxiv, 63,
and *De divinat.*, II, XVII, 40.

Strato says God is Nature, giving birth, making things wax and wane, but itself formless and insensate; Zeno makes a god of Natural Law: it commands good, forbids evil and is animate; he dismisses the gods accepted by custom – Jupiter, Juno and Vesta; Diogenes of Apollonia says God is Time. Xenophanes makes God round, able to see and hear but not to breathe and having nothing in common with human nature; Ariston thinks that the form of God cannot be grasped: he deprives him of senses and cannot tell whether he is animate or something quite different. For Cleanthes God is sometimes Reason, sometimes the World, sometimes the Soul of Nature, sometimes absolute Heat surrounding and enveloping all things. Perseus, a pupil of Zeno's, maintained that the name *god* was bestowed on people who had contributed some outstandingly useful improvements to the life of Man – or even on the improvements themselves. Chrysippus made a chaotic mass of all these assertions and included among his thousand forms of gods men who had been immortalized. Diagoras and Theodorus bluntly denied that gods exist. Epicurus has shiny gods, permeable to wind and light, who are lodged between two worlds which serve as fortresses protecting them from being battered; they are clothed in human shape, with limbs like ours which are quite useless.

> *Ego deûm genus esse semper duxi, et dicam coelitum;*
> *Sed eos non curare opinor, quid agat humanum genus.*

[Personally I have always thought, and will always say, that a race of gods exists in heaven. But I do not think that they care about the actions of the human race.][202]

So much din from so many philosophical brainboxes! Trust in your philosophy now! Boast that you are the one who has found the lucky bean in your festive pudding!

I have drawn some profit from the confusion of forms in the customs of the world: manners and concepts different from mine do not so much annoy me as instruct me; comparing them does not puff me up with pride but humbles me. There is for me no such thing as a privileged choice, except one coming expressly from the hand of God.

I shall not go into monstrous and unnatural vice but on that subject the legislatures of this world are no less contradictory than the rival schools of philosophy. From that we can learn that Fortune herself is not more varied, fickle, blind and ill-advised than human reason.

[A]  Things we know least about are the ones we find most proper to

202. Ennius *apud* Cicero, *De divinat.* II, 1, 104.

deify.[203]   [C]   Making gods of men   [A]   as Antiquity did surpasses even
the most extreme imbecility of reason. I would rather have followed those
who worship the serpent, the dog and the bull; since the natures of such
animals are less known to us, we are free to imagine them as we like and to
endow them with extraordinary qualities. But the Ancients attributed to their
gods our own condition – the imperfections of which we ought to know; they
gave them desire, wrath, acts of vengeance, marriages, powers of generation
and family trees, love, jealousy, bones and limbs like ours, our own feverish
passions and pleasures,   [C]   our deaths and funerals.   [A]   The human
intellect must have been astonishingly drunk to produce all that!

> [B]   *Quae procul usque adeo divino ab numine distant,*
> *Inque Deum numero quae sint indigna videri.*

[Things far removed from numinous deity, unworthy to appear among the Gods.]

[C]   '*Formae, aetates, vestitus, ornatus noti sunt; genera, conjugia, cognationes*
*omniaque traducta ad similitudinem imbecillitatis humanae: nam et perturbatis*
*animis inducuntur; accipimus enim deorum cupiditates, aegritudines, iracundias*'
[We know their faces, their ages, their vestments and their adornments.
Their families, their marriages and their kinships are all reduced to the model
of human weakness. They are even given troubled minds. We hear of the
desires of the gods, of their sicknesses and of their fits of anger].

[A]   Similarly they made gods   [C]   not only of Faith, Virtue, Honour,
Concord, Freedom, Victory, Piety, but even of Pleasure, Fraud, Death,
Envy, Old Age and Misery,   [A]   of Fear, Fever, Ill-Fortune and the other
evils which beset our fragile and decaying lives:

> [B]   *Quid juvat hoc, templis nostros inducere mores?*
> *O curvae in terris animae et coelestium inanes!*

[What pleasure can be found from introducing our manners into our temples? O souls
bowed earthwards, entirely void of things celestial!][204]

[C]   With what unwise wisdom did the Egyptians forbid, under pain of
hanging, that anyone should let it be known that their Gods Serapis and Isis
had once been human: everybody knew then that they had been so! According

---

203. '88: deify: *for adoring things of our own kind, sickly corruptible and mortal, as all*
Antiquity did, *of men whom they had seen living and dying and disturbed by our passions*
surpasses . . .

204. Lucretius, V, 123 (Lambin, pp. 383–84); Cicero, *De nat. deor.*, II, xxviii, 70
(cited with Augustine, *City of God*, IV, xxx, in mind); Cicero, *De nat. deorum*, II, xxiii,
59 ff.; I, xi. 28; xvi, 42; Persius, *Satires*, II, 62 and 61.

to Varro effigies of these Gods were carved with their fingers on their lips to signify this mysterious command to their priests to hush up their mortal origins (otherwise all worship of them would inevitably be brought to naught).[205]

[A]   Since man was so desirous of making himself the equal of God, it would have been better, said Cicero, to bring the properties of God down to earth and to turn them into human attributes rather than to send our wretchedness and corruption up to heaven.[206] But if you look at it aright, equally vain opinions have led Man, in various ways, to do both.

When philosophers go into the hierarchy of their gods and rush to distinguish the alliances, attributes and powers of each of them, I cannot believe they are serious.

When Plato deciphered for us the myth of the 'Orchard of Dis'[207] telling us of the physical pleasures and pains awaiting us (after our bodies have decayed into nothing!); when he associated them with sensations experienced in this present life –

> *Secreti celant calles, et myrtea circum*
> *Sylva tegit; curae non ipsa in morte relinquunt.*

[They hide away in secret glades, screened by myrtle groves on every side; even when dead their troubles do not leave them] –

and when Mahomet promised his followers a paradise decked out with tapestries and carpets, with ornaments of gold and precious stones, furnished with voluptuous nymphs of outstanding beauty, with wines and choice foods to eat: I realized that they were both laughing at us, stooping low to tempt our brutish stupidity with sweet allurements, enticing us with notions and hopes appropriate to our mortal appetites.

[C]   Even some of our Christians have fallen into a similar error, promising themselves an earthly life after our resurrection, a life within time, accompanied by all kinds of worldly pleasures and comforts.   [A]   Plato's thoughts were all of heaven; his familiarity with things divine was so great

205. St Augustine, *City of God*, XVIII, v.

206. Cicero, *De nat. deorum*, I, xxxii, 90; also *Tusc. disput.*, I, xxvi, 65, *apud* Augustine, *City of God*, IV, xxvi.

207. Plato, *Gorgias*, 524a; *Repub.*, 614E; Plutarch, *De la face qui apparoist dedans le ronde de la lune*, 626 CD. For the implications of this passage for Montaigne's conception of the after-life, see *Montaigne and Melancholy*, pp. 131–32, and note 1.

that the surname *Divine* has clung to him ever since;[208] are we to believe that
even he thought there was, in a wretched creature like Man, something able
to approach such incomprehensible Power? Did he believe that we, with our
feeble grasp, could actually have a share in eternal blessedness or reprobation,
or that our senses were robust enough to do so?[209]

This is what we ought to say to him, on behalf of human reason:

If the pleasures you offer me in the next life are related to ones I have
experienced here on earth, that can have nothing to do with the Infinite.
Even if my five natural senses were overwhelmed with joy; even if this
soul of mine were seized of all the happiness she could ever hope for or
desire, we know her limitations:[210] that would amount to nothing. Where
there remains anything of mine, there is nothing divine. If your promises
merely relate to what can exist in our present condition, they cannot
enter into the reckoning.   [C]  All the pleasures of mortals are mortal.   [A]  Take recognizing parents, children and friends in the next
world: if that can touch us and titillate us, if we grasp at such pleasures
as that, then we still remain within earthbound,[211] finite pleasures. We
cannot condignly conceive those high, divine promises if we are able to
conceive them at all. To imagine them condignly, we must imagine them
unimaginable, unutterable, incomprehensible  [C]  and entirely different from our own wretched experiences.   [A]  'Eye cannot see', says
St Paul, 'nor can there rise up in the heart of man, what God has prepared
for his own.'[212] And if (as you assert, Plato, with your 'purifications') we
have to modify our being in order to render ourselves capable of celestial
joy, that would mean a change so extreme and so total that (as we know
from Physics) we would cease to be ourselves:

> [B]  *Hector erat tunc cum bello certabat; at ille,*
> *Tractus ab Aemonio, non erat Hector, equo.*

208. '88: has *justly* clung to him . . . (From Antiquity onwards we find the term
*Divinus Plato*: in the Renaissance it acknowledges Plato's inspiration and sometimes
his preoccupation with the world of the soul.)

209. '88: a *vile* creature like man . . . our *languishing* grasp . . . or that *our taste was
firm* enough to do so?

210. '88: hope for or *can do, we know the weakness and inadequacy of her forces*:
that . . .

211. '88: within *mortal*, finite . . .

212. I Corinthians II:9, adapted. (*The* text for Pauline ecstasy; see *Ecstasy and the
'Praise of Folly'*, pp. 174–79; *Montaigne and Melancholy*, p. 131.)

[Hector was killed in battle: but it was not Hector who was dragged along by Achilles' horse.]

[A]   Something else would receive our rewards.

> [ B]   *quod mutatur, dissolvitur; interit ergo:*
> *Trajiciuntur enim partes atque ordine migrant.*

[When what is changed is loosened asunder, that is death. The elements are displaced and change their ordered places.][213]

[A]   Pythagoras thought up his metempsychosis in which souls change their dwelling-places: are we to think that the lion which is now housing the soul of Caesar has espoused the passions which moved Caesar,   [C]   or that it really is Caesar? And if it really were Caesar, then victory would lie with those who opposed Plato over this opinion, pointing out, among other absurdities, that a son might well find himself astride his mother, now clothed in the body of a mule.[214]

Do we doubt   [A]   that, in such transmigrations as may take place within the same species, the newcomers are different from their forebears? They say that from the ashes of the Phoenix there is born first a worm and then another Phoenix; can anyone think that the second Phoenix is no different from the first? The worm which produces silk for us can be seen dying and shrivelling up: then, from that same body a butterfly appears; that produces another worm: it would be absurd to think it was still the first one. That which once ceases to be no longer exists.

> *Nec si materiam nostram collegerit aetas*
> *Post obitum, rursumque redegerit, ut sita nunc est,*
> *Atque iterum nobis fuerint data lumina vitae,*
> *Pertineat quidquam tamen ad nos id quoque factum,*
> *Interrupta semel cum sit repetentia nostra.*

[If Time, after we are dead, should gather our matter together and make it as it now is; if the light of life were again granted to us – even that would not concern us, once the thread of our memory has been snapped asunder.]

You assert somewhere or other, Plato, that rewards in the life to come concern the spiritual part of man, but that remains just as unlikely.

213. Ovid, *Tristia*, III, 11, 27; Lucretius, III, 756–57 (Lambin, p. 241).
214. Porphyry in St Augustine, *City of God*, X, xxx.

> [B]  *Scilicet, avolsis radicibus, ut nequit ullam*
> *Dispicere ipse oculus rem, seorsum corpore toto.*

[For an eye torn from its socket and removed from its body can see nothing whatsoever.]

[A]  By your reckoning, it would no longer be Man who is touched by such Joy – no longer us: for we are built of two principal parts, which together form our being; to separate them is death and the collapse of our being.

> [B]  *Inter enim jecta est vitai pausa, vageque*
> *Deerrarunt passim motus ab sensibus omnes.*

[For life has been interrupted. No motions can affect our senses now; they are quite lost.]

When the limbs a man had in life are eaten by worms and turning to dust we never say that the man is feeling pain:

> *Et nihil hoc ad nos, qui coitu conjugioque*
> *Corporis atque animae consistimus uniter apti.*

[That is nothing to us. We are a union formed from the marriage and embrace of body and soul.][215]

Moreover, what just grounds do the gods have for noting and rewarding, after death, a man's good, virtuous deeds? Within that man it is the gods themselves who nurtured and produced them. And why are the gods offended by his vicious deeds? Why do they punish them? They themselves brought him forth in this faulty state; with a mere nod of their will they can prevent his failure?[216]

Surely Epicurus, with every appearance of human rationality, could have raised such objections to Plato, [C]  had he not already covered himself by his oft-repeated conclusion: 'From mortal nature nothing certain can be inferred about the Immortal.'

[A]  Human reason goes astray everywhere, but especially when she concerns herself with matters divine. Who knows that better than we do? For we have supplied Reason with principles which are certain and infallible; we light her steps with the holy lamp of that Truth which God has been pleased to impart to us; yet we can see, every day, that as soon as she is allowed to

215. Lucretius, III, 846 (Lambin, pp. 247–51); III, 563–64 (Lambin, pp. 227–28); III, 860 (Lambin, pp. 251–54); III, 845 (Lambin, pp. 247–50).
216. '88: *our* vicious deeds . . . brought *us* forth . . . prevent *our* failure?

deviate, however slightly, from the normal path, turning and straying from
the beaten track traced for us by the Church, she immediately stumbles and
becomes inextricably lost; she whirls aimlessly about, bobbing unchecked on
the huge, troubled, surging sea of human opinion. As soon as she misses that
great public highway she disintegrates and scatters in hundreds of different
directions.

Man cannot be other than he is; he cannot have thoughts beyond his
reach.   [B]  Plutarch says that it is greater arrogance for mere men to start
talking and arguing about gods and demi-gods than for a man who knows
nothing whatever about music to start criticizing singers, or for a man who
has never been on a battlefield to try and argue about arms and war, from
some trivial conjecture presuming to understand an art which far exceeds his
knowledge.[217]

[A]  I believe that, in the Ancient World, men thought they were actually
enhancing the greatness of God when they made him equal to Man, clothed
him with Man's faculties and made him a present of Man's fair humours
[C]  and even of his most shameful necessities;  [A]  they offered him
our food to eat,  [C]  our dances, mummeries and farces to amuse
him;  [A]  our vestments to clothe him and our houses to dwell in, courting him with odours of incense, sounds of music and garlands of flowers;
[C]  they made him conform to our own vicious passions, subverting his
justice in the name of inhuman vengeance, causing him to rejoice in the
smashing and wasting of the very things he had created and protected (as
Tiberius Sempronius did when he made a burned sacrifice to Vulcan of the
arms and treasures seized as booty from his enemies in Sardinia; as Paul
Aemilius did, when he sacrificed the spoils of Macedonia to Mars and
Minerva, and as Alexander did, when he reached the shores of the Indian
Ocean and sought the favour of Thetis by casting many huge golden jars into
the sea).[218]  More. They loaded his altars with butchered carcases – not only
of innocent beasts but of men,  [A]  following the established custom of
many peoples – including our own; no nation, I believe, is exempt: all have
assayed it.

217. Plutarch, tr. Amyot, *Pourquoy la justice divine differe quelquefois ses malefices*,
259 C.

218. Livy, XLI, 16; XLV, 33; Arrian, *Alexander*, VI, 19.

'88 (in place of [C]): flowers: *once with the pleasure of a blood-drenched vengeance –
witness that widely received notion of sacrifices: and that God took pleasure in murder, and
in the torture of things made, preserved and created by him, and that he can rejoice in the
blood of innocent souls, not only of animals, which are powerless*, but of men . . .

[B]  *Sulmone creatos*
*Quattuor hic juvenes, totidem quos educat Ufens,*
*Viventes rapit, inferias quos immolet umbris.*

[He took alive four young men, begot by Sulmo, and another four bred by Ufens, to immolate them as sacrifices to the Shades.][219]

[C]  The Getae think they are immortal; for them, dying is but a journey to their God Zamolxis. Every five years they dispatch one of their number to him to ask for what they need. The ambassador is chosen by lot. The actual dispatching takes this form: the man is told of his charge by word of mouth; three of those present hold three javelins upright, the others toss the man on to them. If some vital organ is impaled and he dies at once, that is a clear indication of divine approval. If he escapes death, he is thought to be evil and accursed, so another ambassador is similarly dispatched.

On one occasion, when Amestris the mother of Xerxes had grown old and wished to appease some god of the Underworld, she caused fourteen young men from the best families in Persia to be buried alive, in accordance with the religious rites of that country. And even today the cement used to make the idols of Themistitan is mixed with the blood of little children, since the only sacrifices they relish are the pure souls of little boys: Justice hungry for innocent blood!

*Tantum relligio potuit suadere malorum.*

[So great are the evils Religion has encouraged.][220]

[B]  The Carthaginians sacrificed their own children to Saturn; those who had none of their own, bought some; their fathers and mothers had to attend the service, looking happy and contented.    [A]  It is a strange notion to seek to requite divine Goodness with our human affliction; the Spartans did: they courted that Diana of theirs with the suffering of boys who were flogged for her sake – sometimes flogged to death. It was a savage humour which sought to please the Architect by ruining what he had built; to ward off the punishment due to the guilty by punishing the innocent; or to believe that that poor wretched Iphigenia, by her sacrificial death in the port of Aulis, could free the Greek army of the weight of offences they had committed against God.

[B]  *Et casta inceste, nubendi tempore in ipso,*
*Hostia concideret mactatu moesta parentis.*

219.  Julius Caesar, *De bello gallico*, VI, xvi; Virgil, *Aeneid*, X, 517.
220.  Herodotus, IV, 94; VII, 114; Plutarch, tr. Amyot, *De la superstition*, 124 A; Lucretius, I, 102 (Lambin, pp. 13–15). The reference to Themistitan is untraced.

[At the very time of her wedding, the pure was impurely slaughtered, a victim sadly murdered by her father.]

[C]   And there were the fair and noble souls of the two Decii, father and son, who threw themselves wildly into the thick of the enemy, as a propitiation to make the gods favour the affairs of Rome: '*Quae fuit tanta deorum iniquitas, ut placari populo Romano non possent, nisi tales occidissent*' [What great wickedness on the part of the gods to refuse to favour the Roman People unless such men were killed!].[221]

[A]   We might add that it is not for the criminal to decide how and when he will be whipped: it is for the judge, who can only take account of such chastisements as he himself has ordered and who cannot treat as punishment anything that is pleasing to the sufferer. Both for the sake of its own justice and of our punishment, God's vengeance must presuppose our complete resistance to it.

[B]   It was an absurd caprice on the part of Polycrates, the tyrant of Samos, to cast his most precious jewel into the sea to atone for his continuous run of good fortune by interrupting its course; he thought to placate the turning Wheel of Fortune with a carefully arranged disaster.   [C]   Fortune, to mock such absurdity, caused the jewel to be returned into his hands through the belly of a fish.

[A]   And then   [C]   what is the use of all those lacerations and loppings off of limbs practised by the Corybantes and Maenads, or, in our own day, by the Mahometans who slash their faces, their bellies and their limbs, to please their prophet, seeing that   [A]   the offence lies in the will not [C]   in the breast, the eyes, the genitals, a well-rounded belly   [A]   or in the shoulders or the throat.   [C]   '*Tantus est perturbatae mentis et sedibus suis pulsae furor, ut sic Dii placentur, quemadmodum ne homines quidem saeviunt*' [Such is their frenzy, arising from minds disturbed and forcibly unhinged, that it is thought the gods can be placated by surpassing even our human cruelty].

How we treat the natural fabric of our bodies concerns not only ourselves but the service of God and of other men. It is not right to harm it deliberately, just as it is wrong to kill ourselves on any pretext whatsoever. There is, it seems, both great treachery and great cowardice in whipping and mutilating the servile, senseless functions of our bodies in order to spare our souls the trouble of governing them reasonably: '*Ubi iratos deos timent, qui sic propitios habere merentur? In regiae libidinis voluptatem castrati sunt quidam; sed nemo*

---

221.   Plutarch, *De la superstition*, 123 G–124 A; *Les Dicts notables des Lacedemoniens*, 227 EF; Lucretius, I, 98; Cicero, *De nat. deorum*, III, vi, 15.
   '88: to requite divine *justice* with our *torment and our suffering*; the Spartans . . .

*sibi, ne vir esset, jubente domino, manus intulit'* [What do they think the gods are angry about, when they believe they can propitiate them thus? Some have been castrated to serve the lust of kings, but no one has ever emasculated himself, even at the command of his master]. [A] In this way they filled their religion with many bad deeds,

> *saepius olim*
> *Relligio peperit scelerosa atque impia facta.*

[Too often in the past, religion has given birth to impious and wicked actions.]²²²

Nothing of ours can be compared or associated with the Nature of God, in any way whatsoever, without smudging and staining it with a degree of imperfection. How can infinite Beauty, Power and Goodness ever suffer any juxtaposition or comparison with a thing as abject as we are, without experiencing extreme harm and derogating from divine Greatness? [C] *'Infirmum dei fortius est hominibus, et stultum Dei sapientius est hominibus'* [The weakness of God is stronger than men and the foolishness of God is wiser than men].²²³

Stilpon the philosopher was asked whether the gods took pleasure in our homage and sacrifices: 'You are most indiscreet,' he replied; 'if you want to talk about that, let us draw aside.'²²⁴ [A] And yet we prescribe limits in the Infinite and besiege his mighty power with those reasons of ours (I call our ravings and our dreamings 'reasons', under the general dispensation of Philosophy who maintains that even the fool and the knave act madly 'from reason' – albeit from one special form of reason).²²⁵

We wish to make God subordinate to our human understanding with its vain and feeble probabilities; yet it is he who has made both us and all we know. 'Since nothing can be made from nothing: God could not construct the world without matter.' What! Has God placed in our hands the keys to the ultimate principles of his power? Did he bind himself not to venture beyond the limits of human knowledge? Even if we admit, O Man, that you have managed to observe some traces of his acts here in this world, do you think that he has used up all his power by filling that work with every conceiv-

222. Much from St Augustine, *City of God*, VI, 10 (citing a lost book of Seneca's *Against Superstition*). Also, Lucretius, I, 82 (Lambin, pp. 12–15).

223. I Corinthians I:25, a central text for Christian Folly since Augustine, not least for Erasmus.

224. Diogenes Laertius, *Lives*, Stilpon, II, 117.

225. For Platonizing thinkers the fool's soul (being divine in origin) remains rational; the knave reasons incorrectly about what is good but is not irrational (cf. n. 2). With what follows, cf. Ronsard, *Remonstrance*, 119f.

able Form and Idea? You only see – if you see that much – the order and
government of this little cave in which you dwell; beyond, his Godhead has an
infinite jurisdiction. The tiny bit that we know is nothing compared with ALL:

> *omnia cum coelo terraque marique*
> *Nil sunt ad summam summai totius omnem.*

[The entire heavens, sea and land are nothing compared with the greatest ALL of all.][226]

The laws you cite are by-laws: you have no conception of the Law of the
Universe. You are subject to limits: restrict yourself to them, not God. He is
not one of your equals; he is not a fellow-citizen or a companion. He has
revealed a little of himself to you, but not so as to sink down to your petty
level or to make himself accountable for his power to you. The human body
cannot fly up to the clouds – that applies to you! The Sun runs his ordered
course and never stops still; the boundaries of sea and land can never be
confounded; water is yielding and not solid; a material body cannot pass
through a solid wall; a man cannot stay alive in a furnace; his body cannot
be present in heaven, on earth and in a thousand places at once. It is for you
that he made these laws; it is you who are restricted by them. God, if he
pleases, can be free from all of them: he has made Christians witnesses to
that fact. And in truth, since he is omnipotent, why should he restrict the
measure of his power to definite limits? In whose interest ought he to give up
being a Law unto himself?

That Reason of yours never attains more likelihood or better foundations
than when it succeeds in persuading you that there are many worlds:

> [B]  *Terramque, et solem, lunam, mare, caetera quae sunt*
> *Non esse unica, sed numero magis innumerali.*

[The earth, the sun, the moon and all that exists are not unique, but numerous beyond
numbering.]

226. Lucretius, VI, 678 (Lambin, pp. 508–510, reading *sint* not *sunt*). A lesson
against homocentricity, inscribed in Montaigne's library. Platonic-Christian arguments are marshalled against Aristotle's denial of a creation *ex nihilo*. Allusions follow
to biblical miracles: Elijah's rapture to heaven (II Kings 2:11) and/or to Christ's bodily
Ascension; the halting of the Sun in Joshua 10:12; the Flood in Genesis 6–9 (cf. Genesis
1:9, 7:4); Psalm 104 (103):6–9; Christ's walking on the water (Matthew 14:25);
Christ's appearing in an enclosed room (John 20:19 ff.); Shadrach, Meshach and
Abednego in the fiery furnace (Daniel 3:22–27). The final miracle is the Real Presence
of Christ's risen body in Heaven and in each Eucharist. In the background is the
Platonic doctrine of the great chain of being (God created all possible forms). With the
*cave* Montaigne exploits the central Platonic myth: man, living as it were in a cave,
mistakes shadows on the wall for the reality outside his cave which casts those shadows.

[A]   That belief was held by the most famous minds of former ages (and still is by some today), on grounds which, to purely human reason, seem compelling, because nothing else within the fabric of the universe stands unique and alone:

> [B]   *cum in summa res nulla sit una,*
> *Unica quae gignatur, et unica solaque crescat.*

[Since nothing born of Nature is unique, nor when it grows is anything unique or all alone.]

[A]   There is some element of multiplicity within every species; it seems unlikely, therefore, that God made only this one universe and no other like it, or that all the matter available for this Form should have been exhausted on this one Particular:

> [B]   *Quare etiam atque etiam tales fateare necesse est*
> *Esse alios alibi congressus materiai,*
> *Qualis hic est avido complexu quem tenet aether.*

[Such things must be said again and again: there are, elsewhere, other material aggregates than the one which the air enfolds in her keen embrace.]

[A]   That is especially the case if the universe has a soul – something which its movements make credible,   [C]   so credible that Plato was sure of it; many Christians, too, either allow it or dare not disallow it, any more than the ancient opinion that the heavens, all heavenly bodies and other constituent parts of the universe are creatures composed of body and soul, subject to mortality, being composite, but immortal by the decree of their Maker.[227]

[A]   Now, if there are several worlds, as   [C]   Democritus,   [A]   Epicurus and almost the whole of philosophy have opined, how do we know whether the principles and laws which apply to this world apply equally to the others? Other worlds may present different features and be differently governed.   [C]   Epicurus thought of them as being both similar and dissi-

227. Lucretius, II, 1085 f., 1077 f., 1064 f. (Lambin pp. 180–82). Montaigne echoes the commentary ('There is no verisimilitude in this world's having been created alone' etc.) and the commentary on pp. 178–79 (allusions to Democritus after Cicero, *De fin.*, and *Acad.: Lucullus*). In the *Timaeus* (31 A B; 55 D E) Plato *defends* (against the atomists) the essential unity of the Universe but believes in a world-soul, as did the Christian Origen (St Augustine, *City of God*, XI, 23). Augustine (XIII, 16 and 17) did not reject Plato's contention (*Timaeus* 41D–42A) that the stars had souls and could be rendered immortal. Echoes in ...montaigne of Plutarch, tr. Amyot, *Des Opinions des Philosophes*, 446A–F.

milar.[228]  [A]  Even within our own world we can see how mere distance
produces infinite differences and variety. Neither wheat nor wine were found
in those New Lands discovered by our fathers, nor any of our animals:
everything there is different.  [C]  And only think of those parts of the
world which, in times gone by, had no knowledge of Bacchus' grapes or
Ceres' corn.

[A]  Should anyone care to believe Pliny  [C]  and Herodotus,[229]  [A]
there are species of men, in some places, which have very little resemblance
to our own;  [B]  there are some ambiguous, mongrel forms, between the
human and the beast; there are lands where men are born without heads,
having eyes and mouths in their chests; there are androgynous creatures and
creatures who walk on all fours, have only one eye in the middle of their
forehead, or have a head more like a dog's than our own; some are fishes
below the waist and live in water; some have wives who give birth at five and
die at eight; other men have skin on their forehead and on the rest of their
cranium so hard that iron spears cannot dent it but simply blunt themselves;
there are men without beards,  [C]  peoples without the use or knowledge
of fire and others who ejaculate black semen.

[B]  What about those people who, by natural means, can change into
wolves  [C]  and mares  [B]  and back again? And  [A1]  even if you
were to accept as true  [A]  what Plutarch says (that somewhere in the
Indies there are men without mouths who sustain themselves by inhaling
certain smells) how many of our own descriptions today are certainly
wrong![230] If laughter were no longer the property of Man and if Man were
no longer a political animal able to reason, our conception of what our inner
disposition and causations are would be largely irrelevant . . .[231]

To go further, we have imposed our own commandments on Nature and
carved them in stone: yet how many things do we know which defy those
fine rules of ours! And yet we try to bind God by them!

How many things are there which we call miraculous or contrary to Nature?
[C]  All men and nations do that according to the measure of their

228. Diogenes Laertius: *Lives*, Democritus, IX, 45; cf. Epicurus, IX, 85.

229. What follows derives from Pliny, *Hist. Nat.*, VI, 2; VIII, 22; Herodotus,
III, 101; IV, 191. Pliny's 'errors' and Herodotus' 'lies' were often evoked in the
Renaissance.

230. Plutarch, *De la face qui apparoist dedans le rond de la Lune*, 623 F (producing
amused laughter from the hearers).

231. The standard definitions of Man, as a thinking, laughing or 'political' animal,
could not apply to men without brains in their heads or mouths to laugh with or cities
to live in (as political animals).

ignorance. [A] How many quintessences, how many occult properties
have we discovered! For us, following Nature means following our own
intelligence as far as it is able to go and as far as we are able to see.[232]
Everything else is a monster, outside the order of Nature! By that reasoning
the cleverest and wisest men would find everything monstrous, since they
are convinced that reason has no foundation to stand on, not even to determine   [C]   whether snow is white (Anaxagoras said it was black), or
whether there are such things as knowledge and ignorance (Metrodorus of
Chios denied that Man could ever know),   [A]   or even whether we are
alive: Euripides hesitates, 'Is *life* this life that we live now? Or is *life* really
what we call death?' That is:

Τίς δ'οΐδεν εί ζῆν τοῦθ' ὃ κέκληται θανεῖν,
τὸ ζῆν δὲ θνείσκειν ἔστι[233]

[B] There is a degree of probability in that alternative: for why do we
give the name *existence* to that instant which amounts to no more than a
flash of lightning against the infinite course of eternal light, or to that tiny
break which interrupts the condition which is naturally ours for all eternity,   [C]   since death fills everything before that moment and everything
which comes afterwards as well as a large part of the moment itself?

[B] Some swear that nothing moves and that there is no such thing at all
as motion –   [C]   as was believed by the followers of Melissus (since, as
Plato proves, there is no place for spherical motion within strict Unity, nor
even for movement from one place to another) –   [B]   or that there is,
in Nature, no generation and no corruption.   [C]   Protagoras says that in
Nature nothing exists but doubt: that everything is equally open to discussion, including the assertion that everything is equally open to discussion;
Nausiphanes holds that among phenomena there is nothing which *is* rather
than *is not*: that nothing is certain but uncertainty. For Parmenides, within
the world of phenomena there is no such thing as genus: there is only Unity.
For Zeno, there is not even Unity, only Nothing: for if Unity exists it must
exist either within another or within itself; if it exists in another, that makes

232. A miracle is, for Christians, an event 'against the whole order of Nature'. To
recognize such an event by natural reason requires, therefore, a true knowledge of the
limits of Nature.

233. Cicero, *Acad.: Lucullus*, II, xxxi, 100, cf. xxxiii, 105–108; the verses from
Euripides were inscribed in Montaigne's library; they are cited by Sextus Empiricus,
*Hypotyposes*, III, 229, but in a different form; Montaigne's version derives from
Stobaeus, Sermo 119, but there are minor variations in many editions of this text.

two; if it exists within itself, that still makes two – the container and the thing contained.

According to these tenets, Nature is but a shadow, false or vain.[234]

[A]   It has always seemed to me that certain expressions are too imprudent and irreverent for a Christian: 'God cannot die'; 'God cannot change his mind'; 'God cannot do this or cannot do that'. I find it unacceptable that the power of God should be limited in this way by the rules of human language; these propositions offer an appearance of truth, but it ought to be expressed more reverently and more devoutly. Our speech, like everything else, has its defects and weaknesses. Most of the world's squabbles are occasioned by grammar! Lawsuits are born from disputes over the interpretation of laws; most wars arise from our inability to express clearly the conventions and treaties agreed on by monarchs. How many quarrels, momentous quarrels, have arisen in this world because of doubts about the meaning of that single syllable *Hoc*.[235]

[B]   Take the proposition which Logic asserts to be the clearest of all. If you say 'The weather is fine' and you say it truly, then the weather is fine. That seems to be clear enough; and yet such a formula can lead us astray. You can see that from the following example: if you say, 'I lie', and you say it truly, then you lie! In both cases, the art, reason and force of the conclusion are the same: yet the second leaves you stogged in the mud![236]

[A]   Pyrrhonist philosophers, I see, cannot express their general concepts in any known kind of speech; they would need a new language: ours is made up of affirmative propositions totally inimical to them – so much so that when they say 'I doubt', you can jump down their throats and make them admit that they at least know one thing for certain, namely that they doubt. To save themselves they are constrained to draw an analogy from medicine: without it their sceptical humour would never get purged! When they say *I know not* or *I doubt* that affirmation purges itself (they maintain) along with all the

234. Plato, *Theaetetus*, 180E–183E; Seneca, *Epist.*, LXXXVIII, 43–46; Plato, *Parmenides*, 138.

'88 (In place of [C]): *I do not know whether Ecclesiastical teaching judges otherwise – and I submit myself, in all things everywhere to its ordinance, but* it has always seemed to me . . .

235. Matthew XXVI:26. Disputes over the eucharistic formula 'This (*Hoc*) is my body' are central to Christian controversy. Cf. H. C. Agrippa, *On the Vanity of all Learning*, III.

236. Cicero, *Acad.: Lucullus*, xxix, 95.

others, exactly like a dose of rhubarb, which evacuates all our evil humours, itself included.[237]

[B] (Scepticism can best be conceived through the form of a question: 'What do I know?' – *Que sçay-je*, words inscribed on my emblem of a Balance.)[238]

[A] See how people avail themselves of such forms of speech as are full of irreverence. In our present religious strife, if you press your adversaries too hard they will bluntly reply that it exceeds God's power to make his body be in paradise and in several places on earth all at the same time. How that scoffer[239] among the Ancients exploited similar assertions! 'At least', he said, 'it is no light comfort for Man to know that God cannot do everything! God cannot kill himself when he wants to (which is the greatest prerogative attached to the human condition); he cannot bring the dead back to life; he cannot make someone not to have lived who has lived, or not to have received honour who has received honour; he has no jurisdiction over the past other than to make it merge into oblivion; finally (so that this equality of status in God and Man can be further strengthened with amusing examples), God cannot even stop ten and ten from making twenty!' That is what he says – and what should never pass a Christian's lips. Whereas, on the contrary, men seem to me to go looking for such insane and arrogant terms in order to cut God down to their own size:

> *cras vel atra*
> *Nube polum pater occupato,*
> *Vel sole puro; non tamen irritum*
> *Quodcumque retro est, efficiet, neque*
> *Diffinget infectumque reddet*
> *Quod fugiens semel hora vexit.*

[Tomorrow the Father can cover the pole with black clouds or with pure sunlight, but he cannot change the past, he cannot undo or annul anything that fleeting time has borne away.]

When we say that countless ages – ages past and ages yet to come – are but a moment to God and that God's essence consists in goodness, wisdom,

237. Diogenes Laertius, *Lives*, Pyrrho, IX, 76 (for 'rhubarb' the text gives *medicamenta*).

238. In 1576 (doubtless under the influence of Pyrrho), Montaigne struck a medal with a Balance, poised, bearing the device *Que sçay-ie?*

239. '88: that *scoffer* Pliny exploited

(Pliny, *Hist. Nat.*, II, 7; the two following quotations are from Horace, *Odes*, III, 29, 43; Pliny, *ibid.*, II, 23.)

power, we utter words, but our intelligence cannot grasp the sense. Despite that, we, in our arrogance, want to force God through human filters. All the raving errors that this world possesses are bred from trying to squeeze on to human scales weights far beyond their capacity: [C] *'Mirum quo procedat improbitas cordis humani, parvulo aliquo invitata successu'* [It is astonishing how far the impudence of the human heart can go, once encouraged by the least success].

How insolently the Stoics taunt Epicurus for holding that essential goodness and happiness belong to God alone, so that the Sage can only possess some shadowy likeness of them. [A] How rashly they subject God to Destiny (would that some who bear the name of Christians did not do so still);[240] Thales, Plato and Pythagoras even make God the slave of Necessity. This fierce desire to scan the Divine through human eyes even brought one of our own great Christian figures to endow God with a corporeal shape;[241] [B] it also explains why we daily assign to God a peculiar responsibility for any event, the outcome of which seems important to us. We attach particular weight to such events, so God must do so too, paying more attention to them than to others which seem unimportant to us or simply part of the regular order: [C] *'magna dii curant, parva negligunt!'* [The gods take care of great matters and neglect the small!]. Listen to the example given and you will see more clearly what is meant: *'nec in regnis quidem reges omnia minima curant'* [Even kings in their kingdoms do not concern themselves with every tiny detail]. As though it were more difficult for God to shake an empire than to shake a leaf, or as though his Providence were exercised differently when influencing the outcome of a battle and the jump of a flea.

The hand of God's governance supports all things with an equal and unchanging sway, with the same order, the same power. Our concerns contribute nothing to this; our human activities and standards are quite irrelevant: *'Deus ita artifex magnus in magnis, ut minor non sit in parvis'* [In great things God is a great artificer, but in such a way that he is no less great in little things].

Our arrogance constantly finds fresh ways of blasphemously equating man with God: our jobs are a burden to us men, so Strato endows the gods – and their priests – with complete immunity from work! For Strato it is Nature who produces and maintains all things, Nature who constructs every part of the universe with her weights and her forces. In this way he frees mankind

---

240. Seneca, *Epist.*, XCII, 275. The Stoics 'subject God to destiny': the Christians who are alleged to do so are doubtless, for Montaigne, Calvinists – cf. Cicero, *Acad.: Lucullus*, II, 29.

241. Tertullian, apparently, while still a Catholic; he became a Montanist.

of a burden: the fear of divine judgement: '*Quod beatum aeternumque sit, id nec habere negotii quicquam, nec exhibere alteri*' [A blessed and eternal Being has no duties and imposes none on others].[242]

'Nature's will is that like things should have like correlatives; for example: the fact that mortals are innumerable leads to the conclusion that the immortals are too; the vast number of things which kill or do harm leads to the conclusion that an equivalent number preserve and do good'; so, just as the souls of the gods have no tongue, eyes or ears yet can understand each other and also judge what we are thinking: so too the souls of men, when free from the bonds of the body in sleep or any kind of ecstasy, have powers of divination, can foretell the future and see such things as they could never see when joined to their bodies . . . [A] 'Men', says St Paul, 'have become fools, professing to be wise, and have changed the glory of the incorruptible God into the image of corruptible man'.[243]

[B]   Only consider what jugglers' farces those 'deifications' were among the Ancients. After the stately pride and pomp of the funeral procession, just as the fire was taking hold of the apex of the pyre and about to engulf the litter with the dead man on it, they would release an eagle which flew upwards, representing the soul making its way to Paradise. We still possess a thousand medallions (above all, the one of that – oh, so honourable – woman Faustina) where the eagle is portrayed bearing off the deified soul, which is slung over its shoulder just like a dead goat! It is pitiful the way we deceive ourselves with the monkey-tricks that we invent;

*Quod finxere timent*

[They are terrified of their own creations]

– like children who are scared by the very face of the friend they have just daubed with black.   [C]   '*Quasi quicquam infelicius sit homine cui sua figmenta dominantur*' [As though anything were more pitiful than a man overmastered by his own figments].[244]

242. Cicero, *De nat. deorum*, II, lxvi, 167; III, xxxv, 86; St Augustine, *City of God*, XI, 22; Cicero, *Acad.*, II, xxviii, 121.

243. Epicurus' principle of *isonomia* (Cicero, *De nat. deorum*, I, xix, 50) and the contentions of Cicero's brother in *De divinat.* I, lvii, 129, are here countered by Romans I:22–23.

244. Lucan, *Pharsalia*, I, 486. (For ancient deifications and medals, cf. G. du Choul, *De la religion des anciens Romains*, 1556, p. 75, etc.; also Joachim Du Bellay, *Regrets*, TLF, *Songe* XI and illustration.) Seneca, *Epist.*, XXIV, 13; St Augustine, *City of God*, VIII, 23–24.

We are far from honouring him who made us when we honour a creature we ourselves have made.

[B] Augustus had more temples than did Jupiter, in which he was served with just as much devotion and just as much belief in his miracles.

The Thasians, wishing to repay the benefits they had received from Age-silaus, came to tell him that they had put him on the canonical list of their gods. 'Are you a people', he asked, 'who have the power to make a god of anyone you please? Just to see, first make a god of one of yourselves; and then, [C] when I have learned how he has prospered, [B] I will come and thank you heartily for your offer.'

[C] Man is indeed out of his mind. He cannot even create a flesh-worm, yet creates gods by the dozen. Just listen to Hermes Trismegistus praising our sufficiency: 'Among all the things which can astonish us, one thing has surpassed astonishment itself: Man's capacity to discover what the Divine nature is and then proceed to create it.'

Here are some arguments from the very school in which Philosophy learned her lessons:

> *Nosse cui Divos et coeli numina soli,*
> *Aut soli nescire, datum*

[Philosophy, she to whom alone it is given to know the gods and the numinous powers of heaven, or, alone, to know that they cannot be known!][245]

– If God exists, (she says) he is animate; if he is animate he has senses; if he has senses, he is subject to corruption! If he is incorporeal, he has no soul and consequently is without activity; if he is corporeal, then he is mortal! What a triumph! – [C] We could never make this world; therefore a Nature *even more excellent than ours* must have taken the task in hand! – It would be stupid arrogance to esteem ourselves the most perfect object in the universe: there must therefore be *one* thing better: God! – When you see a rich and stately dwelling you may not know who the master of it is, but at least you could say that it was not built for rats: take the divine architecture of the palaces of heaven, which we ourselves can see; does it not oblige us to believe that it is the dwelling-place of a Master greater *even than we are*? – Is not the higher always more worthy – and we are at the bottom. – Nothing without reason and soul can beget an animate creature capable of reason: the world has begotten us: therefore it has both reason and soul! – Each part of

---

245. Plutarch, *Les Dicts notables des Lacedemoniens*, 210 GH; Hermes Trismegistus, *Asclepius*, 37, *apud* St Augustine, *City of God*, VIII, 24; Lucan, *Pharsalia*, I, 452 (adapted).

us is less than the whole: we are part of the world: the world is, therefore, provided with wisdom and reason more abundantly than we are. – It is a fair thing to hold great powers of government: the government of the world must, therefore, belong to some happy Nature. – The heavenly bodies do us no harm: they are, therefore, full of goodness. – [B] We need food: so do the gods, who feed on vapours rising up from here below! – [C] Worldly goods are not goods to God: therefore they are not goods to us. – To do harm and to experience harm are equal proofs of weakness: it is therefore mad to be afraid of God! – God is good by nature, man by industry: which makes man superior! – There is no difference between divine wisdom and human wisdom, except that the divine is eternal: but time adds nothing to the quality of wisdom: therefore we and God are on equal footing! – We enjoy life, reason, freedom and we esteem goodness, love and justice: therefore these qualities must be in God!

In short, both constructively and destructively, we forge for ourselves the attributes of God, taking ourselves as the correlative. What a model, what a pattern! Take human qualities and stretch them, raise them, magnify them as much as you please! Wretched little Man, puff yourself up as much as you like! More. More. More still: '*Non si te ruperis, inquit*' . . . ['Not even', he said, 'if you burst.']. [C] '*Profecto non Deum, quem cogitare non possunt, sed semet ipsos pro illo cogitantes, non illum sed se ipsos non illi sed sibi comparant*' [Indeed, Men cannot conceive of God, so they base their conceptions on themselves instead; they do not compare themselves to him, but him to themselves].[246]

[B] Even within Nature, effects barely suggest half their causes. But what of this Cause? God is a Cause completely above the order of Nature. His mode of being is too high, too distant, too magisterial to allow our logical conclusions to judge or to bind him. We shall never get that far by our own efforts: our path is too lowly. We are no nearer the heavens on the top of Mount Cenis than we are at the bottom of the sea. Your astrolabe will tell you that.

Yet men even reduce God to having sexual intercourse with women, noting how often he did it and for how many births.

Paulina, the wife of Saturninus, was a Roman matron of great reputation; she thought she was lying with a god, Serapis, but through the pimping of

246. Several Stoic commonplaces and major borrowings from Cicero (*De nat. deorum*, II, vi, 16–VIII, 22) and others (cf. Pontus de Tyard, *Second Curieux* in *Discours philosophiques*, 1587, 310); Horace's fable of the puffed-up frog (*Satires*, II, iii, 319); finally St Augustine, *City of God*, XII, 18.

the temple-priests she found herself in the arms of a lover.[247]  [C]  In his treatises on theology, Varro, the most subtle and learned of Latin authors, wrote of a sexton in the temple of Hercules who cast dice with both hands, one for himself, the other for Hercules. The stakes were a supper and a woman: if he won, he paid for them out of the collection; if he lost, he paid for them himself. He lost; so the cost of the woman and dinner fell to himself. Now the woman was called Laurentina; lying that night with this 'god' in her arms, she heard him volunteer the remark that the first man she met when she left in the morning would see that she received from heaven the money she had just earned. She did in fact meet a rich young man called Taruntius who took her back home and eventually left her all his money. She in her turn, hoping to do an action pleasing to this god, left her inheritance to the Roman People, who then bestowed divine honours upon her.[248]

As though it were simply not enough that Plato should be descended, on both sides, from the gods, with Neptune as the common ancestor, it was believed as a fact in Athens that, when Ariston had wished to consummate his love for the fair Perictione, he could not bring it off; he was warned in a dream by the god Apollo not to deflower her but to leave her a virgin until she had given birth . . . And they were Plato's father and mother![249]

How many other accounts are there of similar cuckoldries procured by the gods against wretched human beings, or of husbands unjustly defamed to honour their children! In the religion of Mahomet the people believe that there are 'Merlins' in plenty – children, that is, begot without fathers, spiritual children divinely conceived in virgins' wombs. (They are given a special name which, in their language, means just that.)[250]

[B]  We should note that no creature holds anything dearer than the kind of being that it is  [C]  (lions, eagles, dolphins value nothing above their own species)  [B]  and that every species reduces the qualities of everything else to analogies with its own. We can extend our characteristics or reduce them, but that is all we can do, since our intellect can do nothing and guess nothing except on the principle of such analogies; it is impossible for it to go beyond that point.  [C]  That explains Ancient philosophical conclusions such as these: Man is the most beautiful of all forms, so God must also have that form! – No one can be happy without virtue; virtue cannot be without

247. Commonplace deriving from Josephus, *Jewish Antiquities*, XVIII, 4 (but in the temple of Anubis not Serapis).

248. Varro *apud* St Augustine, *City of God*, VI, 7; tale current since Antiquity.

249. Diogenes Laertius, *Lives*, Plato, III, ii, 185.

250. Guillaume Postel, *Des Histoires Orientales (De la République des Turcs)*, 1575, 919 r°.

reason: no reason can dwell elsewhere but in the human shape: therefore God is clad in a human shape! '*Ita est informatum, anticipatum mentibus nostris ut homini, cum de Deo cogitet, forma occurrat humana*' [The mould and prejudice of our minds are such that when we think of God it is the human form which occurs to them].[251]

[B]   That is why Xenophanes said with a smile that if the beasts invent gods for themselves, as they probably do, they certainly make them like themselves, glorifying themselves – as we do.[252] For why should a gosling not argue thus: 'All the parts of the universe are there for me: the earth serves me to waddle upon, the sun to give me light; the heavenly bodies exist to breathe their influences upon me; the winds help me this way, the waters, that way: there is nothing which the vault of Heaven treats with greater favour than me. I am Nature's darling: does not Man care for me, house me, serve me? It is for me that Man sows and grinds his corn; it is true that he eats me, but he also eats his fellow-men, and I eat the worms which kill him and eat him.'

A crane could say the same – even more majestically on account of the freedom of its flight and its secure enjoyment of those fair and higher regions: [C]   '*Tam blanda conciliatrix et tam sui est lena ipsa natura*' [So flattering a procuress is Nature, such a seductress of herself].[253]

[B]   Well, if that is how it goes, the Universe and the Fates are all for us! The lightning flashes for us; the thunder crashes for us; the Creator and all his creatures exist just for us. We are the end which the entire Universe is aiming towards. Just examine the records of celestial affairs which Philosophy has kept for two thousand years and more: the gods have acted and spoken only for Man. Philosophy attributes no other concern to them, no other employment: they go to war against us,

> *domitosque Herculea manu*
> *Telluris juvenes, unde periculum*
> *Fulgens contremuit domus*
> *Saturni veteris.*

[The Sons of Earth, those Titans at whose assault the shining house of ancient Saturn shook with fear, are defeated by the hand of Hercules.]

251. Cicero, *De nat. deorum*, I, xxvii, 76–78.

252. Eusebius Pamphilus, *Preparatio evangelica*, XIII, 13, perhaps via Ph. Duplessis-Mornay, *De la Verité de la religion chrestienne*, chapters 1 (end), 4 (beginning).

253. Developments inspired by Cicero, *De nat. deorum*, I, xxvii, 78: 'Suppose animals possessed reason: would they not attribute superiority to their own kind?' Latin quotation: *ibid.*, 77.

The gods side with us in our civil disturbances, [C] to return our services, since we have so often taken sides in theirs:

[B] *Neptunus muros magnoque emota tridenti*
*Fundamenta quatit, totamque a sedibus urbem*
*Eruit. Hic Juno Scaeas saevissima portas*
*Prima tenet.*

[With his mighty trident Neptune shakes the walls of Troy to their foundations and dashes the whole city to the ground; here, implacable Juno holds the Scaean gates.]

On their feast-days, the Caunians, jealous for the hegemony of their own gods, load weapons on their shoulders and charge around the outskirts of their city stabbing their swords into the air, fighting the foreign gods to the finish and driving them out of their lands.[254]

[B] The powers of the gods are tailored to meet our human needs: this one cures horses, another, men; [C] this one, the plague, [B] that one, the ring-worm, that one, the cough; [C] this one cures one sort of mange; that one, another: '*adeo minimis etiam rebus prava relligio inserit deos*' [Thus does religion, when depraved, bring the gods even into the most trivial affairs]; this god makes grapes to grow, another, garlic; this god is responsible for lechery, that one, for trade, [C] (each tribe of craftsmen has its god!); [B] this god's sway and reputation lie in the East; that god's lie in the West.

*hic illius arma,*
*Hic currus fuit;*

[Here were her arms, here stood her chariot;]

[C] *O Sancte Apollo, qui umbilicum certum terrarum obtines;*

[O holy Apollo, thou that holdest sway in the Navel of the world;]

*Pallada Cecropidae, Minoia Creta Dianam,*
*Vulcanum tellus Hipsipilea colit,*
*Junonem Sparte Pelopeiadesque Mycenae;*
*Pinigerum Fauni Maenalis ora caput;*
*Mars Latio venerandus.*

[The descendants of Cecrops worship Pallas in Athens; Minoan Crete worships Diana;

254. Horace, *Odes*, II, 12, 6; Virgil, *Aeneid*, II, 610; Herodotus, I, 172. (For the gods of grapes and garlic, cf. Cardinal Robert Bellarmine, *On the Loss of Grace and the State of Sin*, book X, chapter ix, 'An enumeration of the maladies and wounds of the human mind', § 6, in *Opera*, 1593, 487B.)

Lemnos, Vulcan; Sparta and Peloponnesian Mycenae, Juno. Pan, crowned with pine leaves, is venerated in Maenalus; and Mars in Latium.]

[B]   This god has only a single town or family under his sway,   [C]   that one lives alone, but the other one, willingly or from necessity, lives with his peers:

> *Junctaque sunt magno templa nepotis avo.*

[The grandson's temple is amalgamated with the temple of his grandsire.]²⁵⁵

[B]   Some of these gods are so mean and so lowly (for their number amounts to thirty-six thousand) that you need a pile of five or six of them to make a grain of corn – their various names are taken from this –   [C]   you need three for a door (one for the wood, one for the hinge, one for the doorstep); then you need four for an infant (protecting its cradle, its drink, its food and its sucking). The functions of some are uncertain and doubtful; others are not allowed into Paradise yet:

> *Quos quoniam coeli nondum dignamur honore,*
> *Quas dedimus certe terras habitare sinamus.*

[Since some are not yet worthy to be honoured with paradise, we at least allow them to dwell in the lands we have given them.]

There are nature-gods, poetic gods, civic gods; there are intermediary beings, half-way between the divine nature and the human, who are mediators, doing business between us and God and worshipped with an inferior, second-grade worship; they have innumerable titles and duties. Some are good: some are bad.   [B]   There are gods who are old and decrepit; there are gods who are mortal; for Chrysippus considered that all gods died in the last great conflagration of the world, except Jupiter.

[C]   Man invents a thousand amusing links of fellowship between himself and God. Is God not a fellow-countryman! *'Jovis incunabula Creten'* [Crete, cradle of Jupiter].²⁵⁶

Here is the justification given after reflection by Scaevola, a great Pontifex, and by Varro, a great theologian (both 'great' in their time): it is necessary (they said) that people should not know many things which are true and

255. Livy, XXVII, xxiii; Virgil, *Aeneid*, I, 16; Anon, cited Cicero, *De divinatione*, II, lvi, 115; Ovid, *Fasti*, III, 81 and I, 294.
256. Echoes of St Augustine, *City of God*, IV, 8; VI, 5 and 7; III, 12 etc.; quotation from Ovid, *Metam.*, I, I, 194 in Vivès's commentary (*ibid.*, III, 12); Plutarch, *Contre les Stoïques*, 583A (cf. Rabelais, *Quart Livre*, T L F, XXVII, p. 135); Ovid, *ibid.*, VIII, 99.

should believe many things which are false, '*cum veritatem qua liberetur, inqui-rat, credatur ei expedire, quod fallitur*' [since man only wants to find such truth as sets him free, it can be thought expedient for him to be deceived].²⁵⁷

[B]   Human eyes can only perceive things in accordance with such Forms as they know.   [C]   We forget what a tumble the wretched Phaëton took when, with a mortal hand, he tried to manage the reins of his father's horses: our rashness causes our minds to take a similar plunge and to be bruised and broken as he was.²⁵⁸   [B]   Ask Philosophy what the Sky and the Sun are composed of; what will she answer, if not iron, or,   [C]   with Anaxago-ras,   [B]   stone, or some such everyday material? If you ask Zeno what Nature is, he replies Fire – an artificer having as its properties generative powers and regularity; if you ask Archimedes (the master of geometry, that science which grants itself precedence over all others in matters of truth and certainty) he replies that the Sun is a god of burning iron. What a fine idea to come out of geometrical demonstrations, with their beauty and compelling necessities! Not so compelling   [C]   and useful, though, but that Socrates thought you only need to know enough geometry to survey any land given or acquired;   [B]   the illustrious Polyaenus (formerly a famous teacher of geometry) came to despise its demonstrations as false and manifestly vain; that was after tasting the sweet fruits of the idle gardens of Epicurus.²⁵⁹

[C]   In Antiquity Anaxagoras was believed to have excelled all others in treating matters celestial and divine; but in Xenophon, Socrates, talking of his teaching, said that the brain of Anaxagoras finally became disturbed: that often happens to those who immoderately pore over matters which do not appertain to them.²⁶⁰

As for Anaxagoras' making the Sun a burning stone, he failed to realize that stone does not glow in the fire, or, what is worse, that it is consumed by fire; as for his making the Sun and Fire one, he further failed to realize that fire does not blacken those who simply look at it, that we can gaze fixedly at fire, or that fire *kills* plants and grasses. Socrates' verdict – and mine as well

257. St Augustine, *City of God*, IV, xxxi and xxxvii.

258. Phaëton was the son of Helios and Clymene. Seeking to reach the heavens he was drowned: the symbol of hubris. (The 'forms', or 'Ideas', exist in the heavenly regions; Man only knows those which God makes accessible to him: to try and discover more is to court disaster.)

259. Xenophon, *Memorabilia*, IV, vii, 2; Cicero, *De nat. deorum*, II, xxii, 57–58; for Archimedes and the compelling power of geometry, Cicero, *Acad.: Lucullus*, II, xxxvii, 116–17 (influenced by a reading of S. Bodin, *De la démonomanie des sorciers*); Guy de Brués, *Dialogues*, p. 90.

260. Xenophon, *Memorabilia*, IV, vii, 7.

– is that the best judgement you can make about the heavens is not to make any at all.[261]

When Plato in the *Timaeus* was about to talk about *daemons* he declared: This is an undertaking which is beyond our range; we are obliged to have faith in men of old who said they were born of *daemons*: it is not reasonable to refuse to believe these children of the gods – even though what they say is not supported by compelling reasons or by verisimilitude – since they swear they are talking about matters known within their homes and families . . .[262]

[A] Now let us see whether we have a little more light than that concerning our knowledge of Man and Nature.

When treating objects which, by our own admission, exceed our knowledge, is it not stupid to go forging bodies for them and imposing on them false Forms of our own invention? – as in the case of the movement of the planets: since our minds cannot manage to conceive what makes them move naturally, we impose on them our own heavy corporeal, material principles:

> *temo aureus, aurea summae*
> *Curvatura rotae, radiorum argenteus ordo.*

[The shaft was of gold; so too the rim of the wheels and the spokes were made of silver.][263]

It is almost as though we had sent coach-smiths, carpenters [C] and painters [A] up there, preparing mechanical contrivances with diverse movements [C] and then, in accordance with Plato's instructions, arranging, round about the spindle of Necessity, sets of wheels and interlaced courses for the heavenly bodies, variously painted.[264]

> [B] *Mundus domus est maxima rerum,*
> *Quam quinque altitonae fragmine zonae*
> *Cingunt, per quam limbus pictus bis sex signis*
> *Stellimicantibus, altus in obliquo aethere, lunae*
> *Bigas acceptat.*

[The Universe is an edifice, immense, encircled by five thundering belts and crossed

261. *Ibid.*, IV, vii, 7; Socrates' verdict was proverbial (Erasmus, *Adages, Quae supra nos, nihil ad nos*).

262. Plato, *Timaeus*, 40 DE (not evidently ironical in Ficino's Latin rendering, p. 710).

263. Ovid, *Metam.*, II, 107.

264. Plato, *Republic*, X, xii, 616.

obliquely by an aethereal sash, decorated with twice half-dozen constellations and the paired horses of the Moon.][265]

These are dreams   [C]   and frantic folly.   [A]   If only Nature would deign to open her breast one day and show us the means[266] and the workings of her movements as they really are   [C]   (first preparing our eyes to see them).   [A]   O God, what fallacies and miscalculations we would find in our wretched science!   [C]   Either I am quite mistaken or our science has not put one single thing squarely in its rightful place, and I will leave this world knowing nothing better than my own ignorance. It was in Plato (was it not?) that I came across the inspired adage, 'Nature is but enigmatic poetry,' as if to say that Nature is intended to exercise our ingenuity, like a painting veiled in mists and obscured by an infinite variety of wrong lights. '*Latent ista omnia crassis occultata et circumfusa tenebris, ut nulla acies humani ingenii tanta sit, quae penetrare in coelum, terram intrare possit*' [All things lie hidden, wrapped in a darkness so thick that no human mind is sharp enough to pierce the heavens or to sound the earth].[267] Certainly, philosophy is poetry adulterated by Sophists. Where do all those Ancient authors get their authority from, if not from the poets? The original authorities were themselves poets; they treated philosophy in terms of poetic art. Plato is but a disjointed poet. As an insult, Timon called him a great contriver of miracles.[268]

[A]   When their natural teeth are missing, women use false ones made of ivory; they replace their real complexion by one contrived from borrowed materials; they pad out their thighs with cloth or felt, round out their bellies with cotton-wool and, as everyone knows and sees, enhance themselves with a false and borrowed beauty.

Learning does the same;   [B]   even our system of Law, they say, bases the truth of its justice upon legal fictions. Learning pays us in the coin of suppositions which she confesses she has invented herself. Those eccentric and concentric epicycles by which Astrology tries to make sense out of the motions of the heavenly bodies are presented to us merely as the best she can

265. Varro: known only from Probus' commentary on Virgil, *Eclogue*, VI.

266. '88: principles (*ressorts*) for *moiens* (means).

267. Plato, *Alcibiades*, II, 147: 'For poetry as a whole is inclined to be enigmatic'; Ficino's Latin rendering (p. 47) is ambiguous, giving rise to Montaigne's rendering, also found (for example) in Cognatus' adage, '*Multa novit, sed male novit omnia*' (cf. *Adagia, id est proverbiorum . . . omnium*, Wechel, 1643, *index rerum* s.v. *natura*).

268. Cicero, *Acad.: Lucullus*, II, xxxix, 122.

'95: disjointed poet. *All superhuman sciences bedeck themselves in the style of poetry.* When their natural . . . (Timon of Athens' insult, repeated by Montaigne in vol. II, chapter 16, 'On Glory'; Diogenes Laertius, *Lives*, Plato, III, xxvi, 119.)

produce; all Philosophy does the same, presenting us not with what really is, nor even with what she believes to be true, but with the best probabilities and elegancy she has wrought.[269]     [C]   Take Plato, explaining the attributes of the bodies of men and beasts, 'We would be certain that what we say is true, if we could have it confirmed by an oracle; as it is, we can only be certain that I have spoken with the greatest appearance of truth that I can find.'[270]

[A]   Philosophy does not only impose her ropes, wheels and contrivances on to the high heavens. Just think for a while what she says about the way we humans are constructed. For our tiny bodies she has forged as many retrogradations, trepidations, conjunctions, recessions and revolutions as she has for the stars and the planets. They are right to call our bodies *Microcosms* ('little worlds') seeing all the various pieces and angles they need to build them up and cement them together. To house all the activities which they find in Man and all the various functions and faculties which we are aware of within us, think of all the sections into which they have subdivided our souls and how many organs they have ascribed to them; think of all the storeys and levels and all the duties and activities they have assigned to us, over and above the natural ones which our poor humanity can actually perceive! They have invented an entire Republic! Man is an object to be seized and handled. Each philosopher, according to his fancy, has been left entirely free to unstitch him, rearrange him, put him together again and furnish him out afresh.

Yet even now they have not overmastered him. They cannot even dream up an ordinance for Man – let alone find out a true one – without there being some sound or cadence which they cannot quite fit in, however abnormal[271] they make their contrivance and however much they try and botch it up with a thousand false and fantastical patches.     [C]   It is wrong to find excuses for them. We do indeed condone artists who represent the sky and far-off lands, seas, mountains or islands with a few slight brush-strokes; we do not know what they are like so are happy with the shadowy imitations that they feign; but when they paint from nature on a known subject – one which we are familiar with – we require of them a perfect, detailed representation of the lines and colours. If they fail, we despise them.[272]

[A]   I have always felt grateful to that girl from Miletus who, seeing the local philosopher Thales with his eyes staring upwards, constantly occupied

269. Astronomy, for example, was concerned to 'save the appearances' – that is, to account for observed phenomena; it did not claim to be describing fact but 'appearances' (*phenomena*), which may or may not really be true.

270. Plato, *Timaeus*, 72D (Ficino, p. 724).

271. '88: monstrous (*monstrueuse*) for abnormal (*enormale*).

272. Plato, *Critias*, 107, CD (adapted) (Ficino, p. 107).

in contemplating the vault of heaven, made him trip over, to warn him that
it was time enough to occupy his thoughts with things above the clouds when
he had accounted for everything lying before his feet. It was certainly good
advice she gave him, to study himself rather than the sky;   [C]   for, as
Democritus says through the mouth of Cicero, *'Quod est ante pedes, nemo
spectat: coeli scrutantur plagas'* [Nobody examines what is before his feet: they
scrutinize the tracts of the heavens].

[A]   But in fact, the human condition is such that where our understanding is concerned, the things we hold in our hands are as far above
the clouds as the heavenly bodies are!   [C]   As Socrates says in Plato,
you can make against anyone concerned with Philosophy exactly the same
reproach as that woman made against Thales: he fails to see what lies
before his feet. No philosopher understands his neighbour's actions nor
even his own; he does not even know what either of them is in himself,
beast or Man.[273]

[A]   These people, now, who find Sebond's arguments to be too feeble,
these know-alls who are ignorant of nothing and make rules for the whole
Universe –

> *Quae mare compescant causae; quid temperet annum;*
> *Stellae sponte sua jussaeve vagentur et errent;*
> *Quid premat obscurum lunae, quid proferat orbem;*
> *Quid velit et possit rerum concordia discors;*

[What limits the seas to their confines, what regulates the years: whether the heavenly
bodies travel and wander freely or by constraint; what makes the dark orb of the
Moon to wax or wane, or what the discordant concord of all things can mean or bring
about][274] –

have they never, among all their books, plumbed the difficulties which confront them in understanding their own being? Some things can be seen easily
enough: our finger and foot are capable of motion; some of our members
move on their own while others move only when we make them do so; certain
impressions produce a blush, others pallor; some thoughts act on the spleen,
others on the brain; some make us laugh, others weep; some stun our minds
into ecstasies and arrest the movements of our limbs;   [C]   there are objects
which make our gorges rise, others which raise up something lower
down.   [A]   But no man has yet discovered how purely mental impressions

273. Erasmus, *Adages: Ad pedes* (but the servant-girl did not trip him up: he fell);
Cicero, *De div.*, II, xiii, 30 (a verse from the *Iphigeneia* of Ennius); Plato, *Theaetetus*,
174 B (Ficino, p. 149).

274. Horace, *Epistles*, I, xii, 16.

like these can effect such deep incursions into objects as massively solid as
our bodies nor the nature of the linking sutures by which these astonishing
stimuli are transmitted:   [C]   '*Omnia incerta ratione et in naturae majestate
abdita*' [All things remain unknown to reason and are hidden in the majesty
of Nature], says Pliny; and St Augustine: '*Modus quo corporibus adhaerent
spiritus, omnino mirus est, nec comprehendi ab homine potest: et hoc ipse homo
est*' [How the spirit adheres to the body is entirely a matter of wonder and
cannot be understood by Man; nevertheless this union of body and spirit *is*
Man].[275]

[A] And yet everybody knows the answer! Merely human opinions
become accepted when derived from ancient beliefs, and are taken on authority and trust like religion or law! We parrot whatever opinions are commonly held, accepting them as truths, with all the paraphernalia of supporting
arguments and proofs, as though they were something firm and solid; nobody
tries to shake them; nobody tries to refute them. On the contrary, everybody
vies with each other to plaster over the cracks and prop up received beliefs
with all his powers of reason – a supple instrument which can be turned on
the lathe into any shape at all. Thus the world is pickled in stupidity and
brimming over with lies.

We do not doubt much, because commonly received notions are assayed
by nobody. We never try to find out whether the roots are sound. We argue
about the branches. We do not ask whether any statement is true, but what
it has been taken to mean. We ask whether Galen said this or said that: we
never ask whether he said anything valid.

It is understandable that this curb on our freedom of judgement and this
tyranny over our beliefs should spread to include the universities and the
sciences: Aristotle is the god of scholastic science: it is heresy to discuss his
commandments (as it once was to discuss those of Lycurgus in Sparta). What
Aristotle taught is professed as law – yet like any other doctrine it may be
false. Where the first principles of Nature are concerned I cannot see why I
should not accept, as soon as the opinions of Aristotle, the 'Ideas' of Plato,
the atoms of Epicurus, the plenum and vacuum of Leucippus and Democritus, the water of Thales, the infinity of Nature of Anaximander, or the
aether of Diogenes, the numbers and symmetry of Pythagoras, the infinity
of Parmenides, the Unity of Musaeus, the fire and water of Apollodorus, the
homogeneous particles of Anaxagoras, the discord and concord of Empedocles, the fire of Heraclitus, or any other opinion drawn from the boundless
confusion of judgement and doctrines produced by our fine human reason,

275. Pliny, *Hist. nat.*, II, xxxvii; St Augustine, *City of God*, XXI, 10.

with all its certainty and perspicuity, when it turns its attention to anything whatever.

Aristotle based the principles of Nature on three elements: matter, form and privation. Yet what is more silly than actually to make a vacuum into one of the causes of the production of material objects? Privation is a negative: what fanciful humour led Aristotle to make it the original cause of objects which actually exist? Yet, except as an exercise in logic, nobody dares to shake that belief. Nobody debates anything to increase doubt but only to defend the founding author of their school against outside objections; his authority marks the goal; beyond it, no further inquiry is permitted.[276]

Base yourself on admitted postulates and you can build up any case you like; from the rules which order the original principles the remainder of your construction will follow on easily without self-contradiction.

This method allows us to bowl our arguments with the jack in view (and so be satisfied that our foundations are rational ones); before they even begin, our professors (like geometricians with their postulated axioms) establish such a hold over our beliefs that they can subsequently reach any conclusion they want. We give them our agreement and consent: they can then pull us this way and that way, spinning us about at will. Once we accept anyone's postulates he becomes our professor and our god: for his foundations he will grab territory so ample and so easy that, if he so wishes, he will drag us up to the clouds. In the practice and business of scholarship we have accepted Pythagoras' contention as legal tender: every expert, he says, must be believed in his own speciality. So, for the meaning of words the logician turns to the grammarian; for the matter of his arguments the rhetorician borrows from the logician; the poet takes his rhythms from the musician; the geometer takes his propositions from the arithmetician; the metaphysicians make their foundations out of the conjectures of physics. For their principles, all branches of learning take admitted postulates, which restrain human judgement on every side. If you come up against the barrier behind which their error of principle is sheltering, they have an axiom ready on their lips: Never argue with those who deny first principles.[277] But there can be no first principles unless God has revealed them; all the rest – beginning, middle and end – is dream and vapour.

Whenever a case is fought from preliminary assumptions, to oppose it

276. Criticism of Aristotle's doctrine of the creative force of privation was current: e.g. in Ramus and in Guy de Brués, *Dialogues*, 161. Cf. also Cicero, *Acad.: Lucullus*, II, xxxvii (118–19); *De nat. deorum*, I, X, xi.

277. H. C. Agrippa, *De Vanitate*, III (*ad fin.*). The axiom cited above was not Pythagorean: cf. Cognatus' adage, '*Peritis in sua arte credendum*'.

take the very axiom which is in dispute, reverse it and make that into your preliminary assumption. For any human assumption, any rhetorical proposition, has just as much authority as any other, unless a difference can be established by reason. So they must all be weighed in the balance – starting with general principles and any tyrannous ones.   [C]   To be convinced of certainty is certain evidence of madness and of extreme unsureness: no people are more insane or less philosophical than the 'lovers of opinion' whom Plato dubbed *philodoxoi*.[278]   [A]   We want to find out by reason whether fire is hot, whether snow is white, whether anything within our knowledge is hard or soft. There are ancient stories of the replies made to the man who doubted whether heat exists – they told him to jump into the fire – or to the one who doubted whether ice is cold – they told him to slip some into his bosom: but a reply like that is quite unworthy of the professed aims of philosophy. Philosophers could have spoken in this way only if they had left us in a state of nature, simply accepting external appearances as they offer themselves to our senses, or if they had left us to follow our basic appetites, governed only by such modes of being as we are born with. But they themselves have taught us to make judgements about the universe; they themselves have fed us with the notion that human reason is the Comptroller-General of everything within and without the vault of heaven; they themselves say that it can embrace everything, do everything and is the means by which anything is known or understood. Such replies would be good among the Cannibals who live long and happy lives, in peace and tranquillity, without the benefits of Aristotle's precepts and without even knowing what the word 'physics' means. Perhaps such a reply could even be better and more firmly based than all the ones which philosophers owe to reason or discovery. Such arguments would be within the capacity of ourselves, of all the animals and of all for whom the pure and simple law of Nature still holds sway. But they themselves have renounced such arguments. They must not tell me: 'This is true; you can see it is; you can feel it is.' What they must tell me is whether I really and truly feel what I think I feel; and if I do feel it, they must go on and tell me why and how and what: let them tell me the name, origin, connections and frontiers of heat or of cold and what qualities are found in the agents and patients of heat and of cold. Otherwise, let them abandon their professional intention, which is to accept nothing and approve nothing except by following the ways of reason. When they have to assay anything, reason is their touchstone. But it

278. Plato, *Republic*, V, 460 E. (For what follows, cf. Erasmus, *Apophthegmata*, III, *Diogenes*, L: when Zeno was proving 'by most acute arguments that there is no such thing as motion', Diogenes got up and walked away. 'What are you doing, Diogenes?' asked Zeno in surprise. 'I am confuting your arguments,' he replied.)

is, most surely, a touchstone full of falsehood, error, defects and feebleness. How better to test that than by reason itself. If we cannot trust reason when talking about itself, it can hardly be a judge of anything outside itself.

If human reason knows anything at all, it must be its own essence and its own domicile. It is domiciled within the soul, being either a part of it or one of its activities – as for the permanent home of that true and essential Reason, whose name we steal under false colours, it is in the bosom of God: that is the habitation where it dwells; that is where it comes from when it pleases God to allow us to have a glimmer of Reason, like Pallas leaping from the head of her Father to make herself known unto the world.

Now let us see what human reason can tell us about itself and about the soul! [C] I am not talking now of that generic soul, in which virtually all philosophy makes the heavenly bodies and the elements to share; nor of that soul which Thales, prompted by his study of the magnet, attributes to objects normally considered inanimate; I am concerned with the soul which belongs to us, the one we should know best:

> [B] *Ignoratur enim quae sit natura animai,*
> *Nata sit, an contra nascentibus insinuetur,*
> *Et simul intereat nobiscum morte dirempta,*
> *An tenebras orci visat vastasque lacunas,*
> *An pecudes alias divinitus insinuet se.*

[The nature of the soul is not known; whether it is innate or, on the contrary, slipped into creatures at the moment of their birth; does it die when we die, does it visit the darkness and the vast depths of Orcus, or else does it, under divine guidance, slip into animals different from ouselves?][279]

[A] Reason taught Crates and Dicaearchus that there is no soul (bodies being endowed with natural power of movement); it taught Plato that the soul is a self-moving substance; Thales, that soul is a natural substance, never in repose; Asclepiades, an exercising of the senses; Hesiod and Anaximander, a substance composed of fire and water; Parmenides, of earth and fire; Empedocles, of blood:

> *– Sanguineam vomit ille animam*
>
> [He vomits up his soul of blood] –

279. Lucretius, I, 112 (Lambin, p. 16). The following list of opinions combines commonplaces from Sextus Empiricus, Cicero and, especially, H. C. Agrippa, *De Vanitate*, II. But one of the most influential studies of the soul in the Renaissance was Melanchthon's *De anima*. Some of the matter of the following pages can be found there or may derive from there.

Possidonius, Cleanthes and Galen, that the soul is heat or a hot complexion –

*Igneus est ollis vigor, et coelestis origo*

[Souls have a fiery vigour and a heavenly origin] –

Hippocrates, a spirit spread throughout the body; Varro, air, infused through
the mouth, warmed in the lungs, refreshed in the heart and spread throughout
the body; Zeno, the quintessence of four elements; Heraclides of Pontus,
light; Xenocrates and the Egyptians, number in motion; the Chaldeans, a
power of indeterminate form:

[B]    *habitum quemdam vitalem corporis esse,*
*Harmoniam Graeci quam dicunt.*

[There is a certain life-giving quality in the body which the Greeks call Harmony.][280]

[A]   And let us not overlook Aristotle, who said the soul was that power
which naturally moved the body and which he called *entelechia* (as dull an
idea as anyone else's, for he does not mention the essence, origin or nature
of the soul but merely notes what it does). Lactantius, Seneca and the better
part of the Dogmatists all confessed that they did not know what it
was.   [C]   And after running through all these opinions, Cicero comments:
'*Harum sententiarum quae vera sit, deus aliquis viderit*' [It is up to some god or
other to say which of these is true].   [A]   'I know from myself', said St
Bernard, 'how incomprehensible God is: I cannot even comprehend the con-
stituents of my own being.' Heraclitus held that everything is full of souls
and daemons; he nevertheless maintained that whatever advances we may
make in our knowledge of the soul, we would never get to the end, since its
essence is too profound.[281]

[A]   There is just as much disagreement and argument about the seat of
the soul: Hippocrates and Hierophilus lodge it in the ventricle of the brain;
Democritus and Aristotle, throughout the body –

[B]   *Ut bona saepe valetudo cum dicitur esse*
*Corporis, et non est tamen haec pars ulla valentis.*

280. Virgil, *Aeneid*, IX, 349 and VI, 730. Both cited in Melanchthon, *De anima*
(*Opera*, 1541, III, 9); Lucretius, III, 99 (Lambin, pp. 198–99).
281. For entelechy (*actuality* or *activity*) as principle of soul, see Aristotle, *De
anima*, 2, 1 and *Metaph.*, 8. 3; discussed, similarly, in Melanchthon, *De anima*, 11 ff.
(Cf. Tertullian, *De anima*, 32); Cicero, *Tusc. disput.* I, xi; St Bernard, *De anima seu
meditationes devotissimae*, I, *in princ.*; Diogenes Laertius, *Lives*, Heraclitus, IX, vii.
What follows may be influenced by H. C. Agrippa, *De Vanitate*, LII; for Renaissance
scholarship, see Melanchthon, *De anima*, 17 ff. (*Quid est organum?*).

[As we often say that a man has a healthy body, without implying that health is part of a healthy man.] –

[A]   Epicurus lodges it in the stomach –

> [B]   *Hic exultat enim pavor ac metus, haec loca circum*
> *Laetitiae mulcent;*

[For terror and fear make the stomach tremble, while joys soothe its pains;][282]

[A]   the Stoics lodge it within and around the heart; Erasistratus, adjoining the membrane of the epicranium; Empedocles, in the blood – like Moses, who for this reason forbade men to 'eat the blood' of beasts (whose soul is within the blood);[283] Galen thought that each part of the body had its own soul; Strato lodged it between the eyebrows: [C]   *'Qua facie quidem sit animus, aut ubi habitet, ne quaerendum quidem est'* [As for the aspect of the soul and the place wherein it dwells, we should not even try to inquire]. – I gladly let that fellow Cicero use his own words (should I dare to contaminate the utterances of Eloquence!) And there is little to gain from stealing the substance of his own ideas, which are neither frequent, sound nor unknown.[284]

[A]   But the reason which led Chrysippus and others of his sect to make a case out for the heart is not to be forgotten: it is (he says) because, when we want to swear an oath, we place our hand upon our bosom, and when we want to pronounce the word ἔγω (which means 'I') we lower our jaw towards our chest. This passage should not be allowed to slip by without a remark about such silliness in so great a person. Even if you leave aside the total lack of weight in the argument as such, his last proof could only convince Greeks that their soul is where he said it is. No man's judgement is so alert as never to nod off to sleep![285]   [C]   Why are we afraid to say so? Here are the Stoics, the fathers of human wisdom, finding that, when a man is buried under the weight of a fallen building, his soul cannot extricate itself but makes lengthy struggles to get free – like a mouse in a trap!

282. Lucretius, III, 102; 142 (Lambin, pp. 198–99, 201–204).

283. A basic interdict of the Law of Moses, e.g. Leviticus 7:26–27; but it is the *anima* (life) not *animus* (mind) which is 'in the blood': *ibid.*, 17:11. Cf. Melanchthon, *De anima*, 16.

284. Cicero, *Tusc. disput.* I, xxvii, 67. Montaigne used Cicero as a source, but he was impatient with his wordiness and credited him with no originality as a thinker.

285. Galen, *De placitis Hippocratis et Platonis*, II, ii; Stoics, rejected by Seneca, *Epist.*, LVII, 7–8. In the original French, Montaigne confusingly uses *estomach* in both its Latin sense (stomach) and its Greek sense (breast).

Some[286] maintain that the world was made specifically to give bodies to souls, as a punishment for having wilfully fallen from their original purity; at first they were simply incorporeal; they are given light or heavy bodies, depending upon how far they have withdrawn from their original spiritual state (which explains the great variety of created matter). The spirit who, as a punishment, was invested with the body of the Sun must have fallen off in some very rare and special way!

The frontiers of our research are lost in dazzling light. Plutarch, writing of the fountain-heads of history, says that when we push our investigations to extremes, they all fall into vagueness, rather like maps where the margins of known lands are filled in with marshes, deep forests, deserts and uninhabitable places.[287] That explains why the most gross and puerile of rhapsodies are to be found among thinkers who penetrate most deeply into the highest matters: they are engulfed by their curiosity and their arrogance. The beginnings and the ends of our knowledge are equally marked by an animal-like stupor: witness Plato's soarings aloft in clouds of poetry and the babble of the gods to be found in his works. Whatever was he thinking about when he   [A]   defined Man as an animate creature with two legs and no feathers? He furnished those who wanted to laugh at him with an amusing opportunity for doing so. For, having plucked a live capon, they went about calling it 'Plato's Man'.[288]

And the Epicureans too. With what simple-mindedness they first imagined that the universe had been formed by their atoms (which, they said, were bodies having some weight and a natural downward movement) until their opponents reminded them that, by their own description, it was impossible for these atoms to link up together: their fall, being straight and perpendicular, could only be effected along parallel lines. This obliged them to add a quite fortuitous sideways motion, and to furnish their atoms with curved hooks on their tails by which they could link themselves firmly to each other. [C]   Even then, they were in trouble from others, who hounded them with another consideration: if atoms do, by chance, happen to combine themselves into so many shapes, why have they never combined together to form a house or a slipper? By the same token, why do we not believe that if innumerable letters of the Greek alphabet were poured all over the market-place they would eventually happen to form the text of the *Iliad*?

286. Platonists, including Origen (criticized by St Augustine, *City of God*, XI, 23).

287. Plutarch, *Life of Theseus*, I, 1.

288. Diogenes Laertius, *Lives*, Diogenes, VI, 40.

That which is capable of reasoning, argued Zeno, is superior to that which is not: nothing is superior to the Universe, therefore the Universe is capable of reasoning. Cotta used the same argument to make the Universe into a mathematician and another argument of Zeno's to make it into a musician – an organist: The whole is greater than the part: we, who are parts of the Universe, are capable of wisdom: therefore the Universe is wise.[289]

[A]  One can find innumerable examples[290] of similar arguments which are not only false but inept and unable to hold together, emphasizing that their inventors were not so much ignorant as silly; you can find them in the criticisms which philosophers make of each other in their clashes of opinion and in the disagreements between Schools.

[C]  Anyone who made an intelligent collection of the asinine stupidities of human Wisdom would have a wondrous tale to tell. I like collecting such things as evidence which, from some angles, can be studied as usefully as sane and moderate opinions.  [A]  We can judge what we should think of Man, of his sense and of his reason, when we find such obvious and gross errors even in these important characters who have raised human intelligence to great heights. Personally I prefer to believe that they treated knowledge haphazardly, sporting with it, in any fashion, like a toy and that they played with reason as if it were some vain and frivolous instrument, putting forward all kinds of thoughts and fantasies, some forceful, others, weak. The selfsame Plato who defined Man as a capon, elsewhere follows Socrates and says that, in truth, he does not know what Man is, and that Man is one of the hardest things in the world to understand.[291] With such varied and unstable opinions they lead us tacitly by the hand to inconclusive conclusions. They profess that they do not present the face of their thought openly and unveiled; they hide it beneath obscurities of poetic fable or behind some other mask. Our imperfection is such that raw meat is not always proper food for our stomachs: it first has to be dried, treated or hung. They do the same: they sometimes take their straightforward opinions and judgements and hide them behind obscurity [C] and season them with falsehood, [A] so as to prepare them for public consumption. They do not want to make an express avowal of the ignorance and weakness of human reason – [C] they want to avoid

289. Cicero, *De fin.*, I, v, 13–vi, 21; *De nat. deorum*, II, xxxvi, 93–94 (adapted); III, ix, 20–23. Cotta is mocking Zeno.

290. '88: find *many similar* examples . . .; (in place of [C], below): schools, *as you can see in the infinite examples in Plutarch, against the Epicureans and Stoics: and in Seneca against the Peripatetics.* We . . .

291. Plato, *Alcibiades*, I, 129 A.

frightening the children – [A] but they give us a good glimpse of it beneath the appearance of confused and unstable erudition.

[B] When I was in Italy, I advised a man who was at pains to learn Italian that if it were merely to be understood, without excelling in any other way, he should simply use the first words which came to his lips, Latin, French, Spanish or Gascon, and stick an Italian ending on them; he would never fail to hit on some local dialect, Tuscan, Roman, Venetian, Piedmontese or Neapolitan: there are so many forms that he was bound to coincide with one of them. I say the same about Philosophy. She has so many faces, so much variety and has been so garrulous, that all our ravings and our dreams may be found within her. Human fancy can conceive nothing, good or evil, which is not there already. [C] '*Nihil tam absurde dici potest quod non dicatur ab aliquo philosophorum*' [Nothing can be so absurd that it has not already been said by one of the philosophers].[292] [B] So I am all the more ready to give a free run to my own whims in public: I know they were born to me, not modelled on others, but you can always find some Ancient or other whose fantasies are akin to them. There will always be somebody to say, 'Look, he got it from there.'

[C] My ways of life are natural to me: in forming them I have never called in the help of any erudite discipline; but when I was seized with the desire to give a public account of them, weak as they are, I made it my duty to help them along with precepts and examples, so that I could publish them more decorously. I was then astonished myself to find that, by sheer chance, they were in conformity with so many philosophical examples and precepts. Only after my life was settled in its activity did I learn which philosophy was governing it! A new character: a chance philosopher, not a premeditated one!

[A] To get back to our souls,[293] Plato placed reason in the brain, anger in the heart, desire in the liver; but that probably resulted from an interpretation of the emotions of the soul rather than from any desire to divide the soul up into separate parts; it was more like one body with several members. The most likely of all these opinions states that the human soul is one single entity with the faculties for ratiocinating, remembering, comprehending, judging and desiring; it exercises its other functions through the instrumentality of the various parts of the body (just as the seaman sails his vessel according to his experience of it, at times tightening or slackening a sheet, at others hoisting the yard or pulling the oar, one single power organizing all these actions); the seat of this power is the brain, as is clearly shown by the

292. Cicero, *De divinat.*, II, lviii, 119.
293. '88: souls, (*for I have chosen this one example as being the most convenient for witnessing to our feebleness and vanity*) Plato . . . (Cf. Melanchthon, *De anima*, 29 f.)

fact that wounds and accidents affecting the head immediately harm the
faculties of the soul; it is not inappropriate, therefore, that this power should
extend from the brain to the rest of the body[294] –

> [C]   *medium non deserit unquam*
> *Coeli Phoebus iter; radiis tamen omnia lustrat.*

[Phoebus never deserts his path through the sky, yet bathes all things with light from
his rays] –

just as the Sun in the sky pours out its light and its powers and fills the whole
universe:

> *Caetera pars animae per totum dissita corpus*
> *Paret, et ad numen mentis nomenque movetur.*

[The remainder of the soul, scattered throughout the body, obeys, and is activated by
the majesty and authority of the mind.][295]

Some said that there is a general Soul, like some huge body, from which
individual souls were extracted, later returning there to be re-absorbed in
that universal matter:

> *Deum namque ire per omnes*
> *Terrasque tractusque maris coelumque profundum:*
> *Hinc pecudes, armenta, viros, genus omne ferarum,*
> *Quemque sibi tenues nascentem arcessere vitas;*
> *Scilicet huc reddi deinde, ac resoluta referri*
> *Omnia: nec morti esse locum;*

[For God is said to spread through all lands, all tracts of sea and highest heaven; from
him all flocks and herds and men and every race of beast all take, at birth, their tenuous
lives, and to him all things eventually return, when they are loosened asunder: and so
there is no place at all for death;][296]

others said that the individual souls merely rejoined this general Soul –
attached to it, but as individuals; others said that souls were produced from
the divine substance itself; others, from fire and water, by angels; some said
they existed from the earliest times; others, that they were created only when
actually required. Some said they came down from the circle of the Moon
and later returned there. Most of the Ancients held that, exactly like all other

294. Diogenes Laertius, *Lives*, Plato, III, lxvii, 224 *apud* Guy de Brués, p. 79 f.

295. Claudian, cited in the *Politici* of Justus Lipsius, IV, ix; then Lucretius, III,
143 (Lambin, pp. 201–202). Montaigne misreads *momen* (impulse) as *nomen* (name,
authority) despite Lambin's explanation.

296. Aristotelian opinions, backed by Virgil, *Georgics*, IV, 221.

natural things, they were engendered from father to son, adducing as an argument the resemblance of sons to their fathers:[297]

> *Instillata patris virtus tibi:*
> *Fortes creantur fortibus et bonis.*

[Your father's virtue is transmitted to you; strong men are born from strong men and good.][298]

Not only physical characteristics were held to flow like this from father to son but similar humours, complexions and inclinations of the soul:

> *Denique cur acris violentia triste leonum*
> *Seminium sequitur; dolus vulpibus, et fuga cervis*
> *A patribus datur, et patrius pavor incitat artus;*
> *Si non certa suo quia semine seminioque*
> *Vis animi pariter crescit cum corpore toto?*

[Finally, why is impetuous ferocity the hereditary mark of the dire lion family, trickery of the fox and swiftness of the deer (which inherits the paternal instinct towards timorous flight) if not because the soul is born from semen and grows with the rest of the body?]

This was held to be the basis of divine Justice which readily visits upon the children the sins of the fathers, because the pollution of the fathers' vices is to some extent imprinted upon the souls of their children, who are influenced by their fathers' unruly desires.[299]

Moreover if souls do not come from natural succession but by some other way – if, say, they existed beforehand as entities independent of their bodies – they would have had some memory of their former state, given that reflection, reason and memory are the natural properties of the soul:

> [B]   *si in corpus nascentibus insinuatur,*
> *Cur superante actam aetatem meminisse nequimus,*
> *Nec vestigia gestarum rerum ulla tenemus?*

297. This doctrine (traducianism) is discussed by Melanchthon, *De anima*, along with other notions mentioned by Montaigne.

298. First line, anon., second, Horace, *Odes*, IV, iv, 29.

299. Lucretius, III, 741 (Lambin, 241–42). Cf. Andreas Tiraquellus, *De legibus connubialibus*, VII, 1–4. It was accepted that sensitive and vegetative souls could be transmitted in semen: the human rational soul was individually created (Melanchthon, *De anima*, 15).

[If souls are only introduced into the bodies at birth, why cannot we fully remember what happened before nor retain any trace of the things which we did?][300]

[A]   If we are to give the value we wish to the attributes of our souls, we are obliged to assume that, even in their natural simplicity and purity, they are full of knowledge; free from the prison of the body, our souls, therefore, must be such, before they entered their bodies, as we hope they will be once they have gone forth from them; so, while they are in the body, they must continue to remember that knowledge: hence Plato's assertion that whatever we learn is really the recollection of what we once knew. But we all know that to be false from our own experience. First: we remember nothing save what we have been taught; if memory did its duty 'purely', it would at least hint at something beyond our apprenticed knowledge. Second: what the soul knew in her pure state was true knowledge: since her intelligence was divine, she knew things as they really are; here below you can make the soul accept lies and errors, if you teach them to her. She cannot be using her powers of recollection in that case, since she had never accommodated such Forms and concepts!

But to say that her imprisonment in the body smothers her native faculties so completely as to snuff them right out, runs, first of all, contrary to that other belief: that we can recognize her powers to be so great, and those of her workings which we are conscious of in this life to be so wonderful, that they allow us to conclude that she is divine, has existed from all eternity and will enjoy immortality.

> [B]   *Nam, si tantopere est animi mutata potestas*
> *Omnis ut actarum exciderit retinentia rerum,*
> *Non, ut opinor, ea ab leto jam longior errat.*

[For if all the faculties of the soul are so completely changed that no memory of the past remains, that seems to me to be no different from extinction.][301]

[A]   Moreover, the powers and actions of our souls must be examined not elsewhere but here, at home in our bodies. Any other perfections they may have are useless and irrelevant; it is for their present state that their whole

300. Lucretius, III, 671 (Lambin, p. 235: criticism of Pythagoreans, citing Aristotle). There follows criticism of the Platonic doctrine that all learning is recollection of knowledge pre-dating the imprisonment of the soul in the body (*Phaedo*, XVIII, 73E). Similar refutations are found elsewhere (e.g. in L. Joubert's *Erreurs populaires*, 1578 (Preface), exploited above, p. 24, on natural language). Christianity avoids the problem of rewards and punishments in the afterlife by making them depend on the presence or absence of imputed merits (Christ's not Man's).

301. Lucretius, III, 674 (Lambin, pp. 265–67, reading *longior* for *longiter*).

immortality will receive its acknowledged rewards: each is entirely account-able for the life of a human being. But it would be an act of gross injustice to lop off the soul's powers and resources, to strip her of all her weapons and then to take the very time when she lies weak and ill in prison – a time of repression and constraint – and to make that the basis for a judgement leading to endless, everlasting punishment; it would be unjust to limit consideration to so short a span, to a life that may have lasted a mere two hours or, at the very worst a hundred years – an instant in proportion to infinity – and then, from that momentary interlude, to order and establish, once and for all, the whole state of her future existence. To reward or punish on the basis of so short a life would be disproportionate and iniquitous.

[C]   To get out of this difficulty, Plato wants future rewards and punish-ments never to exceed a hundred years and always to be proportionate to the actual length of a man's life. Quite a few Christians too have imposed temporal limits on to them.[302]

[A]   As a result of all this men followed Epicurus and Democritus (whose opinions were most widely received); they concluded that the generation and life of the soul shared all the usual characteristics of things human. Many striking features make this seem probable: they could see that the soul was born precisely when the body was capable of receiving her; that her strength increased as the body's did: it was observed that the soul was weak in infancy and then, eventually, experienced a vigorous maturity, a decline into old age and, finally, decrepitude:

> *gigni pariter cum corpore, et una*
> *Crescere sentimus, pariterque senescere mentem.*

[We can feel that the soul is born with the body, grows up with it and then grows old.][303]

Man perceived that the soul can experience various passions and be disturbed by several emotions which subject her to pain and lassitude; she is capable of change, including change for the worse; she is capable of joy, tranquillity, languor; like the stomach or the foot, she is subject to wounds and illness:

302. Plato, *Republic*, X, 615. Origen and the Universalists held that, eventually, Hell would be empty and all would be saved. Montaigne may also be alluding to misconceptions of Purgatory (as a modification of Hell, rather than of Heaven).

303. A series of sustained borrowings from Lucretius, III, 445 f.; 510 f.; 175 f.; 499–501; 492 f.; 463 f.; 800 f.; 458; 110 f. Throughout, the comments of Lambin are relevant (pp. 190–272). For a Christian answer in the dedication of Book III of Lucretius, see the Introduction, p. xxv.

[B]  *mentem sanari, corpus ut aegrum*
*Cernimus, et flecti medicina posse videmus.*

[We see that the mind can be cured like the body and be modified by drugs.]

[A]  She can be confused and dazed by the powers of wine, be upset by the vapours of a burning fever; be lulled to sleep by certain drugs and aroused by others:

[B]  *corpoream naturam animi esse necesse est,*
*Corporeis quoniam telis ictuque laborat.*

[The nature of the mind is necessarily corporeal, for it can be hurt by physical cuts and blows.]

Men saw that all the soul's faculties can be stunned and overthrown by the mere bite of a sick dog; that the soul has no way of avoiding any of these accidents, even by showing the utmost firmness of mind or any moral quality or virtue, by philosophical determination or by any straining of her forces. Let the saliva of some wretched dog slaver over the hand of Socrates and they knew that it would put a sudden end to all his wisdom and to all his mighty, disciplined thought, reducing them to nothing, so that no trace whatever would remain of his original awareness:

[B]  *vis animai*
*Conturbatur, . . . et divisa seorsum*
*Disjectatur, eodem illo distracta veneno.*

[The power of the soul is disturbed and its parts are broken up and dispersed by that same poison.]

They knew that the poison would find no greater powers of resistance in his soul than in a four-year-old's: if Philosophy herself became incarnate, such a poison would make her lose her senses and drive her insane. Cato could wring the neck of Death and Destiny, but if ever he had been bitten by a mad dog and contracted that illness which doctors call *hydroforbia*,[304] even he would have been overcome with fear and terror, quite unable to bear the sight of water or a looking-glass.

[B]  *vis morbi distracta per artus*
*Turbat agens animam, spumantes aequore salso*
*Ventorum ut validis fervescunt viribus undae.*

[The power of the disease spreading through one's limbs drives the soul to distraction, like stormy winds lashing the waves of the troubled sea.]

304. Ignorant medical deformation of *hydrophobia*.

[A] While we are on this subject, Philosophy has armed Man well against all the other ills which may befall him, teaching him either to bear them or else, if the cost of that is too high, to inflict certain defeat on them by escaping from all sensation. But such methods can only be of service to a vigorous soul in control of herself, a soul capable of reason and decision: they are no use in a disaster such as this, where the soul of a philosopher becomes the soul of a madman, confused, lost and deranged. This can happen from several causes: by some excessive emotion which snatches the mind away; by some strong passion engendered by the soul herself; by a wound in certain parts of the body; by a gastric vapour subjecting the soul to giddiness and confusion:

> [B]   *morbis in corporis, avius errat*
> *Saepe animus: dementit enim, deliraque fatur;*
> *Interdumque gravi lethargo fertur in altum*
> *Aeternumque soporem, oculis nutuque cadenti.*

[During physical illness, the soul often goes astray, becoming mad and talking deliriously; sometimes it plunges into a deep lethargy, into a perpetual sleep, as the eyes close and the head droops down.]

[A] Philosophers, it seems to me, have hardly begun to pluck that particular chord; [C] no more than another one of similar importance. To console us in our mortal state they constantly present us with the following dilemma: The soul is either mortal or immortal; if mortal, she will be without pain; if immortal she will go on improving. But they never touch on the other alternative. What if she goes on getting worse! They simply hand threats of further punishment over to the poets. But that game is far too easy.

I am often struck by these two omissions in their argument: I now go back to the first. [A] The deranged soul loses all taste for the Sovereign Good of the Stoics, so constant and so resolute. On this point our wisdom, fair though she is, really must surrender and lay down her arms.

Meanwhile the vanity of human reason led philosophers to conclude that a composite being, linking in fellowship two elements as diverse as mortal body and immortal soul, is quite inconceivable.

> *Quippe etenim mortale aeterno jungere, et una*
> *Consentire putare, et fungi mutua posse,*
> *Desipere est. Quid enim diversius esse putandum est,*
> *Aut magis inter se disjunctum discrepitansque,*
> *Quam mortale quod est, immortali atque perenni*
> *Junctum, in concilio saevas tolerare procellas?*

[It is mad to think that the mortal is able to be joined to the eternal, to agree together and each to help the other. What can we possibly conceive more different, or, rather, more contrary and incompatible, than these two elements, one mortal, the other immortal and eternal, which you would join together to ride out the wildest storm?]

Moreover the soul, like the body, was thought to be involved in death,

> [B] *Simul aevo fessa fatiscit.*

[She droops down, tired out with age.]

[C] According to Zeno this is shown to us clearly by the image of sleep (which he thought was both the soul and the body dropping down in a faint): '*Contrahi animum et quasi labi putat atque concidere*' [He conceived that the soul contracts, as it were, collapses and falls down in a swoon].[305]

[A] It was recognized that the soul may sometimes retain her force and vigour to the end; that was explained by the different varieties of illness, just as some men retain one or other of their senses intact to the end – their hearing, say, or their sense of touch – nobody being so enfeebled as to have absolutely no part vigorous and whole.

> [B] *Non alio pacto quam si, pes cum dolet aegri,*
> *In nullo caput interea sit forte dolore.*

[In the same way, a sick man's feet may feel sharp pains, without his head feeling anything.][306]

Our mental insight is to Truth what an owl's eyes are to the splendour of the sun. Aristotle says that. Is there any better way of convicting ourselves than by noting such total blindness in so clear a light?

[A] Now for the contrary opinion: that the soul is in fact immortal. [C] Cicero says that, at least as far as books are concerned, it was first introduced by Pherecides of Scyros in the time of King Tullus. Some others attribute it to Thales, and there are other candidates.[307] [A] This branch of human learning is treated with the greatest reservation and doubt. On this matter, even the most confirmed Dogmatists are mainly constrained to shelter behind the shadowy teachings of Plato's Academy. On this subject, nobody knows what Aristotle's conclusions were, [C] no more than those of the Ancients in general, who handle the matter with a kind of vacillating belief: '*rem gratissimam promittentium magis quam probantium*' [a thing most pleasing,

305. Cicero, *De divinat.*, II, lviii, 119. Montaigne takes some of these arguments up again in vol. III, chapter 12, 'On Experience'.

306. The last of this series of borrowings from Sextus Empiricus; then Aristotle, *Metaphysics*, II, 1, 993 b (a *bat* not an *owl*).

307. Cicero, *Tusc. disput.*, I, xvi.

but more in promise than in proof].[308] Aristotle hid behind a cloud of difficult
and incomprehensible words and meanings, leaving his followers arguing as
much about what he meant as about the matter itself.

Two considerations made this opinion plausible to them: first, that without
the immortality of the soul, fame would have no secure basis and so be hoped
for in vain. (By the standards of the world that is a consideration of wonderful
importance.) The second is one of utility: it is useful that people should be
convinced, [C] as Plato says, [A] that even when vices escape the dark
and uncertain vigilance of human justice, they still remain exposed to that of
divine Justice which will pursue them even after the death of the
guilty.[309] [C] Man takes extreme care to prolong his being, providing for
it by all possible means: he has tombs to preserve his body and fame to
preserve his soul.

Dissatisfied with his lot, Man has given free run to his opinions, building
himself up into something else and propping himself up with his own ingenuity. The soul can never find a sure footing; she is too confused and weak
for that. She roams about seeking bases for her hopes and consolations in
conditions which are foreign to her nature. She clings to them and puts down
roots. These notions which she ingeniously forges for herself may be ever so
frivolous and fantastic, but she can find repose in them more surely than in
herself, and much more willingly. [A] But it is a source of wonder that
even those who are most obstinately attached to so just and clear a persuasion
as spiritual immortality fall short, being powerless to establish it by their
human ability. [C] One Ancient writer said, 'Somnia sunt non docentis, sed
optantis' [They are not the dreams of one who demonstrates but of one who
desires].[310] [A] From this evidence Man realizes that such truth as he does
find out for himself is due to Fortune and to chance. Even when truth drops
into his hands, Man has no means of seizing hold of it; his reason does not
have power enough to establish any rights over it. Every single idea which
results from our own reflections and our own faculties – whether it is true or
false – is subject to dispute and uncertainty. In bygone days God produced
the confusion and disorder of the Tower of Babel as a chastisement of our
pride, to teach us our wretchedness and our inadequacy. Everything we
undertake without God's help, everything we try and see without the lamp
of his grace, is vanity and madness. The essence of Truth is to be constant
and uniform: when Fortune arranges for a little of it to come into our pos-

308. Seneca, Epist., CII, 2 (a major treatment of the theme of immortality,
influencing the following argument).

309. Plato, Laws, X, 907.

310. Cicero, Acad.: Lucullus, II, xxxviii, 121 (citing Democritus).

session, out of weakness we corrupt it and debase it. Any course a man may adopt on his own is allowed by God to lead to this same confusion, the idea of which is so vividly portrayed in the just punishment which God visited upon the arrogance of Nembroth, bringing to nought his vain attempts to build that pyramidal Tower:  [C]  *'Perdam sapientiam sapientium et pruden-tiam prudentium reprobabo'* [I will destroy the wisdom of the wise, and the understanding of the prudent I will reject].  [A]  That diversifying of tongues and language by which God threw confusion over the enterprise of Babel, what else does it signify if not the infinite, endless altercation over discordant opinions and arguments which accompanies the vain struc-tures of human knowledge, enmeshing them in confusion.  [C]  Usefully enmeshing them! If we actually possessed one grain of knowledge, there would be no holding us back. I like what that Saint said: *'Ipsa utilitatis occultatio, aut humilitatis exercitatio est, aut elationis attritio'* [Even that which is useful has been rendered obscure: that provides an occasion for exercising our humility and restraining our pride]. To what degree of arrogance and insolence do we not carry our blindness and our brutish stupidity.[311]

[A]  But to get back to our subject: it is truly reasonable that we should be beholden to God alone, to the benefit of his grace, for the truth of so excellent a belief: it is from God's bountiful liberality that we receive the fruition of everlasting life, which is the enjoyment of eternal blessedness.

[C]  We should freely admit that God alone tells us this, and faith.[312] It is not a lesson we have been taught by Nature or Reason. Anyone who makes repeated examinations of himself, internally and externally, as a human being, with human powers but bereft of the divine privilege of grace; anyone who sees Man as he is, without flattery, will find no quality or faculty in Man which is not redolent of death and dust. The more we attribute, grant and refer to God, the more Christianly we act. Would the Stoic philosopher not be better advised to owe to God what he said he owed to the chance agreement of the Voice of the People? *'Cum de animarum aeternitate disserimus, non leve momentum apud nos habet consensus hominum aut timentium inferos, aut colen-tium. Utor hac publica persuasione'* [When treating the immortality of the soul we attach no little weight to the general agreement among those who fear

311.  Nembroth (Nimrod) was King of Babel; the Tower of Babel, sometimes por-trayed as pyramidal, sought to 'reach unto heaven'; God overthrew it and confounded men's language, 'that they may not understand another's speech': Genesis 10:9–11:9; I Corinthians 1:19; St Augustine, *City of God*, XI, 22.

312.  Points made in Lambin's dedication of Book III of Lucretius to 'Germano Valenti Pimpuntio': no human arguments assure us of immortality, not even Plato's: only Christ does. Cf. Introduction, p. xxv.

or worship the gods of the Underworld. I make good use of this general conviction].[313]

[A]   The feebleness of human reasoning on this subject is particularly noticeable from the fabulous details which men have added to it in their efforts to discover the characteristics of our future immortality.   [C]   We may leave aside the Stoics, who grant that souls do have a future life, but only a finite one: '*usuram nobis largiuntur tanquam cornicibus: diu mansuros aiunt animos; semper, negant*' [They allow us to live as long as crows: our souls last a long time, they say, but not for ever].[314]

[A]   The most universally received opinion (which still subsists today in some places) was the one attributed to Pythagoras – (not that he was the first to hold it, but because his approval and authority gave great weight and credence to it); it was that our souls, when they depart from us, go the rounds from one body to another, from a lion, say, to a horse; from a horse, to a king, ceaselessly driven from one abode to another.[315]   [C]   Pythagoras said he distinctly remembered having previously been Aethalides, then Euphorbus, then Hermotimus and finally Pyrrhus, before his soul eventually passed into himself, with recollections covering two hundred and six years.

Some added that these souls sometimes go back to heaven, and then come down again:

> *O pater, anne aliquas ad coelum hinc ire putandum est*
> *Sublimes animas iterumque ad tarda reverti*
> *Corpora? Quae lucis miseris tam dira cupido?*

[O Father, must we believe that some exalted souls go from here to heaven and then come back again to sluggish bodies? Why do those wretches still yearn for the light of day?][316]

Origen has souls everlastingly shuttling back and forth between wretchedness and bliss. Varro's opinion relates how souls rejoin their original bodies after four hundred and forty years have rolled; for Chrysippus that happens after

313. Seneca, *Epist.*, CXVII, 6.

314. Cicero, *Tusc. disp.*, I, xxxi; cf. Rabelais, *Quart Livre*, XXVII, *ad fin.*

315. Diogenes Laertius, *Lives*, Diogenes, VIII, 526.

'88 (in place of [C]): another. *Socrates, Plato and virtually all those who wished to believe in the immortality of souls, allowed themselves to be convinced by that discovery, as well as whole nations, our own among them.* But . . . Cf. Caesar, *De bello gallico*, VI, 18.)

316. Virgil, *Aeneid*, VI, 719 (cf. St Augustine, *City of God*, XIV, 5). Platonic teachings: cf. Plutarch, *De la face qui apparoist dedans le rond de la Lune*, 626 C–H (the 'orchard of Dis').

an undefined period.[317] Plato says that it was from Pindar and the old poets that he acquired his belief in the endless succession of changes by which the soul is purified (in the World to Come her rewards and punishments are temporary, since her life on earth is lived within time); he drew the conclusion that the soul must possess a detailed knowledge of the affairs of heaven, hell and earth (having sojourned in them during her many journeys to and fro): for her, it is a matter of recollection.[318]

Elsewhere, the soul's progression is like this: if a man has lived well he joins the star to which he is assigned; if badly, he becomes a woman; if even then he does not amend, he changes once more, this time into a beast with attributes appropriate to his vices; he will know no end to his punishments until he returns to his native condition, having rid himself, by force of reason, from all the gross, dull and material qualities within him.[319]

[A] But I must not forget the objection raised by the Epicureans against this transmigration of souls from body to body. It is quite entertaining. They pose the question: What order could be maintained if the crowds of the dying proved greater than the number being born? The souls turned out of house and home would all be jostling each other, trying to be the first to get into their new containers! They also ask how souls would spend their time while waiting for their new lodgings to be got ready. The Epicureans maintain that if, at the other extreme, more animate creatures were born than died, their bodies would be in a parlous state, having to wait for souls to be poured into them: some would die before they had started to live:

> *Denique connubia ad veneris partusque ferarum*
> *Esse animas praesto deridiculum esse videtur,*
> *Et spectare immortales mortalia membra*
> *Innumero numero, certareque praeproperanter*
> *Inter se, quae prima potissimaque insinuetur.*

[It seems absurd that souls should have to wait for the connubial embraces and parturitions of beasts – innumerable immortal beings looking out for mortal limbs and struggling among themselves to see who is strong enough to slip in first.][320]

Others make our souls remain in the body after death, so as to animate the snakes, worms and other creatures which are said to be produced by spontaneous generation in our rotting flesh or even from our ashes. Others

---

317. St Augustine, *City of God*, XXI, 16–17; XXII, 28 (including note by Vivès).
318. Plato, *Meno*, 82 (Ficino, p.19).
319. Plato, *Timaeus*, 42 E D (Ficino, p. 710).
320. Lucretius, III, 776 f. (Lambin, pp. 243–45). The following passage draws on III, 712–40 (Lambin, pp. 237–41).

split the soul into two parts, mortal and immortal. Others make it corporeal yet immortal. Others make it immortal, but without knowledge or awareness. There have been those who thought that the souls of the damned become devils [C] (and some of us Christians have thought that, too). [A] Similarly, Plutarch thinks that those who are saved become gods. There are few things that Plutarch asserts with more conviction (everywhere else his manner is one of sustained doubt and indecision). 'We must think', he says, 'and firmly believe that the souls of men who have been virtuous by the standards of Nature and divine Justice, change from men into saints and from saints into demi-gods; finally these demi-gods become gods, once they are perfectly cleansed and purified (as in the sacrifices of purgation), and delivered in this way from death and passability. They do not become gods by some decree of the Senate but are gods in very truth, such as one could rationally expect them to be, full and perfect gods, to whom is granted a most blessed and most glorious apotheosis.'[321] Plutarch is the most reticent and most moderate of the whole bunch, but if you would like to see him indulging in some bolder skirmishing and spinning some miraculous yarns about all this, I refer you to his treatises *On the Moon* and *On the Daemon of Socrates*; there, more clearly than anywhere, you can confirm that the mysteries of philosophy have plenty of oddities in common with poetry; human understanding in its strivings to plumb the depths of everything and to give an account of it, destroys itself, just as we ourselves, tired and exhausted by life's long race, fall back into childishness.[322]

With that we come to the end of all the fine doctrines which we can distill from human science about our souls.

There is no less rashness in what science tells us about our bodily parts. We had better choose one or two examples, otherwise we shall drown in the vast and troubled sea of medical error. We can at least find out whether there is any agreement over the material from which Man reproduces himself.[323]

321. Plutarch, *Life of Romulus*, XIV, ad. fin.

322. In Amyot's Plutarch, *De la face qui apparoist dedans le rond de la Lune*, 614–27, and *Du Demon ou esprit familier de Socrates* (636–49). (This is a reminder of a revolution in thought; the generation of Rabelais still sought mystical religious truths in these treatises.)

323. Discussion of the body, and of the various theories of human reproduction form a major element in Melanchthon's *De anima* (cf. 39 ff.). Since the human egg had yet to be discovered, all theories of generation turned on the nature of semen and of the womb. Rival schools, especially those of Hippocrates and Galen, clashed from Antiquity (cf. Rabelais, *Tiers Livre*, TLF, VIII; XXXIII; and notes). Montaigne draws on H. C. Agrippa, *De Vanitate*, LXXXII, and Plutarch, tr. Amyot, *Des opinions des philosophes*, 456 G–459 D. Cf. also Tiraquellus, *De legibus connubialibus*, XV, 10–11.

[C]  As for the way Man was originally produced, that is a very deep and ancient problem: small wonder, then, that it leaves the human mind troubled and distraught. Archelaus the natural philosopher of whom Socrates was the disciple (and, according to Aristoxenus, the paramour) taught that men and animals were made of milky sludge, exuded from the earth under the influence of heat.

[A]  Pythagoras said that our semen is the foam of our purest blood; Plato, a liquid draining from the marrow of the spinal column (supporting this with the argument that our backs are the first of our members to feel tired when we are on the job); Alcmeon says it is a part of the substance of the brain (proving this by the fact that men's vision becomes troubled when they work immoderately at that particular exercise); for Democritus it is a substance extracted from the whole mass of the body; for Epicurus, a substance extracted from the soul as well as from the body; for Aristotle, the final excretion drawn from the nutriment of blood which spreads through all our limbs; for others it is concocted blood, digested by heat in the testicles – because extreme exertions can make us ejaculate drops of blood: there may be a little more probability here if, that is, any probability at all can be drawn from confusion so infinite.

How does this semen achieve its purpose? Opinions are as numerous and as contradictory. Aristotle and Democritus hold that women have no semen, but only a kind of sweat which they exude when they bounce about in the heat of their enjoyment: it plays no role in generation. Galen, on the contrary, and those who follow him assert that generation can only occur when semen from male and female come into contact.

And then, see how the doctors, philosophers and lawyers are all disputing and quarrelling with our women about how long a pregnancy can last! Personally I support, from my own case, those who assert that a pregnancy can last eleven months: the whole world is full of such experiences; any simple, uneducated woman could give advice on these disputed questions. And still we cannot reach agreement![324]

That suffices to demonstrate that Man has no more knowledge of his own body than of his own soul. We have shown Man to himself – and his reason to his reason, to see what it has to tell us. I have succeeded in showing, I think, how far reason is from understanding even itself.

324. The duration of pregnancies was a question of great actuality: in general doctors accepted as legitimate children born after eleven (or even thirteen) months; some lawyers denied the possibility. Cf. Rabelais, *Gargantua*, TLF, III and notes. Also discussed in Melanchthon, *De anima* (cf. my study, *The Rabelaisian Marriage*, 1958). Montaigne was born after a prolonged pregnancy of eleven months.

[C]  And what can anyone understand who cannot understand himself?
'*Quasi vero mensuram ullius rei possit agere, qui sui nesciat*' [As though one
could measure anything and not know how to measure oneself].[325] Protagoras
was really and truly having us on when he made Man the measure of all things
– Man, who has never known even his own measurements. If Man cannot
have it, then his dignity will not let any other creature have it: yet Man is so
full of contradictions and his ideas are so constantly undermining each other
that so favourable a proposition is simply laughable: it leads to the inevitable
conclusion that both measure and the measurer are nothing.[326]

When Thales reckons that a knowledge of Man is very hard to acquire, he
is telling him that knowledge of anything else is impossible.[327]

For your sake, Patroness,[328] I have abandoned my usual practice and have
taken some pains to make this into a very long chapter. Sebond is your author:
you will, of course, continue to defend him with the usual forms of argument
in which you are instructed every day; that will exercise your mind and your
scholarship. The ultimate rapier-stroke which I am using here must only be
employed as a remedy of last resort. It is a desperate act of dexterity, in which
you must surrender your own arms to force your opponent to lose his. It is
a covert blow which you should only use rarely and with discretion. It is
rashness indeed to undo another by undoing yourself.   [B]  We must not
seek to die as an act of revenge, as Gobrias did when locked in close combat
with a Persian nobleman: Darius arrived on the scene, sword in hand, but
was afraid to strike for fear of killing him; Gobrias shouted to him to strike
boldly, even if he had to run both of them through.[329]

[C]  I have seen the proffered terms of a duel condemned in cases where
the weapons or the circumstances left no room for hope that either of the
combatants could survive.

The Portuguese took fourteen Turkish prisoners in the Indian Ocean,
who, impatient of their captivity, decided to reduce themselves, their masters
and the vessel to ashes; they succeeded in doing so by rubbing some of the

325. Pliny, II, 1.

326. For Protagoras, the arch-Sceptic and agnostic who introduced total relativism
by making each individual man the measure of all things, see Plato, *Theaetetus*, 152
A–C; 166D; 174 A–B; Aristotle, *Metaph.*, XI, v, 6 (1062 b). Later, Montaigne draws
on these pages as well as on Sextus, *Hypotyposes*, I, XXXII, 216 ff.

327. Thales (Diogenes Laertius, *Lives*, Thales, I, XXXV, 36), as cited by Erasmus
in his Socratic adage *Nosce teipsum*. (For Justus Lipsius, Montaigne was 'our Thales'.)

328. See above, p. 40. Montaigne undermines the case for deriving knowledge
from sense-data – a central contention of Pyrrhonism.

329. Herodotus, III, 73, cited by Plutarch, tr. Amyot, *Comment on pourra discerner
le flatteur d'avec l'amy*, 41 B–C.

ship's nails together until a spark fell among the barrels of gunpowder which were there.[330]

[A] Here we have now reached the limits and very boundaries of knowledge, where (as in the case of Virtue) extremes become vices. [A1] Keep to the beaten track: it can hardly be good to be so subtle and so clever. Remember the Tuscan proverb, *'Chi troppo s'assottiglia si scavezza'* [He who becomes too clever is lost]. [A] My advice to you is to cling to moderation and temperance, as much in your opinions and arguments as in your conduct, fleeing what is merely new or odd. All roads which wander from the norm displease me. You, by the authority of your high rank as well as by virtue of qualities which are more strictly your own, can, with a glance, command anyone you please; you ought to have entrusted this task to a professional scholar, who would have been able to make a very different defence of these ideas and to have enriched them more effectively.[331] Nevertheless there is ample material here for what you have to do.

When talking of Law, Epicurus said that even the harshest laws were necessary: without them men would start eating each other. [C] Plato is a mere finger's breadth away from that; he says that, without laws, we would live like wild animals: and he makes a good assay at proving that true.[332] [A] Our minds are dangerous tools, rash and prone to go astray: it is hard to reconcile them with order and moderation. We have seen during my lifetime virtually all outstanding men, all men of abnormally lively perception, breaking out into licentiousness of opinion or behaviour. It is a miracle if you find one who is settled and civilized. We are right to erect the strictest possible fences around the human mind. In the march of scholarship or anything else the mind must needs have its footsteps counted and regulated; you must supply artificial hedges and make it hunt only within them. [A1] We rein it in, neck and throat, with religions, laws, customs, precepts, rewards and punishments (both mortal and immortal), and we still find it escaping from all these bonds, with its garrulousness and laxity. It is an empty vessel: we can neither grasp it nor aim it; it is bizarre and misshapen and suffers no knot and no grapple.

[B] Certainly few souls are so powerful, so law-abiding and so well

330. Cf. S. Goulard, *Hist. du Portugal*, XII, xxiii, 366r°; similar but not identical account.
'95: gunpowder, which were *in the place where they were kept*. Here we have now . . .
331. Petrarch, *Canzoniere*, XXII, 48.
'88: effectively *and who would have used, in piling up his case, other authors besides our Plutarch. When* . . . (Cf. Erasmus' adages *Ne quid nimis* and *Medium sequere*.)
332. Epicurus, cf. p. 53; Plato, *Laws*, 874 (tr. Ficino, p. 862).

endowed that we can trust them to act on their own, allowing them liberty of judgement to sail responsibly and moderately beyond accepted opinion. It is more expedient to keep them under tutelage. What an outrageous sword [C] the mind is, even for its owner, [A] unless he knows how to arm himself ordinately and with discretion. [C] No beast more rightly needs blinkers to compel it to restrict its gaze to what lies before its feet, and to stop it from wandering about, this way and that, outside the ruts which custom and law have trodden out for it. [A] That is why it would be better for you to keep closely to your usual ways, whatever they may be, rather than to fly off like this with such frantic licence. Nevertheless, if one of those newfangled 'doctors' comes into your presence and starts acting clever, putting your spiritual health at risk as well as his own, you can, in the last resort, call on this remedy as a prophylactic against the deadly plague which is daily spreading through your courts: it will stop that poisonous contagion from infecting you and those about you.[333]

The freedom and vigour of minds in Antiquity created many Schools holding different opinions in philosophy and the humanities; before taking sides, each individual was responsible for judging and choosing for himself. But nowadays [C] men are all in step, '*qui certis quibusdam destinatisque sententiis addicti et consecrati sunt, ut etiam quae non probant, cogantur defendere*' [bound by vows to certain definite opinions, so that they are forced to defend even those which have not won their assent];[334] [A] our studies are accepted according to the decrees of civil authority, [C] with the result that our Schools have only one model, all having the same circumscribed form of basic instruction and teaching; we now no longer try and find out what weight and value such coins have: each of us in his turn accepts them at the going rate with the generally approved value. Nobody defends the alloy, only its currency. Every discipline becomes equally acceptable. Medicine is accepted as though it were as valid as geometry; jiggery-pokery, enchantments, magic spells producing impotence, communication with the spirits of the dead, prognostications, casting horoscopes and even that absurd hunt for the philosopher's stone, all pass without contradiction. You merely have to know that the seat of Mars lies at the centre of the triangle of the palm, Venus in the thumbs and Mercury in your little finger; or know that, if the line of Fortune cuts across the protuberance of the forefinger, that is a sign of cruelty, but when it stops short at a point below the middle finger and

333. R. Sebond is a prophylactic against the 'poison' of Lutheranism (see p. 2ff.). The rest of the *Apology* uses scepticism as the ultimate defence of catholicism.
'88: a *dangerous* sword . . .
334. Cicero, *Tusc. disput.* II, ii.

the median line forming an angle with the line-of-life just below it, that is the sign of a pitiful death; in the case of a woman, if the line-of-nature is 'open' (not forming an angle with the line-of-life) that portends unchastity. Witness for yourself whether a mastery of this particular science does not win a man favour and respect in any company.

Theophrastus said that the human intellect, guided by the senses, could go only so far towards understanding natural causes; but when it reached the original first causes it proves blunt and has to stop, either because of its own weakness or else because of the difficulty of the subject.[335]

That is a moderate and modest opinion which holds that our intellect is adequate enough to bring us to the knowledge of some things but that there are definite limits to its power, beyond which it is rash to use it.

It is a plausible opinion, set forth by conciliatory men (but it is difficult to fix boundaries for the human mind: it is avidly curious and sees no more reason for stopping after a mile than after fifty yards); it says: 'The assays of experience have taught me that where one man fails another succeeds; that what is unknown to one century is clarified by the next; that the sciences and the arts are not just cast in a mould all at once, but have to be gradually shaped by repeated handling and polishing, just as the mother-bear takes time to lick her cub into shape; I may not be strong enough to uncover anything but I can still take soundings and make assays; by kneading and working the dough of this new subject-matter, by blending it and warming it through, I make it easier for my successor to enjoy it at leisure; I render it more pliable for him, more manageable.

*ut hymettia sole*
*Cera remollescit, tractataque pollice, multas*
*Vertitur in facies, ipsoque fit utilis usu.*

[As wax from Mt Hymettos can be softened in the sun and kneaded with the thumb to form various shapes, becoming more useful with usage.][336]

A second man will do the same for the third: that is why no difficulty should drive me to despair – nor should my own powerlessness, for it is merely my own; Man is capable of understanding everything as well as something.'

Yes; but if Man admits, like Theophrastus, that he has no knowledge of first causes and principles, then let him boldly give up all the rest of his knowledge; without foundations, his argument collapses; discussion and inquiry have only one aim: to establish first principles; if Man's course is not

335. Cf. H. C. Agrippa, *De Vanitate*, I.
336. Ovid, *Metam.*, X, 284.

stopped by his reaching that goal, he is thrown into boundless uncertainty. [C] '*Non potest aliud alio magis minusve comprehendi, quoniam omnium rerum una est definitio comprehendendi*' [One thing cannot be better understood, or less understood, than another: 'understanding' anything always means the same].[337]

[A]    It is probable that if the soul knew anything, she would first know herself; then, if she knew anything outside herself, she would first of all know her bodily sheath. Yet we can see the gods of the medical schools still quarrelling over human anatomy:

> *Mulciber in Trojam, pro Troja stabat Apollo.*
>
> [Vulcan against Troy: Apollo for Troy.][338]

Can we ever expect them to agree! We are closer to ourselves than to the whiteness of snow or the weight of a stone: if Man does not know himself, how can he know what his properties and powers are? Some true knowledge may perhaps find lodgings in us; if so, that is by chance, since error is received into the soul in the same way and in the same fashion; souls have no means of telling one from the other, no means of separating truth from falsehood.

The Academic philosophers accepted that our balance of judgement may be swayed one way or the other; they found it too crude to say that it is no more likely that snow be white than black, or that we no more understand the movement of a stone thrown by our own hand than the movement of the Eighth Sphere. These are bizarre difficulties and our intellect can hardly find room for them (even though they had established that we are incapable of knowing anything and that Truth is swallowed up in deep abysses where Man's vision cannot penetrate); to avoid them they admitted that some things are more likely than others and concede to judgement the power to incline towards one probability rather than other. They grant it this propensity, but they deny it conclusions.

The Pyrrhonists' idea is bolder, yet, at the same time, more true-seeming.[339] For what is this Platonic *inclination*, this *propensity* towards one proposition rather than another, than the recognition of there being more apparent truth in this than in that? But if our minds could grasp the form, lineaments, stance and face of Truth, then they would see whole truths as easily as partial truths, nascent and imperfect. Take that apparent verisimilitude which

337. Cicero, *Acad.: Lucullus*, II, xli, 128 (adapted).
338. Ovid, *Tristia*, I, ii, 5.
339. '88: more *true and more firm*. For . . .

makes the scales incline to the left rather than to the right – then increase it; take that ounce of verisimilitude which turns the scales: multiply it a hundredfold or a thousandfold; in the end the balance will come down definitely on one side, deciding on one choice, on one whole truth.

But how can they bring themselves to yield to verisimilitude if they cannot recognize verity? How can they know there to be a resemblance to something the essence of which they do not know? We judge entirely, or entirely not. If our intellectual faculties and our senses have no foundation to stand on but only float about in the wind, then it is pointless to allow our judgement to be influenced by their operation, no matter what 'probabilities' it seems to present us with;[340] and so the surest position for our intellect to adopt, and the happiest, would be the one where it could remain still, straight, inflexible, without motion or disturbance.   [C] *'Inter visa vera aut falsa ad animi assensum nihil interest'* [Where the assent of the mind is concerned, there is no difference between true impressions and false ones].[341]

[A]   Things do not lodge in us with their form and their essence; they do not come in by the force of their own authority: we can see that clearly; if they did, we would all react to them in the same way: wine would taste the same in the mouth of a sick man and a healthy one; a man whose hands were calloused or benumbed would find the same hardness in the timber or iron he was handling as anyone else. External objects therefore throw themselves on our mercy; we decide how we accept them.[342]

Now, if we, for our part, could receive anything without changing it, if our human grasp were firm and capable of seizing hold of truth by our own means, then truth could be passed on from hand to hand, from person to person, since those means are common to all men. Among so many concepts we could at least find one which all would believe with universal assent. But the fact that there is no single proposition which is not subject to debate or controversy among us, or which cannot be so, proves that our natural judgement does not grasp very clearly even what it does grasp, since my judgement cannot bring a fellow man's judgement to accept it, which is a sure sign that I did not myself reach it by means of a natural power common to myself and to all men.

Let us leave aside that infinite confusion of opinions which we can see

340. St Augustine advanced such arguments against Academic theories of probability (*Contra academicos*, e.g., II, 7); they had long been current.

341. Cicero, *Acad.: Lucullus*, II, xxviii, 90.

342. From here Montaigne takes on Lucretius, the defender of the senses as true guides. Cf. Introduction, p. xxiv. He relies mainly on his own experience, in sickness and in health, against which he judges the established Classical authorities.

among the philosophers themselves and that endless, world-wide debate about knowledge. It really is the truest of presuppositions that men – I mean the most learned, the best-endowed and the cleverest of men – never agree about anything, not even that the sky is above our heads. Those who doubt everything doubt that too. Those who deny that we can ever know anything say we cannot know whether the sky is above our heads or not. Those two opinions are by far the strongest, numerically.

Apart from this infinite diversity and disagreement, we can easily see that the foundations of our powers of judgement are insecure from the worry it personally causes us and from the lack of certainty each man feels within himself. How our judgements vary! How frequently we change our ideas! What I hold and believe today, I hold and believe with the totality of my belief. All my faculties, all my resources hold tight to that opinion and vouch for it with all their might. It would be impossible for me to embrace and maintain any truth more strongly. I am wholly for it, truly for it. But – not once, not a hundred times, not a thousand times, but every day – have I not embraced something else with the same resources and under the same circumstances, only to be convinced later that it was wrong? At least we should acquire wisdom at our own expense! If this appearance has once deceived me, if my touchstone regularly proves unreliable and my scales wrong and out of true, why should I trust them this time, rather than all the others? Is it not stupid to let oneself be deceived so often by the same guide? Fortune may shift us five hundred times, may treat our powers of belief like a pot to be endlessly emptied and filled with ever-differing opinions: nevertheless, the present one, the last one, is always sure and infallible! For this last one we must abandon goods, honour, life, health, everything.

> *posterior res illa reperta,*
> *Perdit, et immutat sensus ad pristina quaeque.*

[When we find something new, the recent destroys the older and makes us change our taste for it.][343]

[B] Whatever people preach to us and whatever we may learn from them, never forget that the giver is a man and so is the taker; a mortal hand presents it to us: a mortal hand takes it from him. Only such things as come to us from Heaven have the right and the authority to carry conviction; they alone bear the mark of Truth; but even they cannot be seen with our human eyes, nor do we obtain them by our own means: so great and so holy an Image

343. Lucretius, V, 1414 (Lambin, pp. 462–63 – explained with Montaigne's sense).

could never dwell in so wretched a dwelling, unless God first makes it ready for that purpose, unless he forms it anew and fortifies it by his special grace and supernatural favour.

[A]   Our condition is subject to error: that ought, at very least, to lead us to be more moderate and restrained in making changes. We ought to admit that, no matter what we allow into our understanding, it often includes falsehoods which enter by means of the same tools which have often proved contradictory and misleading.

It is not surprising that they should prove contradictory, since they are so easily biased and twisted by the lightest of occurrences. It is certain that our conceptions, our judgement and our mental faculties in general are all affected by the changes and alterations of the body. Those alterations are ceaseless. Are our minds not more alert, our memory more ready, our reasoning powers more lively when we are well rather than ill? Does not everything present a different aspect to our minds under the influence of joy and gaiety or of chagrin and melancholy? Do you think that the poems of Catullus or Sappho delight a miserable old miser as they do a vigorous and ardent youth?   [B]   Cleomenes the son of Anaxandridas being ill, his friends reproached him with having new and unaccustomed humours and ideas. 'I am not surprised,' he replied; 'I am not the same person when I am well: being different, my opinions and ideas are different too.'³⁴⁴

[A]   There is a saying current in the legal chicanery of our law-courts applied to a criminal who comes before judges who happen to be in a good, gentle, generous mood: GAUDEAT DE BONA FORTUNA 'Let him enjoy this good luck': for it is certain that we sometimes come across minds whose judgement is prickly, sharp and poised to condemn and which, at other times, are less difficult, more affable, more given to finding excuses. A judge may leave home suffering from the gout, jealous, or incensed by a thieving valet: his entire soul is coloured and drunk with anger: we cannot doubt that his judgement is biased towards wrath.   [B]   The august Senate of the Areopagus held their sessions at night, lest the sight of the plaintiff should influence their justice.   [A]   The very air and calm weather have power to change us – as that Greek poem says which Cicero cited:

> Tales sunt hominum mentes, quali pater ipse
> Juppiter auctifera lustravit lampade terras.

---

344. Plutarch, *Les Dicts notables des Lacedemoniens*, 218 C; also a general influence of Pyrrhonism (*Hypotyposes*, I, xxxii, 217–19 etc.). *Chagrin* was a technical word for melancholic depression.

[The minds of men are such as Father Jupiter wills them to be, as he bathes the earth in fruitful light.]³⁴⁵

It is not only fevers, potions and great events which upset our judgement: the lightest thing can send it spinning. If a continual fever lays our minds prostrate, you can be sure that a three-day fever will have a proportionately bad effect on them, even though we are not aware of it. If apoplexy can dim and totally snuff out our mental vision, you can be sure that even a cold will confuse it. Consequently, there can hardly be found a single hour in an entire lifetime when our powers of judgement are settled in their proper place; our bodies are subject to so many sustained changes and are composed of so many kinds of principles that there is always one pulling the wrong way – I trust the doctors over that!

This malady, moreover, is not so easy to detect unless it is extreme and past all cure; Reason always hobbles, limps and walks askew, in falsehood as in truth, so that it is hard to detect when she is mistaken or unhinged.

By *reason* I always mean that appearance of rationality which each of us constructs for himself – the kind of reason which can characteristically have a thousand contrary reactions to the same subject and is like a tool of malleable lead or wax: it can be stretched, bent or adapted to any size or to any bias; if you are clever, you can learn to mould it.

Take a judge; however well-intentioned he may be, he must watch himself carefully (and not many people spend much time doing that), otherwise some inclination toward friend, relation, beauty or revenge (or even something far less weighty, such as that chance impulse which leads us to favour one thing rather than another, or which enables us to choose, without any sanction of reason, between two identical objects – or even some more shadowy cause, equally vain) will encourage some sneaking sympathy or hostility toward one of the parties to slip, unnoticed, into his judgement and tip the balance.

I spy closely on myself and keep my eyes constantly directed on myself alone – I do not have much else to do:

> *quis sub Arcto*
> *Rex gelidae metuatur orae,*
> *Quid Tyridatem terreat, unice*
> *Securus*

345. Homer, *Odyssey*, XVIII, 135, translated by Cicero, *apud* St Augustine, *City of God*, V, 8. (Montaigne has already cited this in vol. II, chapter 1, 'On the Inconstancy of our Actions'.)

[Quite indifferent to what ruler of the frozen North inspires great fear, or what dangers frighten Tiridates][346] –

yet even I hardly dare to tell of the vanity and the weakness which I find in myself. I have such wobbly legs, I am so unsteady on my feet, I totter about so and cannot even trust my eyesight, with the result that I feel quite a different person before and after a meal; when good health and a fine sunny day smile at me, I am quite debonair; give me an ingrowing toe-nail, and I am touchy, bad-tempered and unapproachable. [B] My horse's gait seems sometimes rough, sometimes gentle; the very same road, now short, now much longer, and the same form of action more agreeable or less so. [A] Now, I am ready to do anything; later, ready to do nothing; what is nice now can be nasty later on. [A1] A thousand chance emotions, unbidden, are in turmoil within me; sometimes a melancholic humour gets hold of me; at others, a choleric one; sometimes grief or joy dominate me, for reasons of their own. [A] I pick up some books: I may have discovered outstanding beauties in a particular passage which really struck home: another time I happen upon the same passage and it remains an unknown, shapeless lump for me, however much I twist it, and pat it and bend it or turn it. [B] Even in the case of my own writings I cannot always recover the flavour of my original meaning; I do not know what I wanted to say and burn my fingers making corrections and giving it some new meaning for want of recovering the original one – which was better. I go backwards and forwards: my judgement does not always march straight ahead, but floats and bobs about,

*velut minuta magno*
*Deprensa navis in mari vesaniente vento.*

[Like a tiny boat buffeted on the ocean by a raging tempest.][347]

Many's the time I have taken an opinion contrary to my own and (as I am fond of doing) tried defending it for the fun of the exercise: then, once my mind has really applied itself to that other side, I get so firmly attached to it that I forget why I held the first opinion and give it up. Almost any inclination, no matter which, takes me with it and carries me along by my own weight. Almost anybody could say much the same of himself if he watched himself [C] as I do. [B] Preachers know that the emotion which comes upon them as they speak moves them towards belief; and we know that when we

346. Horace, *Odes*, I, xxvi, 3.
347. '88: does not always *get better, but floats and rolls about,* . . . (Catullus, XXV, 12.)

are in a temper we devote ourselves to defending an assertion, impressing it upon ourselves and embracing it with furious approbation, far more than we ever do in cold-blooded calm.

You give your lawyer a simple statement of your case; he replies, hesitantly, doubtfully: you feel that he is quite indifferent which side he is to defend. But if you offer him a good fee to get stuck into it and all worked up about it, does he not begin to take a real interest and, once his will is inflamed, do not his arguments and forensic skills become inflamed as well? A clear and indubitable truth comes and presents itself to his understanding. He finds that your case sheds quite a new light: he really believes in it and convinces himself accordingly. I even wonder whether ardour, born of despite and of obstinacy, when confronted by pressure from a magistrate or by violent threats –

[B]  (or even simply a concern of reputation) –   [A]  has not brought some men to be burned in defence of an opinion for which, when at liberty among friends, they would never even have burned their finger-tips.

The jolts and shocks which our soul receives from the passions of the body greatly affect her, but her own proper passions do so even more. They have such a hold on her that it could perhaps be maintained that her motions and propulsion come from her own tempests: without those agitations she would be becalmed like a ship on the open sea, abandoned by the helpful winds.[348] Anyone who did maintain that, [C] following the Peripatetics, [A] would do us little wrong, since it is recognized that most of the finer actions of the soul require – and can only arise from – such passionate impulses. It is said that valour cannot be achieved without the help of anger –

[C]    *Semper Ajax fortis, fortissimus tamen in furore*

[Ajax was always brave, but bravest when mad with fury][349] –

that we do not attack the wicked or our foes vigorously enough, unless we are angry; and that, to get justice out of judges, counsel must move them to anger. Strong desires motivated Themistocles; they motivated Demosthenes and forced philosophers to travel far and work late: and they lead us too towards useful ends: honour, learning, health.

In addition, our soul's weakness when faced with pain and suffering serves to nurture repentance and remorse within our conscience and to feel the chastisements with which God scourges us as well as the chastisements of political punishment.   [A]  Compassion acts as a stimulus to  [B]  clem-

348. Cf. Plutarch, tr. Amyot, *De la Vertu Morale*, 37 F–G.

349. Cicero, *Tusc. disput.*, IV, xxiii; the rest of [C] follows closely *ibid.*, xix. For the role of passion and anger in bravery, cf. Aristotle, *Eudemian Ethics*, III, 15–19, 1229a.

ency; prudent self-preservation[350]   [C]  and self-control  [A]  are awakened by our fear; and how many fair actions are awakened by ambition?
And how many by arrogance?   [A]  In short, not one eminent or dashing
virtue can exist without some strong, unruly emotion. Was this one of the
considerations which moved the Epicureans to relieve God of all care and
concern for the affairs of men, since even the very actions of his goodness
could not be directed towards us without disturbing his repose with passions
– which are the goads and incitements which drive the soul towards virtuous
actions?   [C]  Or else did they think differently, taking the passions to be
like storms, shamefully deflowering the soul of her tranquillity? '*Ut maris
tranquillitas intelligitur, nulla ne minima quidem aura fluctus commovente: sic
animi quietus et placatus status cernitur, quum perturbatio nulla est qua moveri
queat*' [We know the sea is tranquil when not even the slightest breath of
wind ruffles the surface; so too the soul is calm and at peace when there is no
emotion seeking to disturb it].[351]

What varied thoughts and reasons, what conflicting notions, are presented
to us by our varied passions! What certainty can we find in something so
changeable and unstable as the soul, subject by her condition to the dominance of perturbations,   [C]  and who never moves except under external
constraint.   [A]  If our judgement is in the hands of illness itself and of
turbulence; if it is obliged to receive its impressions from foolhardiness and
madness: what certainty can we expect from it?

[C]  Is it not somewhat bold of Philosophy to think that men perform their
greatest deeds, those nearest to the divine, when they are beside themselves,
frenzied and out of their senses? Our amendment comes when our reason
slumbers or when we are deprived of it; the two natural ways of entering into
the council chamber of the gods and to have foreknowledge of Destiny are
sleep and frenzy.[352]

Here is a pleasant thought: when the passions bring dislocation to our
reason, we become virtuous; when reason is driven out by frenzy or by sleep,
that image of death, we become prophets and seers. I have never been more
inclined to believe Philosophy! It was a pure enthusiasm – breathed into the

350. '80 (in place of [B]): stimulus to *liberality and justice* . . .
351. Cicero, *Tusc. disput.*, V, vi.
'88 (in place of [C]): actions? *At least we know only too well that the passions produce
innumerable and ceaseless changes in our soul and tyrannize over it wondrously; is the
judgement of an angry man or a fearful one the same judgement as he will have later when
he has calmed down?* What varied . . .
352. The ideal of *tranquillity of mind* is indeed, for Platonizing philosophers, subordinated to philosophical ecstasy; cf. Rabelais, *Tiers Livre*, TLF, XIIII and XXXVII.

spirit of Philosophy by holy Truth herself – which wrenched from her, against her normal teaching, that the tranquil state of our soul, the quiet state, the sanest state that Philosophy can obtain for her, is not her best state. Our waking sleeps more than our sleeping; our wisdom is less wise than our folly; our dreams are worth more than our discourse; and to remain inside ourselves is to adopt the worst place of all.

But does Philosophy not realize that we are clever enough to notice that that maxim which makes the spirit so great, so perfect, and so clear-sighted when detached from Man, and yet so dark, so ignorant and so earthy when it remains in Man, is produced by the very spirit which itself forms part of dark, ignorant and earthy Man. And so, for that very cause, is neither to be trusted nor believed?[353]

[A]  Being of a soft and heavy complexion, I do not have much experience of those disturbances which bear the mind away and which mostly take our souls by surprise without giving them time to know themselves. But there is a passion in the heart of the young (induced, they say, by idleness); those who have assayed resisting its power, even when it takes an untrammelled, moderate course, find that it gives a good idea of the abrupt changes and deteriorations which our judgement can suffer. There was a time when I tensed myself to resist and parry its assaults (for I am so far from being one who welcomes vices, that I never give in to them unless they compel me to); despite my resistance, I would feel it within me as it was born, and as it grew and developed; I was lively: my eyes were open. Yet it would seize me, possess me. It was like a kind of drunkenness; everything took on an unaccustomed appearance; I would see the woman I yearned for becoming manifestly more attractive, her qualities swelling and growing as the wind of my imagination blew upon them; the difficulties facing my courtship would seem to become easy and smooth; my reason and conscience would withdraw into the background. Then, with lightning speed, at the very instant when my fire had burned itself out, my soul would recover another state, another judgement, another way of looking at things; it was now the difficulties of getting out of it which seemed immense and insurmountable; the very same things took on very different tastes and appearances from the ones offered me by inflamed desire.

Which was right? Pyrrho knows nothing about that!

We are never free from illness: fevers blow hot and cold; we drop straight

---

353.  That is, philosophical ecstasy cannot claim to reveal infallible truth. Montaigne proceeds to emphasize the 'asinine' aspect of his own melancholy complexion (an antidote to all melancholic ecstasies).

from symptoms of a burning passion into symptoms of a shivery one.   [B]
The more I jumped forward, the more I now leap back:

> Qualis ubi alterno procurrens gurgite pontus
> Nunc ruit ad terras, scopulisque superjacit undam,
> Spumeus, extremamque sinu perfundit arenam;
> Nunc rapidus retro atque aestu revoluta resorbens
> Saxa fugit, littusque vado labente relinquit.

[Thus does the sea with alternate tides now dash up the beach, covering the rocks with
its foaming billows, and seeking out the deep recesses of the sand; and then it quickly
turns, sucking back the shingle and fleeing the rocks, as its sinking waters relinquish
the beach.][354]

[A]   This very awareness of my mutability has had the secondary effect of
engendering a certain constancy in my opinions. I have hardly changed any
of my first and natural ones, since whatever likelihood novelty may appear
to have, I do not change easily, for fear of losing in the exchange. As I do not
have the capacity for making a choice myself, I accept Another's choice and
remain where God put me. Otherwise I would not know how to save myself
from endlessly rolling.

[A1]   And thus, by God's grace, without worry or a troubled conscience,
I have kept myself whole, within the ancient beliefs of our religion, through
all the sects and schisms that our century has produced.   [A]   The writings
of the Ancients – I mean the good, ample, solid ones – tempt me and stir me
almost at will; the one I am reading always seems the most firm. All appear
right in their turn, even though they do contradict each other. The ease with
which good minds can make anything they wish seem likely, so that there is
nothing so strange but that they will set about lending it enough colour to
take in a simple man like me, shows how weak their proofs really are. For
three thousand years the skies and the stars were all in motion; everyone
believed it; then   [C]   Cleanthes of Samos, or according to Theophrastus,
Nicetas of Syracuse   [A]   decided to maintain that it was the Earth which
did the moving,[355]   [C]   revolving on its axis through the oblique circle of
the Zodiac;   [A]   and in our own time Copernicus has given such a good
basis to this doctrine that he can legitimately draw all the right astronomical
inferences from it. What lesson are we to learn from that, except not to worry

354. Virgil, Aeneid, XI, 624.
355. Plutarch, De la face qui apparoist dedans le rond de la Lune, 615 E; Cicero,
Acad.: Lucullus, II, xxxix, 123 (reading Nicetas for Hicetas). Montaigne's three thousand
years means from the Creation (dated about 4000 BC) to the time of Cleanthes and
Nicetas.

about which of the two opinions may be true? For all we know, in a thousand years' time another opinion will overthrow them both.[356]

> Sic volvenda aetas commutat tempora rerum:
> Quod fuit in pretio, fit nullo denique honore;
> Porro aliud succedit, et e contemptibus exit,
> Inque dies magis appetitur, floretque repertum
> Laudibus, et miro est mortales inter honore.

[Thus the rolling years give various things their time; what used to be highly esteemed is now worthless; something else comes out from discredit and succeeds the old; it is daily sought for; everyone praises it and it is wondrously honoured among mortal men.][357]

Thus, whenever some new doctrine is offered to us we have good cause for distrusting it and for reflecting that the contrary was in fashion before that was produced; it was overturned by this later one, but some third discovery may overturn that too, one day. Before the principles which Aristotle introduced came into repute, other principles satisfied human reason just as his satisfy us now. What letters-patent do Aristotle's principles have, what exclusive privilege, that the course of our inquiries should stop with them and that they have the right to our assent for all time? They are not exempt: they can be kicked out as their predecessors were. When some new argument presses me hard, it is up to me to decide whether someone else may find a satisfactory reply even if I cannot; for to believe everything that may look true just because we ourselves cannot refute it, is very simple-minded. From that it would follow that the belief of the common people – [C]  and all of us are common people –  [A]  would blow about like a weathercock: for their minds, soft and non-resistant, would constantly be forced to accept different impressions, each one effacing the trace of the other. Anyone who feels too weak to resist should follow legal practice and reply that he will consult counsel – or refer to the wiser heads who trained him.

How long has medicine been in the world? They say that some newcomer called Paracelsus is changing or reversing the entire order of the old rules, maintaining that, up to the present, medicine has merely served to kill people. He will be able to prove that easily enough, I believe, but it would not be very wise for me, I think, to test his new empiricism at the risk of

356. The theory of Copernicus 'saved the appearances' as did that of Ptolemy: but Galileo later claimed to describe reality.

357. Lucretius, V, 1276 (Lambin, pp. 454–55).

my life. [A1] 'Believe nobody,' as the saying goes. 'Anyone can *say* anything.'[358]

One of those men who champion novelties and reformations in natural science told me recently that all the Ancients had evidently been wrong about the nature and movements of the winds; if I would only listen he would make me clearly see the palpable truth. After showing some patience in hearing his arguments (which looked extremely probable) I said, 'What! Those who were navigating according to the rules of Theophrastus, were they really going West when steering East? Were they sailing sideways or astern?' – 'That is as may be,' he replied, 'but they certainly got it wrong.' I then retorted that I would rather be guided by results than by reason – for they are always clashing! I have even been told that in geometry (which claims to have reached the highest degree of certainty among the sciences) there are irrefutable demonstrations which overturn truth based on experience. Jacques Peletier, for example, in my own home, told me how he had discovered two lines drawing ever closer together but which, as he could prove, would meet only in infinity.[359] And the sole use Pyrrhonists have for their arguments and their reason is to undermine whatever experience shows to be probable; it is wonderful how far our supple reason will go along with their project of denying factual evidence: they can prove that we do not move, that we do not speak and that there is no such thing as weight or heat, with the same force of argument as we have when we prove the most likely things to be true.

Ptolemy was a great figure; he established the boundaries of the known world; all the ancient philosophers thought they had the measure of it, save for a few remote islands which might have escaped their knowledge. A thousand years ago, if you had questioned the data of cosmography, you would have been accused of Pyrrhonizing – of doubting opinions accepted by everybody; [B] it used to be heresy to allow the existence of the Antipodes![360] [A] But now that in our century new discoveries have revealed, not the odd island or the odd individual country, but an infinite land-mass, almost equal in size to the part we already knew, geographers today proceed to assure us that everything has really been seen and discovered this time.

358. Paracelsus (1493–1541). His works appeared posthumously (1575–88). He scorned traditional medicine absolutely.

359. Peletier, a poet and mathematician, doubtless explained the conic hyperbola and asymptotes (lines which draw ever nearer to a given curve but do not meet it within a finite distance). He was actively opposed to the renewal of Pyrrhonism.

360. Cicero suspended judgement over the Antipodes (*Acad.: Lucullus*, II, xxxix, 123); St Augustine rejected the idea (*City of God*, XVI, 9); but it never was heretical to believe in them.

*Nam quod adest praesto, placet, et pollere videtur.*

[For we are pleased with what is to hand; it works its spell.][361]

Since Ptolemy was once mistaken over his basic tenets, would it not be foolish to trust what moderns are saying now?[362]   [C]  Is it not more likely that this huge body which we call the Universe is very different from what we think? Plato holds that its entire aspect changes – that there comes a point when the heavens, the stars and the sun reverse the motions which we can see there and actually rotate from East to West.[363] The Egyptian priests told Herodotus that since the time of their first king, some eleven thousand years ago – (and they showed him the statues of all these kings, portrayed from life) – the Sun had changed its course four times, and the sea and land had changed places. They also said that no date within time can be ascribed to the origin of the world;[364] Aristotle and Cicero agree with that; and one of our own people maintained that the world exists from all eternity but has a cycle of deaths and rebirths; he cited Solomon and Isaiah as witnesses, his aim being to counter objections to God's having been a Creator who had once never created anything, an idle God who only cast aside his idleness when he set his hand to this enterprise and therefore a God subject to change.[365]

In the most famous of the Greek Schools of Philosophy the Universe is considered to be a god made by a greater one; it is composed of a body, with a soul situated in the centre but extending to the circumference by means of musical Numbers; it is divine, most blessed, most great, most wise and eternal. Within this 'god' there are other gods (the earth, the sea, the heavenly bodies) all maintained by the harmonious and perpetual movement of a sacred dance as they draw together then draw apart, hide then reveal themselves, or move to and fro and change their rows.[366]

361. Lucretius, V, 1412 (Lambin, pp. 462–63).

362. '88 (in place of [C]): *saying now? Aristotle says that all human opinions have existed in the past and will do so in the future an infinite number of other times: Plato, that they are to be renewed and come back into being after thirty-six thousand years. Epicurus . . .* (Taken from Varchi, *L'Hercolano*. Montaigne replaces this with authorities taken from St Augustine or thought of because of him.)

363. Plato, *Politicus*, XIII, 270 AC; cf. St Augustine, *City of God*, XII, 14.

364. Herodotus, II, 142–43 (cf. St Augustine, *City of God*, XII, 13; J. Bodin, *Methodus ad Hist. cognit.*, 1595, p. 293).

365. Origen, *De Princ.*, 3, 5, 3; cf. St Augustine, *City of God*, XII, 14 (citing Solomon and Ecclesiastes; Isaiah is in the notes of Vivès), and XI, 23. The doctrine of a Creator who had not yet created was rejected by Neo-Platonists such as Proclus.

366. Plato, in the *Timaeus*, 33D–41E.

Heraclitus laid down that the Universe was composed of fire and was destined one day to burst into flames and burn itself out: it would be born again some other time. Apuleius said that Men were '*sigillatim mortales, cunctim perpetui*' [individually mortal, collectively eternal]. Alexander gave his mother the written record which one of the Egyptian priests had taken from their monuments; it bore witness to the boundless antiquity of that people and included a true account of the birth and growth of other countries. Cicero and Diodorus say that, in their own days, the Chaldaeans kept records going back some four hundred thousand years; Aristotle, Pliny and others date Zoroaster six thousand years before the time of Plato. Plato says that the citizens of Saïs possess written records covering eight thousand years, adding that the city of Athens was built a thousand years before the foundation of that city.[367]

[B]   Epicurus taught that there exist in several other worlds objects very like the ones we can see here, fashioned the same way.[368] He would have said that with even greater assurance if he could have seen those strange examples of past and present similarities and resemblances to be found between our world and that New World of the West Indies.

[C]   In truth, when I consider what we know about the course of social life on this earth, I have often been struck with wonder at the resemblances there are – separated by immense spaces of place and time – between many savage beliefs or fantastic popular opinions which, whatever way you look at them, do not seem to arise from our natural reasoning. The human mind is a great forger of miracles, we know that: but this relationship has something abnormal about it which I cannot define; you can even see it in names, events and thousands of other ways.   [B]   For we have newly discovered peoples who, as far as we know, have never heard of us, yet where they believe in circumcision; where countries or great states are entirely governed by women, without men; where you can find something like our Lenten fasts, with the addition of sexual abstinence. We have found peoples where our Crosses are honoured in various ways (in one place they even displayed them prominently on their graves); in another crosses were used (especially the cross of St Andrew) to ward off nocturnal visions; they also put them on their children's beds against enchantments. Elsewhere was discovered a wooden cross, immensely tall, which was worshipped as the god of rain – and that was very far from the coast. Also found there were the express image of our penitents,

367. Texts cited after St Augustine, *City of God*, VIII, 5; XII, 10, 11, including the notes of Vivès.

368. Plutarch, *Des oracles qui ont cessé*, 342 D.

the use of mitres, the practice of priestly celibacy, the art of divination from
the entrails of sacrificed animals,   [C]   a total abstention from all kinds of
fish and flesh,   [B]   the custom for priests to make liturgical use of a special
tongue not the common one; the idea that the first god was driven away by
a second, his younger brother; the belief that they were created with all kinds
of advantages which were subsequently cut off because of their sin; their land
changed and their natural condition made harsher; they were submerged by
a heaven-sent flood, only a few families being saved who had taken refuge in
high mountain caves, which they blocked up to stop the waters getting in;
various species of animals were shut in there too; when they thought the rain
had ceased, dogs were sent out: they came back dripping wet and clean, so
it was judged that the waters had only begun to subside; later other dogs were
sent out. When they returned all covered in mud the humans emerged to re-
people the world, which they found to be full of nothing but snakes.

In one case the inhabitants were convinced of a Day of Judgement. When
the Spaniards scattered the bones of their dead about as they plundered
their graves in search of treasure, they were beside themselves with anger,
declaring that such scattered bones could not easily be put together again.
They have trade by barter (but no other) with fairs and markets for this
purpose; they have dwarves and deformed people to enliven the banquets of
their princes; falconry they have, but with their own native birds; they have
tyrannous taxation, elegant gardens, acrobats, dancing, musical instruments,
coats-of-arms, tennis-courts, games of dice and chance – at which they get so
carried away that they stake themselves and their freedom; they have medicine based entirely on magic charms, pictorial writing, a belief in one first
man who was father of all peoples; they have the worship of a god who once
lived as a Man in perfect celibacy, abstinence and penitence, preaching the
law of Nature and liturgical ceremonies and who disappeared from the world
without a natural death; a belief in giants, the custom of getting drunk on
their local drink and seeing who can down the most, religious ornaments
painted with bones and death's heads, surplices, holy water and aspergilla,
women and servants who gaily volunteer to be burnt or buried alive with
their husband or masters, laws of inheritance which leave everything to the
eldest son and set nothing but obedience aside for the younger one, the
custom that a man promoted to high rank adopts a new name and abandons
his old one, the custom of sprinkling chalk on the knee of a new-born babe,
saying to him: 'Dust thou art, and to dust thou shalt return'; and they have
the art of augury.

Such vain shadows of our religion as may be seen in some of these examples
witness to its dignity and holiness: it has penetrated into infidel nations on

our side of the world by a kind of imitation, but to those natives of far-off lands it came by a shared supernatural inspiration. For we found a belief in Purgatory but of a different style: they attribute to cold what we attribute to heat, thinking that the souls of the dead are punished and purged by the rigours of extreme cold.

That reminds me of another pleasing example of diversity: some peoples like to uncover the end of the penis, circumcising the foreskin like Jews or Moslems, whereas others have such conscientious objections to ever uncovering it that, lest the top of it should ever see the light of day, they scrupulously stretch the foreskin right over it and tie it together with little cords.

And here is another one: just as we honour kings and festive days by putting on our best clothes, there are regions where they emphasize the disparity between themselves and their king and mark their total submission to him by appearing in their shabbiest clothing; as they go into the palace they put a tattered robe over their good one, so that all pomp and glory should belong to the king alone.[369]

But to get on.

[A1]   If Nature includes among her normal activities – along with everything else – the beliefs, judgements and opinions of men; and if such things have their cycles, seasons, births and deaths, every bit as much as cabbages do, the heavens changing them and influencing them at will: what permanent, magisterial authority should we go on attributing to them?[370]

[B]   Now if experience makes it clear that the very form of our being – not only our colour, build, complexion and behaviour but our mental faculties as well – depends upon our native air, climate and soil   ([C]   as Vegetius said: 'et plaga coeli non solum ad robur corporum, sed etiam animorum facit' [the heavenly regions contribute not only to the strength of men's bodies but of their souls as well]);[371] and if the goddess who founded Athens chose for her city a country of temperate climate which made men wise – that is what the priests of Egypt told Solon: 'Athenis tenue coelum, ex quo etiam acutiores putantur Attici; crassum Thebis, itaque pingues Thebani et valentes' [the air of Athens is not oppressive, which is why the Athenians are considered most intelligent; that of Thebes is oppressive, therefore the Thebans are considered heavy and tough][372] –   [B]   then men must vary as flora and fauna do: whether they are more warlike, just, equable, clever or dull, depends on where they were born. Here they are addicted to wine: there, to robbery and lechery; here

369. All the above compiled from Lopez de Gomara, L'Histoire générale des Indes.
370. A regular theme for reflection. Cf. J. Bodin, Methodus, V.
371. Vegetius, I, ii, apud Justus Lipsius, Politicorum, V, 10.
372. Cicero, De fato, IV, 7.

they are inclined towards superstition: there to disbelief;   [C]   here, to freedom: there, to slavery;   [B]   they may be more suited to learn one particular
art of science than another; they may be slow or intelligent, obedient or
rebellious, good or bad, all depending on inclinations arising from their
physical environment. Change their location, and, like trees, they take on a
new character. That was why Cyrus refused to allow the Persians to give up
their squat and rugged land and emigrate to softer plains;   [C]   he said that
rich soft lands make for soft men, that fertile lands make for barren minds.³⁷³
Now, if we can see that the influence of the stars makes an art or an opinion
to flourish; and if a particular age produces a particular kind of nature and
inclines the human race towards some particular trait of character (their
spirits producing good crops then lean crops, as fields do): what happens to
all those special privileges which we pride ourselves upon? A wise man can
be mistaken; a hundred men can; indeed, according to us, the whole human
race has gone wrong for centuries at a time over this or that: so how can we
be sure that human nature ever stops getting things wrong,   [C]   and that
she is not wrong now, in our own period?

[A]   Among other considerations witnessing to Man's weakness, it seems
to me that we should not overlook that even his desires cannot lead him to
discover what he needs; I am not talking about fruition, but about thinking
and wishing: we cannot even agree on what we need to make us contented.
Even if we let our thoughts tailor everything to their wishes, they cannot
even desire what is proper to them   [C]   and so be satisfied:

> [B]   *quid enim ratione timemus*
> *Aut cupimus? quid tam dextro pede concipis, ut te*
> *Conatus non poeniteat votique peracti?*

[Is it reason that governs our fears and our desires? What have you ever conceived,
even auspiciously, without being sorry about the outcome – even of its success?]³⁷⁴

[A]   That is why   [C]   Socrates prayed the gods to give him only what they
knew to be good for him. The Spartans, in public as in private, simply prayed
that good and beauteous gifts be vouchsafed to them; they left the choice and
selection to the gods:³⁷⁵

373. Plutarch, tr. Amyot, *Les Dicts notables des Anciens Roys* . . . 188 E; Herodotus,
IX, 121.

374. Juvenal, *Sat.*, X. 4.

375. Xenophon, *Memorabilia*, II, iii, 2: Plato, *Alcibiades*, II, 148 B–C.

'88: That is why *the Christian, wiser and more humble and more aware of what he is,
refers himself to his Creator to choose and command what he needs.* Conjugium . . .

[B]   *Conjugium petimus partumque uxoris; at illi*
     *Notum qui pueri qualisque futura sit uxor.*

[We pray to have a wife and children, yet only Jupiter knows what the children and
that wife will be like.][376]

In his supplications the Christian says, 'Thy will be done', in order not to
suffer that unseemly state which poets feign for King Midas: he prayed to
God that all he touched should turn to gold. His prayer was granted: his
wine was gold, his bread was gold, so were the very feathers in his bed, his
undershirt and all his garments. In this way he found that the enjoyment of
his desires crushed him and that he had been granted a boon no man could
bear. He had to unpray his prayers:

     *Attonitus novitate mali, divesque miserque,*
     *Effugere optat opes, et quae modo voverat, odit.*

[Thunderstruck by so new an evil, rich and wretched both at once, he hates what once
he prayed for.][377]

I can cite my own case. When I was young I begged Fortune, as much as
anything, for the Order of St Michael: it was then the highest mark of honour
for the French nobility, and very rare. Fortune granted it to me, but with a
smirk: instead of elevating me, instead of lifting me up so that I could reach
it, she used greater condescension: she debased the Order, and brought it
right down to my neck – lower still in fact.

[C]   Cleobis and Bito asked their god, Trophonius and Agamedes their
goddess, for rewards worthy of their piety; the gift they were given was death:
so different from ours, where our needs are concerned, are the opinions of
heaven.[378]

[A]   It is sometimes to our detriment that God vouchsafes us riches,
honour, life and health itself: the things which please us are not always
good for us. If, instead of a cure, he sends us death or a worsening of
our ills – '*Virga tua et baculus tuus ipsa me consolata sunt*' [Even thy rod
and thy staff do comfort me] – God acts thus by reason of his Providence,
which knows our deserts far more accurately than we can ever do; whatever
comes from a hand most loving and omniscient we must accept as
good:

376. Juvenal, *Sat.*, X, 352. Then   [B]: *he says . . . done' and may perhaps
chance* to
377. The Lord's Prayer ('Thy will be done') glossed with Ovid, *Metam.*, XI,
128.
378. Cicero, *Tusc. disput.*, I, xlvii.

> *si consilium vis*
> *Permittes ipsis expendere numinibus, quid*
> *Conveniat nobis, rebusque sit utile nostris:*
> *Charior est illis homo quam sibi.*

[If you want my advice, allow the gods to judge what is best for us and most advantageous for our affairs; a man is dearer to them than he is to himself.][379]

For to ask the gods for honour and high office is like begging them to send you into battle, into a game of dice or into some other situation where the outcome is unknown and the gain dubious.[380]

[A]  No quarrel among philosophers is more violent or so bitter as the one which looms over the question of Man's sovereign good;  [C]  according to Varro's calculation, 288 sects were produced by it:[381] *'Qui autem de summo bono dissentit, de tota philosophiae ratione dissentit'* [Whoever disagrees over the sovereign good disagrees about the whole of philosophy].[382]

> [A]  *Tres mihi convivae propre dissentire videntur,*
> *Poscentes vario multum diversa palato:*
> *Quid dem? quid non dem? Renuis tu quod jubet alter;*
> *Quod petis, id sane est invisum acidumque duobus.*

[For me it resembles three men disagreeing at a feast, each liking very different dishes and asking for them. What am I to give them? What am I not to give them? You reject what delights another: what you like is tart and unpleasant to the other two.][383]

That is the way Nature ought to answer their disputes and their quarrels.

There are those who say that our good is to be found in virtue; some who say in pleasure; some, in conforming to Nature; one says in knowledge  [C]  or freedom from pain;[384]  [A]  another, in not letting oneself be deceived by appearances, a notion rather like that other one  [B]  taught by Pythagoras of old:

> [A]  *Nil admirari prope res est una, Numaci,*
> *Solaque quae possit facere et servare beatum;*

379. Psalm 23 (22): 4; Juvenal, *Sat.*, X, 346.
380. Xenophon, *Memorabilia*, I, iii, 2.
381. St Augustine, *City of God*, XIX, 1 – also exploited in the following paragraphs (*ibid.*, 1–4).
382. Cicero, *De fin.*, V, v, 14.
383. Horace, *Ep.*, II, ii, 61.
384. Cicero, *De fin.*, V, v, 14, citing Hieronymus, the pupil of Aristotle.

[Be astonished by nothing; it is almost the one and only way, Numacius, which leads to lasting happiness;]³⁸⁵

that is the aim of the Pyrrhonists.   [C]  (To be astonished by nothing is, for Aristotle, the attribute of greatness of soul.)³⁸⁶  [A]  Archesilus said that suspending the judgement and keeping it upright and inflexible are good actions, whereas acts of consent and commitment are vicious and bad. It is true that he left his Pyrrhonism behind when he erected that axiom into a certainty!³⁸⁷ Pyrrhonists say that the sovereign good is *Ataraxia*, which consists in a total immobility of judgement; they consider that not to be a positive affirmation but simply an inner persuasion such as makes them avoid precipices and protect themselves from the chill of the evening; it presents them with this notion and makes them reject any other.

[B]  How I wish that, during my lifetime, someone like Justus Lipsius (the most learned man left, a polished and judicious mind, a veritable brother to my dear Turnebus), had the health, the will and sufficient leisure to compile an honest and careful account which listed by class and by category everything we can find out about the opinions of Ancient philosophy on the subject of our being and our morals; it would include their controversies and their reputations, it would tell us who belonged to which school, and how far the founders and their followers actually applied their precepts on memorable occasions which could serve as examples. What a beautiful and useful book that would be!³⁸⁸

[A]  Moreover, if we draw our moral rules from ourselves, what confusion we cast ourselves into! For the most convincing advice we get from reason is that each and every man should obey the laws of his own country;³⁸⁹  [C]  that is Socrates' precept, inspired (he said) by divine counsel.³⁹⁰  [A]  But what does that mean, except that our rules of conduct are based on chance? Truth must present the same face everywhere. If Man could know solid Rectitude and Justice in their true Essences, he would never restrict them to the

385. Horace, *Ep.*, I, vi, 1.

386. Greatness of Soul is the subject of *Nicomachaean Ethics*, IV, iii, and of *Eudemian Ethics*, III, v (1232a f.).

387. Sextus Empiricus, *Hypotyposes*, I, xxxiii, 223–34 (for Archesilas), I, iv, 8; vi, 12; xii, 25–30 (for *Ataraxia*).

388. Justus Lipsius, the neo-Stoic moralist (1547–1606) was read by Montaigne and admired by him. After a period of conforming to Protestantism he became a Roman Catholic fundamentalist. For Turnebus, see p. 3.

389. '88: country, *as Socrates' oracle had taught him, that to do punctiliously one's duty of piety according to the uses of one's nation is equivalent to serving God.* But . . .

390. Aristotle, *Nicomachaean Ethics*, V, vii, 1–3.

customary circumstances of this place or of that; Virtue would not be
fashioned from whatever notions happen to be current in Persia or in India.

Nothing keeps changing so continuously as the Law. Since I was born I
have seen our neighbours, the English, chopping and changing theirs three
or four times, not only on political matters (where we may wish to do without
constancy) but on the most important subject there ever can be: religion.[391]
It makes me feel sad and ashamed, since the English are a people with whom
we used to be so familiarly acquainted in my part of the world that traces of
their former kinship can still be seen in my own house.

[C] And closer to home, I have seen capital offences made lawful; such are
the uncertainties and the fortunes of war that any one of us may eventually be
found guilty of *lèse-majesté* against God and the King, simply for holding fast
to different ideas of legitimacy, once our Justice were to fall to the mercy of
Injustice (which, after a few years of possession, would change its essence).[392]
Could that ancient god have more clearly emphasized the place of ignorance
within our human knowledge of the divine Being, or taught us that religion is
really no more than a human invention, useful for binding societies together,
than by telling those who came before his Tripod to beg for instruction that the
true way of worship is the one hallowed by custom in each locality?[393]

Oh God, how bound we are to the lovingkindness of our sovereign Creator for
making our belief grow up out of the stupidities of such arbitrary and wandering
devotions, establishing it on the changeless foundation of his holy Word![394]

[A] But what has Philosophy to teach us in this plight? Why, that we
should follow the laws of our country! – laws which are but an uncertain sea
of opinions deriving from peoples or princes, who will paint it in as many
different colours and present it, reformed, under as many different faces
as they have changes of heart. I cannot make my judgement as flexible as
that. What kind of Good can it be, which was honoured yesterday but
not today [C] and which becomes a crime when you cross a river!
What kind of truth can be limited by a range of mountains, becoming
a lie for the world on the other side![395]

391. Allusion to religious settlements by Parliaments under Henry VIII, Edward
VI, Bloody Mary and Elizabeth I.
392. Allusions to changing alliances and legitimacies in the French Wars of
Religion.
393. Apollo (n. 389 above); Xenophon, *Memorabilia*, I, iii, 1.
394. The conviction of Lambin also; cf. Introduction, p. xxv.
395. Cf. Erasmus, *The Complaint of Peace* (*Opera*, 1703–1706, IV, 628 DE).

[A] Philosophers can hardly be serious when they try to introduce certainty into Law by asserting that there are so-called Natural Laws, perpetual and immutable, whose essential characteristic consists in their being imprinted upon the human race. There are said to be three such laws; or four – some say less, some say more: a sign that the mark they bear is as dubious as all the rest. How unlucky they are – (for what else should I call it but bad luck, seeing that out of laws so infinite in number, they cannot find even one which luck [C] or accidental chance [A] has allowed to be universally accepted by the agreement of all peoples). They are so pitiful that there is not one of these three – or four – selected laws, which has not been denied and disowned by several nations, not just one. Yet universal approval is the only convincing indication they can cite in favour of there being any Natural Laws at all. For whatever Nature truly ordained, we would, without any doubt, all perform, by common consent: not only all nations but all human beings individually would be deeply aware of force or compulsion when anyone tried to make them violate it. Let them show me just one law with such characteristics: I would like to see it.[396]

Protagoras and Ariston said that the essential justice of any law consists in the will of the law-giver: without it, *good* and *honourable* lose their qualities, simply lingering on as empty words for things indifferent.

In Plato, Thrasymachus thinks that there is no right other than the advantage of the superior.[397]

Nothing in all the world has greater variety than law and custom. What is abominable in one place is laudable somewhere else – as clever theft was in Sparta. Marriages between close relations are capital offences with us: elsewhere they are much honoured:

> *gentes esse feruntur*
> *In quibus et nato genitrix, et nata parenti*
> *Jungitur, et pietas geminato crescit amore.*

[They say there are peoples where the son lies with his mother, the daughter with her father, where family piety is enhanced by a double affection.][398]

396. Aristotle's doctrine of Natural Law came in for increased criticism as new peoples were discovered, but also because of inner inconsistencies; cf. Jeremy Taylor, *Ductor Dubitantium*, 1660, p. 221.

397. Protagoras was allegedly banished for atheistic impiety: Cicero, *De nat. deorum*, I, xxiii, 63; Ariston of Chios was a Stoic enclined to cynicism; Thrasimacus, in Plato, *Republic*, 338 (Ficino, p. 535).

398. Ovid. *Metam.*, X, 331, in Tiraquellus, *De legibus connubialibus*, VII, 38. For context cf. Sextus Empiricus, *Hypotyposes*, III, xxiv, 203–217.

Murdering children, murdering fathers, holding wives in common, making a business out of robbery, giving free rein to lusts of all sorts – in short there is nothing so extreme that it has not been admitted by the custom of some nation or other.

[B]  It is quite believable that natural laws exist: we can see that in other creatures. But we have lost them; that fine human reason of ours is always interfering, seeking dominance and mastery, distorting and confounding the face of everything according to its own vanity and inconsistancy. [C]  'Nihil itaque amplius nostrum est: quod nostrum dico, artis est' [Nothing of ours is left: what I call ours is really artificial].399

[A]  Any object can be seen in various lights and from various points of view: it is chiefly that which gives birth to variety of opinion: one nation sees one facet, and stops there; another sees another.

Nothing can be imagined more horrible than eating one's father: yet the peoples who followed this custom in the Ancient world looked on it as a mark of piety and love, seeking to provide their ancestors with the most worthy and honourable of obsequies, finding a home for their father's remains in their own person, in the very marrow of their bones; they were giving them a kind of new life; they were born again, as it were, by being transmuted into their living flesh as their children ate and digested them. It is easy to think what abominable cruelty it would be for men deeply imbued in such a superstition to leave their parents' remains to rot in the earth, food for beasts and worms.400

The aspects of theft which struck Lycurgus were the quickness, the industry, the boldness and the skill necessary to steal something from a neighbour, as well as of the public good which came from each man carefully guarding his own property. He believed that this gave a grounding in the twin subjects of assault and defence, both of which are useful for training soldiers (the principal virtue and science which he wished to instil into that nation). That outweighed the disorder and injustice of carrying off other people's property.

The tyrant Dionysius offered Plato a long, perfumed, damask robe, fashionable in Persia. Plato refused it saying that, since he was born a man, he would not willingly wear women's clothing. Aristippus, however, accepted it, replying that no apparel could corrupt a chaste heart;401 and  [C]  when his friends taunted him with cowardice for taking so little offence when Dionysius spat in his face, he replied: 'Merely to catch a gudgeon fishermen

399. Cicero: De fin., V, xxi, 60 (now parsed differently).
400. Cf. Montaigne, 'On the custom of not easily changing an accepted law', vol. I, chapter 23, after Herodotus, III, xii, etc.
401. Sextus Empiricus, Hypotyposes, III, xxiv, 204.

suffer the waves to bespatter them from head to foot.' Diogenes was washing some cabbage leaves when he saw Aristippus go by: 'If you knew how to live on cabbage,' Diogenes said, 'you would not be courting a tyrant.' Aristippus retorted: 'You would not be here washing cabbages, if you knew how to live among men.'[402]

[A]  That is how Reason can make different actions seem right.
[B]  Reason is a two-handled pot: you can grab it from the right or the left.

> *bellum, o terra hospita, portas;*
> *Bello armantur equi, bellum haec armenta minantur.*
> *Sed tamen iidem olim curru succedere sueti*
> *Quadrupedes, et frena jugo concordia ferre;*
> *Spes est pacis.*

[You are threatening war; what a hospitable land! Horses are armed for war: war is what these beasts portend! – Yet those same animals are often yoked to carts, plodding tranquilly in harness; there is hope for peace.][403]

[C]  When they lectured Solon for shedding vain and useless tears at the death of his son, he replied, 'It is precisely because they are vain and useless that I am right to shed them.' Socrates' wife exclaimed, increasing her grief: 'Those wretched judges have condemned him to death unjustly!' But Socrates replied, 'Would you really prefer that I were justly condemned?'[404]

[A]  We pierce our ears: the Greeks held that to be a mark of slavery. When we lie with our wives we hide away: the Indians lie with them in public. The Scythians used their temples to execute foreigners: elsewhere temples serve as sanctuaries:[405]

[B]  *Inde furor vulgi, quod numina vicinorum*
*Odit quisque locus, cum solos credat habendos*
*Esse Deos quos ipse colit.*

[The fury of the mob is aroused since everyone hates his neighbours' gods, convinced that the gods he adores are the only true ones.][406]

402. Erasmus, *Apophthegmata, Aristippus* V and I. These *Apophthegmata* supply Montaigne with many anecdotes, especially in [C].
403. Virgil, *Aeneid*, III, 539.
404. Diogenes Laertius, *Lives*, Solon, I, lxiii, 53; Erasmus, *Apophthegmata: Socratica* LIII.
'88 (in place of [C]): *From this diversity of aspects there arises the fact that judgements are variously applied to the choice of objects.*
405. Sextus Empiricus, *Hypotyposes*, III, xxiv, 200–203.
406. Juvenal, *Sat.*, XV, 36.

[A] I have heard tell of a judge who, whenever he came across in his lawbooks a thorny disagreement between Bartolus and Baldus or a subject marked by conflicting interpretations, wrote in the margin, *Question for friend*, meaning by that that the truth was so entangled in controversy that in a similar case he could favour whichever party he wanted to. It was only lack of wit and intellect which stopped him from writing *Question for friend* all over the place! Counsel and judges today find enough bias in their lawsuits to bowl them any way they please. A field of study so limitless, dependent on the authority of so many opinions and subject to such arbitrariness, is bound to give rise to an extreme confusion of judgements. There is no case so clear that it does not provoke controversy. One court judges this way: another reverses the verdict and then, on a later occasion, reverses its own judgement. Familiar examples of this can be seen in an astonishing abuse which stains the splendour and ceremonial authority of our judicial system: the verdict of the parties is *not* to settle for the verdict of the Court: they dash from one judge to another for a decision on the same case.

As for the licence of philosophical opinion about vice and virtue, there is no need to go lengthily into that; it is better to pass over some of the notions in silence than to trumpet them abroad [C] before weaker intellects. [B] Arcesilaus said that in lechery proclivities [C] and occasions [B] were irrelevant.[407] '*Et obscoenas voluptates . . . si natura requirit, non genere, aut loco, aut ordine, sed forma, aetate, figura metiendas Epicurus putat*' [Epicurus thinks that when Nature demands to be satisfied by lascivious pleasures, we need not consider family origin, position or rank but only beauty, youth and figure]. '*Ne amores quidem sanctos a sapiente alienos esse arbitrantur*' [They think that even pure passions of love are not incompatible with being a Sage]. '*Quaeramus ad quam usque aetatem juvenes amandi sint*' [Let us investigate up to what age it is proper to love young men]. The last two quotations are Stoic; together with the reproach which Dicaearchus made to Plato himself on this subject, they show how far even the sanest philosophy will go in tolerating quite excessive licence, far from common practice.[408]

[A] Laws gain their authority from actual possession and custom: it is

407. Plutarch, tr. Amyot, *Les Regles et preceptes de Santé*, 295 DE (condemning all vicious sexuality).

408. Cicero, *Tusc. disput.*, V, xxxiii, 94; *De fin.*, III, xx, 68; Seneca, *Epist.* CXXIII, 15 (condemning Stoic indiscretions); Cicero, *Tusc. disput.*, IV, xxxiv, 71. Dicaearchus reproached Plato for his *Symposium* and *Phaedrus*; but Montaigne seems to have taken all these quotations as allusions to irregular affairs; Marie de Gournay translates *amores sanctos* by *amours illicites* ('illicit love-affairs').

'95 '98, etc.: for *Dicaearchus*, 'Diogarchus'.

perilous to go back to their origins; laws, like our rivers, get greater and
nobler as they roll along: follow them back upstream to their sources and all
you find is a tiny spring, hardly recognizable; as time goes by it swells with
pride and grows in strength. But just look at those Ancient concerns which
gave the original impulse to that mighty stream, famed, full of dignity, awesome and venerable: you then see them to be so light and so delicate that it
is not surprising that these people here – philosophers who weigh everything
and reduce everything to reason, never accepting anything on authority and
trust – reach verdicts far removed from those of the generality. These people,
who model themselves on their concept of Nature as she originally was, not
surprisingly stray from the common path in most of their opinions. Few of
them for example would have approved of the constraints we impose on
marriage;   [C]   most of them wanted a community of wives without binding
obligations.   [A]   Courteous conventions like ours they rejected.[409] Chrysippus said that, for a dozen olives, a philosopher will turn a dozen somer-
saults in public, even with his breeches off.[410]   [C]   He could hardly have
advised Clisthenes against giving his fair daughter Agarista to Hippoclides,
just because he saw him stand on his head on a table with his legs wide apart
in the air.[411]

In the midst of a discussion, and in the presence of his followers, Metrocles
rather injudiciously let off a fart. To hide his embarrassment he stayed at
home until, eventually, Crates came to pay him a visit; to his consolations and
arguments Crates added the example of his own licence: he began a farting
match with him, thereby removing his scruples and, into the bargain,
converting him to the freer Stoic school from the more socially oriented
Peripatetics whom he had formerly followed.[412] What we call 'honourable'

409. '88: rejected. *Everyone had heard tell of the shameless way of life of the Cynic
philosophers.* Chrysippus . . .

410. Cf. Plutarch, tr. Amyot, *Contredicts des philosophes Stoïques*, 569 B ('In the
VII[th] Book of his *Offices* he goes further, saying he will do a somersault three times,
provided he be given a talent.').

'88 (in place of [C]): breeches off. *And that 'honesty' and 'reverence', as we call them,
which make us hasten to hide some of our natural and rightful actions, not to dare to call
things by their name or to fear to mention things we are allowed to do, could they not be said
to be a guileful wantonness, invented in Venus' own chambers so as to give more value and
stimulus to her games? Is it not an allurement, a bait and a stimulus to voluptuousness? For
usage makes us evidently feel that ceremony, modesty and difficulties are means of sharpening
and inflaming such fevers as those.* That is why some say . . .

411. Herodotus, VI, cxxix; Aelian, *Var. hist.*, XII, 24.

412. Erasmus, *Apophthegmata*, VII, *Crates Thebananus Cynicus*, XVII.

behaviour – not to dare to perform openly actions which are 'honourable'
when done in private – they termed silliness. As for ingeniously concealing
or disowning those of our actions which Nature, custom and our very
desires publish and proclaim abroad, they reckoned that to be a vice. They
thought it a desacralizing of Venus' mysteries to take them out from the
discreet sanctuary of her temple and exhibit them to the public gaze: draw
back the curtains, and her sports are debased. (Shame has a kind of weight:
concealment, dissimulation and constraint form part of our esteem.) They
thought that it was most ingenious that Lust, out of regret for the dignity
and convenience of her traditional bedchambers, should don the mask of
Virtue, seeking to avoid being prostituted at the crossroads and trampled
underfoot before the eyes of the mob. That is why   [A]   some say that
abolishing the public brothels would not merely take the fornication at
present restricted to such places and spread it everywhere, but would also
stimulate that vice in men by making it more difficult:

> *Moechus es Aufidiae, qui vir, Corvine, fuisti;*
> *Rivalis fuerat qui tuus, ille vir est.*
> *Cur aliena placet tibi, quae tua non placet uxor?*
> *Nunquid securus non potes arrigere?*

[Corvinus! You used to be the husband of Aufidia; she has married your rival and you
are her lover. Now she has become the wife of another, she pleases you (she never
did when she was your own). Why? Are you unable to get it up without risking a
beating?][413]

You can find a thousand variations on that experience.

> *Nullus in urbe fuit tota qui tangere vellet*
> *Uxorem gratis, Caeciliane, tuam,*
> *Dum licuit; sed nunc, positis custodibus, ingens*
> *Turba fututorum est. Ingeniosus homo es.*

[Caecilianus: when you left your wife free, nobody in the whole of Rome wanted to
touch her: now you have put guards round her, she is besieged by a huge crowd of
fucking admirers. Clever chap!][414]

Once a philosopher was surprised in the very act; asked what he was doing,

413. Martial, III, lxx.
414. Martial, I, lxxiv, cited Tiraquellus, *De legibus connubialibus*, XVI, 11.

he coldly replied: 'I am planting a man'; he no more blushed than if he had been caught planting garlic.[415]

[C] It is, I think, too tender and respectful an opinion when one of our great religious authors holds that Necessity actually compels this act to be carried out in modest seclusion: he could not convince himself that the Cynics actually consummated it in their licentious embraces, but were content with imitating lascivious motions in order to display that absence of shame which formed part of their teachings. He thought that they had to find a secluded place later on, so as to be able to ejaculate what shame had constrained them to hold back. But he had insufficiently plumbed the depths of the Cynics' debauchery: for when Diogenes was masturbating in the presence of crowds of bystanders, he specifically said he wanted to give his belly *complete* satisfaction by rubbing it up like this. To those who asked why his 'hunger' had to be satisfied in the street, not in some more suitable place, he replied, 'I was in the street when I felt hungry.' Women philosophers who joined this school joined in with their bodies – everywhere and indiscriminately: Hipparchia was only admitted into the group of disciples around Crates on condition that she followed the customary practices and rules in every particular.[416]

These philosophers attached the highest value to virtue; they rejected all other disciplines except morals; nevertheless, they attributed ultimate authority, above any law, to the decisions of their Sage: they decreed no restraints on pleasure  [A]  except moderation and the respect for the freedom of others.

Heraclitus and Protagoras noted that wine tastes bitter when you are sick, delightful when you are well, and that an oar looks crooked in the water but straight out of it; from these and similar contradictory appearances they argued that every object contains within itself the causes of such appearances: that there was a bitterness in wine which was related to the taste of the sick man; a quality of bentness in the oar which was related to whoever was looking at it in the water; and so on, for all the rest. That is equivalent to

415. Source unknown.

'88: planting *cabbages. Solon is said to have been the first to give women freedom in his Laws to profit publicly from their bodies. And the philosophical school which most honoured Virtue did not in short impose any bridle on the practising of lust of all sorts* except moderation . . . (Transferred by Montaigne to vol. III, chapter 5, 'On Some Lines of Virgil'.)

416. St Augustine, *City of God*, XIV, 20 (defending the notion that shame is natural); Diogenes Laertius, *Lives*, Diogenes, VI, lxix and lviii (cf. Erasmus, *Apophthegmata*, III, *Diogenes Cynicus*, XLVII) and *Lives*, Hipparchia, VI, cxvi. The same associations, with additional material, are found in Tiraquellus, *De legibus connubialibus*, XV, 159.

saying that everything is in everything; from which it follows that nothing is in anything: for where everything is, nothing is.[417]

It was this opinion which reminded me of an experience which we have all had, that once you start digging down into a piece of writing there is simply no slant or meaning – straight, bitter, sweet or bent – which the human mind cannot find there.

Take that clearest, purest and most perfect Word there can ever be: how much falsehood and error have men made it give birth to! Is there any heresy which has not discovered ample evidence there for its foundation and continuance? That is why there is one proof which the founders of such erroneous doctrines will never give up: evidence based upon exegesis of words.

A man of some rank, deeply immersed in the quest for the philosopher's stone, wanted to justify it to me recently on authority: he cited five or six Biblical texts which he said were the ones he chiefly relied on to salve his conscience (for he is in holy orders). The choice of texts he produced was not only amusing but most applicable to the defence of that egregious science.

That is how divinatory nonsense comes to be believed in. Provided that a writer of almanacs has already gained enough authority for people to bother to read his books, examining his words for implications and shades of meaning, he can be made to say anything whatever – like Sybils. There are so many ways of taking anything, that it is hard for a clever mind *not* to find in almost any subject something or other which appears to serve his point, directly or indirectly.  [C]  That explains why an opaque, ambiguous style has been so long in vogue. All an author needs to do is to attract the concern and attention of posterity. (He may achieve that not so much by merit as by some chance interest in his subject-matter.) Then, whether out of subtlety or stupidity, he can contradict himself or express himself obscurely: no matter! Numerous minds will get out their sieves, sifting and forcing any number of ideas through them, some of them relevant, some off the point, some flat contradictory to his intentions, but all of them doing him honour. He will grow rich out of his students' resources – like dons being paid their midsummer fees at the *Lendit* fair.

[A]  This has lent value to many a worthless piece, making several books seem valuable by loading on to them anything at all; one and the same work is susceptible to thousands upon thousands of diverse senses and nuances –

417. Cf. Sextus Empiricus, *Hypotyposes*, I, xxix, 210–11; xxxii, 218; Cicero, *Acad.*: *Lucullus*, II, vi, 79. (The refraction of a 'bent oar' was a major argument for sceptics.)

as many as we like. [C] Is it possible that Homer really wanted to say all that people have made him say,[418] and that he really did provide us with so many and so varied figurative meanings that theologians, military leaders, philosophers and all sorts of learned authors (no matter how different or contradictory their treatises) can refer to him and cite his authority as the Master General of all duties, works and craftsmen, the Counsellor General of all enterprises?

[A] Anyone on the lookout for oracles and predictions has found plenty of material there! I have a learned friend who is astonishingly good at producing wonderfully apt passages from Homer in favour of our religion: he cannot be easily prised from the opinion that Homer actually intended them (yet he knows Homer as well as any man alive). [C] And the very things he finds favouring our religion were thought in ancient times to favour theirs.

See how Plato is tossed and turned about. All are honoured to have his support, so they couch him on their own side. They trot him out and slip him into any new opinion which fashion will accept. When matters take a different turn, then they make him disagree with himself. They force him to condemn forms of behaviour which were quite licit in his own century, just because they are illicit in ours. The more powerful and vigorous the mind of his interpreters, the more vigorously and powerfully they do it.

[A] Democritus took the very foundations of Heraclitus – his assertion that things bear within themselves all the features we find in them – and drew the contrary conclusion, namely, that objects have none of the qualities we find in them: from the fact that honey is sweet to some and bitter to others, he concluded that it was neither sweet nor bitter. The Pyrrhonists said that they did not know whether it is sweet or bitter or neither or both, for they always reach the highest summit of doubt.[419] The Cyrenaics held that nothing is perceptible which comes from without: the only things perceptible are those which affect us inwardly, such as pain and pleasure. They did not even recognize the existence of tones or colours, but only certain emotional impulses produced by them; on these alone Man must base his judgement: Protagoras thought that whatever appears true is true for the man concerned; the Epicureans place judgement – in the case of both knowledge and pleasure

418. Cf. Rabelais, *Gargantua*, TLF, Prologue, 87 f.

'88 (in place of [C]): like. *Homer is as great as you wish, but it is not possible that he intended to represent as many ideas as people attribute to him. Law-givers have divined in him instructions without number for their own concerns; so have military men; so have those who treat of the arts.* Anyone on the . . .

419. Sextus Empiricus, *Hypotyposes*, I, xxx, 213–14. What follows is from Cicero, *Acad.: Lucullus*, II, xxiv, 76; xlvi, 142.

– in the senses. Plato wanted judgements about Truth, and Truth herself, to be independent of opinion and the senses, belonging only to the mind and thought.[420]

[A]  Such discussion has brought me to the point where I must consider the senses: they are the proof as well as the main foundation of our ignorance.

Without a doubt, anything that is known is known by the faculty of the knower; for, since judgement proceeds from the activity of a judge, it is reasonable that he perform that activity by his own means and by his will, not by outside constraint (as would be the case if the essence of an object were such that it forced us to know it). Now knowledge is conveyed through the senses: they are our Masters:

> [B]    *via qua munita fidei*
> *Proxima fert humanum in pectus templaque mentis.*

[the highway by which conviction penetrates straight to men's hearts and to the temple of their minds.][421]

[A]  Knowledge begins with them and can be reduced to them. After all, we would have no more knowledge than a stone if we did not know that there exist sound, smell, light, taste, measure, weight, softness, hardness, roughness, colour, sheen, breadth, depth. They form the foundations and principles on which our knowledge is built.  [C]  Indeed, for some thinkers, knowledge is sensation.   [A]  Anyone who can force me to contradict the evidence of the senses has got me by the throat: he cannot make me retreat any further. The senses are the beginning and the end of human knowledge.

> *Invenies primis ab sensibus esse creatam*
> *Notitiam veri, neque sensus posse refelli.*
> *Quid majore fide porro quam sensus haberi*
> *Debet?*

[You realize that the conception of truth is produced by the basic senses; the senses cannot be refuted. What should we trust more than our senses, then?][422]

420.  Plato, cited Cicero (n. 419), and *Theaetetus*, 186: knowledge is not in sensation but in reasoning upon sensation. Truth is 'perceived', not apprehended; it is not attainable from 'opinion'.

421.  Lucretius, V, 102 (Lambin, p. 382).

422.  Lucretius, IV, 478, 482 (Lambin, pp. 308–311). This section of Lucretius is aimed at anyone who dares to think that 'nothing is known' (*nil sciri*); Lucretius, 469 ff. This fact lends piquancy to what follows: Montaigne, like Carneades, is about to use his opponent's weapons against him.

Attribute as little to them as you can, but you will have to grant them this: that all the instruction we receive is conveyed by them and through them. Cicero says that when Chrysippus assayed denying their force and power, so many contrary arguments and overwhelming objections occurred to him that he could not answer them. Whereupon Carneades, who maintained the opposite side, boasted of fighting him with his own words and weapons, exclaiming, 'Wretch! You have been defeated by your own strength!'[423]

For us there is absolutely nothing more absurd than to say that fire is not hot; that light does not illuminate; that iron has no weight or resistance. Those are notions conveyed to us by our senses. There is no belief or knowledge in man of comparable certainty.

Now, on the subject of the senses, my first point is that I doubt that Man is provided with all the natural senses.[424] I note that several creatures live full, complete lives without sight; others, without hearing. Who can tell whether we, also, lack one, two, three or more senses? If we do lack any, our reason cannot even discover that we do so. Our senses are privileged to be the ultimate frontiers of our perception: beyond them there is nothing which could serve to reveal the existence of the senses we lack. One sense cannot reveal another:

[B]   *An poterunt oculos aures reprehendere, an aures*
      *Tactus, an hunc porro tactum sapor arguet oris,*
      *An confutabunt nares, oculive revincent?*

[Can the ears correct the eyes; the ears the touch? Can the tastes in our mouths correct the touch? Or will our nostrils and our eyes prove touch to be wrong?]

They all form, each one of them, the ultimate boundary of our faculty of knowledge:

          *seorsum cuique potestas*
          *Divisa est, sua vis cuique est.*

[For each has received its share and power, quite separate from the others.][425]

A man born blind cannot be made to *understand* what it is not to see; he cannot be made to wish he had sight and to regret what he is lacking. (Therefore we ought not to take comfort from our souls' being happy and satisfied

---

423. Cicero, *Acad.: Lucullus*, II, xxvii, 87 and Plutarch, *Contredicts des philosophes Stoïques*, 562H–563A.

424. Sextus Empiricus, *Hypotyposes*, I, xiv, 96–97. The whole of this section (36–163) forms the background to these pages.

425. Lucretius, IV, 486, 490.

with the senses we do have; if we are deprived and imperfect, our souls have
no way of sensing it.) It is impossible to say anything to that blind man by
reason, argument or comparison, which will fix in his understanding what
light, colour and sight really are. There is nothing beyond the senses which
can supply evidence of them. We do find people who are born blind express-
ing a wish to see: that does not mean that they know what they are asking
for. They have learned from us that they lack something which we have, and
they wish that they had it;   [C]   they name it all right, as well as its effects
and its consequences; but they do not know what it is, for all that; they cannot
even get near to grasping what it is.

I have met a nobleman of good family who was born blind, or, at least,
blind enough not to know what sight is. He has so little knowledge of what
he is lacking that he is always using words appropriate to seeing, just as we
do; he applies them in his own peculiar way. When he was presented with
one of his own godchildren, he took him in his arms and said: 'My God, what
a handsome child. How nice to see him! What a happy face he has.' He will
say (like one of us): 'What a lovely view there is from this room! What a clear
day. How bright the sun is.'And that is not all. Hearing how much we enjoy
the sports of hunting, tennis and shooting, he likes them, too; he tries to join
in and believes that he can take part like us. He gets carried away, has a great
deal of fun and yet has no knowledge at all of these sports, except through
the ears. On open ground, where he can use his spurs, somebody shouts,
'There goes a hare.' Then somebody says, 'Look, the hare has been caught.'
You will see him as proud of the kill as other men he has heard.

At tennis he takes the ball in his left hand and hits it with his racket. As
for the harquebus, he shoots at random, and is delighted when his men tell
him he has shot too high or too wide.

How do we know that the whole human race is not doing something just
as silly? We may all lack some sense or other; because of that defect, most of
the features of objects may be concealed from us. How can we know that the
difficulties we have in understanding many of the works of Nature do not
derive from this, or that several of the actions of animals which exceed our
powers of understanding are produced by a sense-faculty which we do not
possess? Perhaps some of them, by such means, enjoy a fuller life, a more
complete life than we do.

We need virtually all our senses merely to recognize an apple: we recognize
redness in it, sheen, smell and sweetness. An apple may well have other
qualities than that: for example powers of desiccation or astringency, for
which we have no corresponding senses.[426]

426. Sextus Empiricus, *Hypotyposes*, I, xiv, 95-96.

Take what we call the occult properties of many objects (such as the magnet attracting iron).[427] Is it not likely that there are certain senses known to Nature which furnish the faculties necessary for perceiving them and understanding them, and that the lack of such faculties entails our ignorance of their true essence? There may be some peculiar sense which tells cocks when it is midday or midnight and makes them crow,   [C]   or which teaches hens (before any practical experience) to fear the sparrow-hawk but not larger animals like geese or peacocks; which warns chickens of the innate hostility of cats but tells them not to fear dogs; which puts them on their guard against a *miaou* (quite a pleasing sound, really) but not against a bark (a harsh and aggressive sound);[428] which tells hornets, ants and rats how to select the best cheese and the best pear, before they even taste them;   [A]   which leads stags [C] elephants and snakes [A] to recognize herbs necessary to cure them.

There is no sense which is not dominant and which does not have the means of contributing vast amounts of knowledge. If we had no comprehension of sounds, harmony and the spoken word, that would throw all the rest of our knowledge into inconceivable confusion. For, quite apart from all that arises from the properties of each individual sense, think of the arguments, consequences and conclusions which we infer about other things by comparing one sense with another. Let an intelligent man imagine human nature created, from the beginning, without sight; let him reflect how much ignorance and confusion such a defect would entail, how much darkness and blindness there would be in our minds. We can see from that how vital it would be for our knowledge of truth if we lacked another sense, or two or three senses. We have fashioned a truth by questioning our five senses working together; but perhaps we need to harmonize the contributions of eight or ten senses if we are ever to know, with certainty, what Truth is in essence.

Those schools which attack Man's claim to possess knowledge base themselves mainly on the fallibility and weakness of our senses: for, since all knowledge comes to us through them and by them, we have nothing left to hold on to if they fail in their reports to us, if they change and corrupt what they convey to us from outside, or if the light which filters through to our mind from them is darkened in the process.

This ultimate difficulty has given rise to many strange notions: that a given

427.  These qualities were classified as 'sympathies' and 'antipathies' within nature and were fundamental to Renaissance science; cf. G. Fracastoro, *De sympathia et antipathia rerum*, 1554. For the magnet, cf. Rabelais, *Quart Livre*, TLF, LXII; for animals recognizing medical simples, *ibid.*, LXII (drawing on Plutarch and Celio Calcagnini).

428.  Seneca, *Epist.*, CXXI, 19.

object does have all the qualities we find in it; that it has none of the qualities which we think we find in it;[429] or, as the Epicureans contend, that the Sun is no bigger than our sight judges it to be –

> [B]   *Quicquid id est, nihilo fertur majore figura*
>      *Quam nostris oculis quam cernimus, esse videtur*

[Be that as it may, its size is no bigger than it seems when we behold it][430] – or, that those appearances which make an object look big when you are close to it and smaller when you are farther from it, are both true –

> [B]   *Nec tamen hic oculis falli concedimus hilum*
>      *Proinde animi vitium hoc oculis adfingere noli*

[We do not at all concede that the eyes can be deceived. Do not attribute to the eyes the errors of the mind][431]

– or, conclusively, that there is no deception whatsoever in our senses, so that we must throw ourselves on their mercy and seek elsewhere the justification for any differences and contradictions which we find in them: that, indeed, we should invent some lie or raving lunacy (yes, they get as far as that!) rather than condemn our senses.

[C] Timagoras said that he did not really see the candle-flame double when he squeezed his eye-ball sideways, but that this appearance arose from a defect of opinion not of vision.[432] [A] The absurdest of all absurdities [C] for Epicureans [A] is to deny [C] the effective power of [A] the senses:

429. Sextus Empiricus, *Hypotyposes*, I, xxix, 210–11.
430. Lucretius, V, 577 (of the Moon, not the Sun; but the section starts (564) '*Nec nimio solis major rota*' [The wheel of the Sun cannot be much larger than as perceived by our senses]). Lambin (p. 410) classes as 'the most stolid and silly of the opinions of Epicurus that the Sun, Moon and Stars have the size they appear to have'. He cites Cicero, *Acad.: Lucullus*, II, xxxix, 124 (cf. Introduction, p. xxx and Cicero, *ibid.*, xxvi, 82).
431. Lucretius, IV, 379; 386. (Lambin, pp. 300–302, explains: 'Lucretius says that, if we are deceived in our seeing things, that is a defect of our minds, not of our eyes . . . For Epicurus wished the senses to be certain and true; see Cicero [*Acad.*] *Lucullus*, II [142 f.]; later we add material from Lucretius himself.')
432. Cicero, *Acad.*, *Lucullus*, II, xxv, 79–80; for the importance of the contention, cf. Aristotle, *Metaph.*, XI, vi, 7 (1063a), a criticism of 'Man as measure' which, if accepted, would imply the truth of the notions for which Lucretius is to be cited – with disapproval.

> *Proinde quod in quoque est his visum tempore, verum est.*
> *Et, si non potuit ratio dissolvere causam,*
> *Cur ea quae fuerint juxtim quadrata, procul sint*
> *Visa rotunda, tamen praestat rationis egentem*
> *Reddere mendose causas utriusque figurae,*
> *Quam manibus manifesta suis emittere quoquam,*
> *Et violare fidem primam, et convellere tota*
> *Fundamenta quibus nixatur vita salusque.*
> *Non modo enim ratio ruat omnis, vita quoque ipsa*
> *Concidat extemplo, nisi credere sensibus ausis,*
> *Praecipitesque locos vitare, et caetera quae sint*
> *In genere hoc fugienda.*

[Consequently, whatever, at any time, has seemed to the senses to be true, is in fact true. If reason cannot unravel the causes which explain why things that are square when you are close to them appear round at a distance, it is better to find some untrue explanation of these two different impressions than to let the evidence of our senses slip through our fingers, violate first principles and shake the foundations on which our lives and their preservation are built. For, if we could no longer trust our senses and so avoid the giddy heights and other dangers Man must shun, not only would our Reason collapse in ruins but our lives as well.][433]

[C] That is a counsel of despair. It is quite unphilosophical. It reveals that human knowledge can only be supported by an unreasonable Reason, by mad lunatic ravings; that, if Man is to make himself worth anything, it is better to exploit 'Reason' such as this or any other remedy, no matter how fantastic it may be, rather than to admit so unflattering a truth that he is, of necessity, as stupid as a beast. Man cannot avoid the fact that his senses are both the sovereign regents of his knowledge, and yet, in all circumstances, uncertain and fallible. So here they must fight to a finish; if legitimate weapons fail us – and they do – they must use stubbornness, foolhardiness or cheek!

[B] Should what the Epicureans say be true (namely, that if the senses play us false we have no knowledge at all);[434] and should what the Stoics say be equally true (that sensible appearances are so deceptive that they can give rise in us to no knowledge whatever); then we are forced to conclude, at the expense of the two great schools of Dogmatists, that there is no such thing as knowledge.

[A] Anybody can provide as many examples as he pleases of the ways our senses deceive or cheat us, since so many of their faults or deceptions are

---

433. Lucretius, IV, 499 (Lambin, pp. 300–302).
434. Cicero, *Acad.: Lucullus*, II, xxxii, 101.

quite banal: a trumpet sounds a league behind us, but an echo in a valley may
make it seem to come from in front:

> [B]   *Extantesque procul medio de gurgite montes*
>    *Iidem apparent longe diversi licet*
> *Et fugere ad puppim colles campique videntur*
>    *Quos agimus propter navim*
>            *ubi in medio nobis equus acer obhaesit*
> *Flumine, equi corpus transversum ferre videtur*
> *Vis, et in adversum flumen contrudere raptim.*

[Distant mountains beetling over the sea may appear as one, yet are in fact many; as
we sail along, hills and plains appear to be rushing towards our prow; if we look down
when our horse stops in mid-stream, the river seems to be forcing it to go up-stream
against the current.][435]

[A]   Hold a musket-ball beneath your second finger, with your middle
finger entwined over it: you will have to force yourself to admit that there is
only one ball, so decidedly do you sense it to be two. We can see every day
that our senses have mastery over our reason, forcing it to receive impressions
which it knows to be false and judges to be false.

I will not go into the sense of touch. Its effects are immediate, lively and
concrete; many a time, as a result of the pain which it causes the body, it
overthrows all those fine Stoic axioms. It takes a man who has resolutely
made up his mind that colic paroxysms are a thing indifferent (like any other
pain or disease) and that they have no power to affect the blessed state of
supreme felicity in which the Sage has been lodged by his Stoic Virtue – and
makes him yell about his belly.

No heart is so flabby that the sounds of our drums and trumpets do not
set it ablaze, nor so hard that sweet music does not tickle it and enliven it;
no soul is so sour that it does not feel touched by some feeling of reverence[436]
when it contemplates the sombre vastness of our Churches, the great variety
of their decorations and our ordered liturgy, or when it hears the enchantment
of the organ and the poised religious harmony of men's voices. Even those
who come to scoff are brought to distrust their opinion by a shiver in their
heart and a sense of dread.

[B]   As for me, I do not think I would be strong enough to remain
unmoved even by verses of Horace or Catullus, if well sung by a good voice
coming from a fair young mouth!   [C]   Zeno was right to claim that the

435. Lucretius, IV, 397; 389; 421 (Lambin, pp. 300–302; but in 390 reading *praeter*
as *propter*); 'defects of the mind are not defects of the senses'.

436. '88: of *religious* reverence . . .

voice is Beauty's flower.[437] Some people have even tried to make me believe
that a famous man known to all Frenchmen had impressed me unduly with
a recital of some of his verses, which seem very different seen on paper than
heard in the air, and that my eyes would contradict my ears, so great is the
power of eloquent delivery to endow any work which accepts its sway with
value and style.

While on the topic, Philoxenus' reaction was not without charm: he heard
a piece he had composed being sung badly, so he jumped on some of the
singer's tiles and smashed them. 'I spoil your things,' (he said) 'you despoil
mine!'[438]

[A] Why did even those who had firmly decided to die avert their gaze
from the very blow which they ordered to be struck? Why do those who have
freely agreed to cauterizations and incisions for the sake of their health find
that they cannot stand the sight of all the preparations, of the surgical instruments or of the actual operation? Sight does not share in the pain.

Are not these appropriate examples for demonstrating the authority of our
senses over our powers of reason? – Even though we know that a lady's tresses
are borrowed from a page or a lackey; that her rosy colour comes from Spain
and her smooth whiteness from the ocean, we still find her person more
attractive and agreeable – quite unreasonably, though, for in all that nothing
is her own:

> Auferimur cultu; gemmis auroque teguntur
> Crimina: pars minima est ipsa puella sui.
> Saepe ubi sit quod ames inter tam multa requiras:
> Decipit hac oculos Aegide, dives amor.

[We are carried away by clothing; ugliness is hidden behind gems and gold; the smallest
part of herself is the actual girl! You can often look in vain for the girl you love
under all these gewgaws. This is the shield with which the rich deceive a lover's
eyes.][439]

What great power our poets attribute to the senses, when they make Nar-
cissus enamoured of his own reflection:

> Cunctaque miratur, quibus est mirabilis ipse;
> Se cupit imprudens; et qui probat, ipse probatur;
> Dumque petit, petitur; pariterque accendit et ardet.

437. Erasmus, Apophthegmata, VII, Zeno, XXIV.
438. Attributed by Diogenes Laertius to Arcesilas (Lives, IV, xxxvi, 270).
439. Ovid, Remedia amoris, 343. ('From the ocean': that is, from pulverized sea-
shells, used as face 'powder'.)

[He is enchanted by his own enchantments; unawares, he loves himself; he both praises and is praised; he yearns and is yearned for; the passion he kindles enflames himself.]

Similarly, Pygmalion's mind was disturbed by the visual impact of his ivory statue: he fell in love with it and sighed for it:

> *Oscula dat reddique putat, sequiturque tenetque,*
> *Et credit tactis digitos insidere membris;*
> *Et metuit pressos veniat ne livor in artus.*

[He kisses her, and believes his kisses are returned; he waits on her, embraces her; he believes her limbs respond to the touch of his fingers; he fears that in his ardour he may bruise her.]⁴⁴⁰

Take a philosopher, put him in a cage made from thin wires set wide apart; hang him from one of the towers of Notre Dame de Paris. It is evident to his reason that he cannot fall; yet (unless he were trained as a steeplejack) when he looks down from that height he is bound to be terrified and beside himself. It is hard enough to feel safe at the top of a church tower, even behind open-work ramparts of stone: some people cannot even bear thinking about it.

Take a beam wide enough to walk along: suspend it between two towers: there is no philosophical wisdom, however firm, which could make us walk along it just as we would if we were on the ground.

I am not particularly afraid of heights, but when I was on the French side of the Italian Alps I made an assay and found that I could not suffer the sight of those boundless depths without a shiver of horror; I was at least my own height away from the edge and could not have fallen over unless I deliberately exposed myself to danger: yet my knees and thighs were trembling. I also noticed that, whatever the height, it was comforting and reassuring if there happened to be some tree or rock jutting out on the slope which could hold our gaze and interrupt our vision: it was as though they could have helped us if we fell. But when the precipices were sheer and smooth we could not even look at them without feeling giddy,   [C]  '*ut despici sine vertigine simul oculorum animique non possit*' [such that no one could look down without vertigo in eyes and mind].⁴⁴¹

Which shows how sight can deceive us.

One fine philosopher even poked out his eyes so as to free his mind from visual debauchery; he could then go on philosophizing in freedom. But by

---

440. Ovid, *Metam.*, III, 424; X, 256.
441. Livy, XLIV, 6.

the same standard he ought to have blocked up his ears[442] – [B] which Theophrastus says are the most dangerous of all our organs when it comes to receiving violent impressions capable of changing and disturbing us.[443] [A] Eventually he would have to deprive himself of every other sense (tantamount to life and being), for all the senses can have this dominant power over our reason and our soul: [C] 'Fit etiam saepe specie quadam, saepe vocum gravitate et cantibus, ut pellantur animi vehementius; saepe etiam cura et timore' [Some visual feature, some grave voice or incantations may often strike the mind most vehemently: worry and care may often do that too].[444]

[A] Doctors maintain that people with some complexions can be driven mad by certain sounds or instruments. I have known people who could not even hear a bone being gnawed under their table without losing control; and there is hardly a person who is not upset by the sharp rasping sound of a file against iron. Some people are moved to anger or even hatred by hearing somebody chewing nearby or talking with some obstruction of their throat or nose.

Gracchus had a prompter who was a flautist; he conducted the voice of his master, softening it or making it firm:[445] what use was he if the rhythm and quality of the sounds did not have the power of moving and swaying the judgement of the listeners? We have good enough reason to make a fuss about this judgement of ours: it lets itself be affected and managed by the modulations and properties of so light a breath of wind!

The senses deceive our intellect; it deceives them in their turn. Our soul sometimes gets her own back: [C] they both vie with each other in lying and deceiving. [A] When we are moved to anger, we do not hear things as they are:

>    Et solem geminum, et duplices se ostendere Thebas.

>    [We see twin suns: two Thebes.][446]

Love someone and she appears more beautiful than she is:

>    [B] Multimodis igitur pravas turpesque videmus
>    Esse in delitiis, summoque in honore vigere.

442. Democritus (whom Montaigne already mentions in vol. I, chapter 14: 'That the taste of good and evil things depends in large part on the opinion we have of them', and vol. I, chapter 39: 'On Solitude'). Cf. Aulus Gellius, Attic Nights, X, xvii; Cicero, De fin., V, xxix, 87 (hesitating to believe it).

443. Plutarch, tr. Amyot, Comment il fault oïr, 24H–25A.

444. Cicero, De divinat., XXXVI, 80.

445. Plutarch, tr. Amyot, Comment il fault refrener la colere, 57H–58A.

446. Virgil, Aeneid, IV, 470.

[Many ugly and deformed women are deeply loved, enjoying, as we see, the highest favour.][447]

[A] And anyone we dislike appears more ugly. When a man is in pain and affliction, the very light of day seems sombre and dark. Our senses are not only changed for the worse, they are knocked quite stupid by the passions of the soul. How many things do we see which we do not even notice when our minds are preoccupied with other matters?

> *In rebus quoque apertis noscere possis,*
> *Si non advertas animum, proinde esse, quasi omni*
> *Tempore semotae fuerint, longeque remotae.*

[Even in the case of things which are clearly visible, you know that if you do not turn your mind to them, it is as though they had never been there or were far away.][448]

It seems, then, that the soul draws the powers of the senses right into herself and makes them waste their time.

And so, both within and without, man is full of weakness and of lies.

[B] Those who have compared our lives to a dream are right – perhaps more right than they realized. When we are dreaming our soul lives, acts and exercises all her faculties neither more nor less than when she is awake, but she does it much more slackly and darkly; the difference is definitely not so great as between night and the living day: more like that between night and twilight. In one case the soul is sleeping, in the other more or less slumbering; but there is always darkness, perpetual Cimmerian darkness.

[C] We wake asleep: we sleep awake. When I am asleep I do see things less clearly but I never find my waking pure enough or cloudless. Deep sleep can sometimes even put dreams to sleep; but our waking is never so wide awake that it can cure and purge those raving lunacies, those waking dreams that are worse than the real ones.

Our rational souls accept notions and opinions produced during sleep, conferring on activities in our dreams the same approbation and authority as on our waking dreams: why should we therefore not doubt whether our thinking and acting are but another dream; our waking, some other species of sleep?

[A] If the senses are our basic judges, we should not merely call upon

447. Lucretius, IV, 1155 (Lambin, pp. 358–59).
448. Lucretius, IV, 811 (Lambin, pp. 331–33, citing Cicero, *Tusc. disput.*, in support).

our own for counsel: where this faculty is concerned, the animals have as
much right as we do, or even more. Some certainly have better hearing, sight,
smell, touch or taste. Democritus said that the gods and the beasts have
faculties of sense far more perfect than Man does.

Now there are extreme differences between the action of their senses and
ours: our saliva cleanses and dries up our wounds: it kills snakes.[449]

> Tantaque in his rebus distantia differitasque est,
> Ut quod aliis cibus est, aliis fuat acre venenum.
> Saepe etenim serpens, hominis contacta saliva,
> Disperit, ac sese mandendo conficit ipsa.

[There are so many differences and variations: one man's food is another man's bitter
poison. Indeed if a snake comes into contact with human saliva, it begins to bite its
own tail and dies.][450]

So what quality are we to give to saliva? Do we follow our own senses or the
snake's? We are trying to discover the truth about its true essence: which of
the two will tell us? Pliny says that there are certain 'sea-hares' in the Indies
which are poison to us and we to them: a touch kills them.[451] Which is truly
poisonous, the fish or the man? Which should we believe: the effect of the fish
on the man or the man on the fish?  [B]  The quality of one kind of air is
infectious to Man but not to cattle; another has the quality of being infectious
to cattle but harmless to men. Which of the two has truly and naturally the
quality of being infectious?  [A]  Sufferers from jaundice see everything
paler and yellower than we do:

> [B]  Lurida praeterea fiunt quaecunque tuentur
> Arquati.

[Those ill from 'rainbow-yellow' see everything in sallow colours.][452]

[A]  There is a suffusion of blood under the skin around the eye which
doctors call Hyposphragma – those who suffer from it see everything blood-
red.[453] How do we know that these humours, which can affect the workings
of Man's eyesight, are not the dominant norm among beasts? Some animals,
as we know, have yellow eyes exactly like sufferers from jaundice and others
have eyes which are blood-red. It is probable that the colours of objects

449. Cf. Rabelais, Quart Livre, TLF, LXIV, derived from Celio Calcagnini.
450. Lucretius, IV, 636 (Lambin, p. 619).
451. Pliny, Hist. Nat., XXXII, 1.
452. Lucretius, IV, 333 (Lambin, pp. 296–97).
453. Medical deformation of hyposphagma; cited after Sextus Empiricus, Hypotyposes, I, xiv, 45. The following is from ibid., 45–47.

appear different to them and to us. Who judges them right? Nobody claims that the essence of anything relates only to its effect on Man. Hardness, whiteness, depth, bitterness – such qualities are of service to animals and are known to them as to ourselves: Nature has granted that they be useful to animals as well as to us men.

If we squeeze one of our eyes, the objects we look at appear thinner and elongated: many beasts have eyes which are always squeezed up like that. For all we know, that elongated form is the true one, not what our eyes see in their normal state.    [B]   If we press up our eyes from the bottom, we see double:

> *Bina lucernarum florentia lumina flammis,*
> *Et duplices hominum facies, et corpora bina.*

[The lamp has twin flowerings of light, men have twin faces and twin bodies.][454]

If our ears are blocked up or if the auricular passage is constricted we hear sounds differently from normal: animals have hairy ears or, in some cases, merely a little hole instead of an ear: consequently, they do not hear what we hear and the sound is perceived differently.[455]

At banquets or in the theatre, when various shades of coloured glass are placed in front of the torches, we know that they can make everything appear green, yellow or violet:

> [B]   *Et vulgo faciunt id lutea russaque vela*
> *Et ferruginea, cum magnis intenta theatris*
> *Per malos volgata trabesque trementia pendent:*
> *Namque ibi consessum caveai subter, et omnem*
> *Scenai speciem, patrum, matrumque, deorumque*
> *Inficiunt, coguntque suo volitare colore.*

[When yellow, red or rust-brown awnings are stretched over our vast theatres, flapping about in the wind on their poles and their frames, it is quite usual for them to impart their colours to the stage and to the whole assembly seated in their seats, to senators and matrons and to the statues of the gods, as their colours dance about.][456]

[A]   It seems likely that the different coloured eyes which we can notice in some animals may impart corresponding colours to what the animals see.

454. Lucretius, IV, 450 (Lambin, pp. 305–307, who alludes to Aristotle, *Proble-mata*, 3, for the explanation); Sextus Empiricus, *Hypotyposes*, I, 47; Plato, *Theaetetus*, 153b–154a.

455. Sextus Empiricus, *Hypotyposes*, I, xiv, 50–51.

456. Lucretius, IV, 74 (Lambin, pp. 278–81) reading *volitare* for *fluitare*.

If we want to judge the activities of the senses we should agree with the
animals and then among ourselves. We are far from doing that. Quarrels
are constantly arising because one person hears, sees or tastes something
differently from another. As much as anything, we quarrel over the diversity
of the images conveyed to us by our senses.[457]

A child, a man of thirty, a sexagenarian, each hears and sees things differently: that is a normal law of Nature. Similarly for taste. Some people's senses
are dullish and dimmer: others are more open and acute. We perceive objects
to be like this or that in accordance with our own state and how they seem to
us.[458] But *seeming*, for human beings, is so uncertain and so controvertible
that it is no miracle if we are told that we may acknowledge that snow seems
white to us but cannot guarantee to establish that it is truly so in essence.
And once you shake that first principle, all the knowledge in the world is
inevitably swept away.

What about our very senses hampering each other? A painting may seem
to have depth, but feels flat. Musk is pleasant to the smell but offensive to
the taste: should we call it pleasant or not? There are herbs and ointments
suitable to one part of the body but injurious to another; honey is pleasant
to taste, unpleasant to look at.[459] Take those rings wrought in the shape of
plumes which are called in heraldry *Feathers without Ends*. Can any eye ever
be sure how wide they are and avoid being taken in by the optical illusion?
For they seem to get wider on one side, narrower and more pointed on the
other, especially if you turn them round your finger; yet to your touch they
all appear to have the same width all the way round.

–  [C]  (In the ancient world some men increased their lust by the use of
distorting mirrors which enlarged whatever was put before them, so that the
organs used on the job pleased them more, because they looked as though
they had grown bigger. But which sense did they allow to win? Was it their
sight, which showed them their members as thick and big as they liked, or was
it their touch, which showed the same members to be tiny and despicable?)[460]

[A]  Is it our senses which endow the object with these diverse attributes,
whereas, in reality, objects only have one? Rather like bread when we eat it;

457. Cf. Sextus Empiricus, *Hypotyposes*, I, xiv, 78–79; 106.

458. *Ibid.*, I, xiii, 33–34.

'88: acute. *Sick people lend a bitter taste to sweet things; from which it transpires that we
do not receive things as they are but,* like this or that . . . (From Aristotle, *Metaph.*, IV,
v, 27 – dropped as a repetition.)

459. Sextus Empiricus, *Hypotyposes*, I, xiii, 91–92.

460. *Ibid.*, I, xiv, 48–49; Seneca, *Quaest. Nat.*, I, xvi.

it is one thing, bread, but we turn it into several: bones, blood, flesh, hair
and nails.

> [B]   *Ut cibus, in membra atque artus cum diditur omnes,*
>        *Disperit, atque aliam naturam sufficit ex se.*

[Like food, which spreads to all our limbs and joints, destroys itself and produces
another substance.][461]

[A]   Moisture is sucked up by the roots of a tree: it becomes trunk, leaf and
fruit; air is one, but when applied to a trumpet it is diversified into a thousand
kinds of sound: is it our senses (I say) which similarly fashion such objects
with diverse qualities or do they really have such qualities? Then, given that
doubt, what conclusion can we reach about their true essence?

And then, to go further still: the attributes of illness, madness or sleep
make things appear different from what they do to the healthy, the sane and
the waking man:[462] is it not likely therefore that our rightful state and our
natural humours also have attributes which can endow an object with a mode
of being corresponding to their own characteristics, making it conform to
themselves, just as our disordered humours do?   [C]   Why should a temperate complexion not endow objects with a form corresponding to itself just
as our distempers can, stamping its own imprint upon them?[463] On to his
wine the queasy man loads tastelessness; the healthy man, a bouquet; the
thirsty man, sheer delight.

[A]   Now, since our state makes things correspond to itself and transforms
them in conformity with itself, we can no longer claim to know what anything
truly is: nothing reaches us except as altered and falsified by our senses.
When the compasses, the set-square and the ruler are askew, all the calcu-
lations made with them and all the structures raised according to their
measurements, are necessarily out of true and ready to collapse.

The unreliability of our senses renders unreliable everything which they
put forward:

> *Denique ut in fabrica, si prava est regula prima,*
> *Normaque si fallax rectis regionibus exit,*

461. Sextus Empiricus, *Hypotyposes*, I, xiv, 33; Lucretius, III, 703 (Lambin, pp.
237–38).

462. Sextus Empiricus, *Hypotyposes*, I, xiv, 100–104.

'88: Waking man: *Since that particular state, by endowing objects with a being different
from the one they have, and since a jaundiced humour changes everything to yellow*, is it not
likely . . . (Then, for *rightful* state, *ordinary* state.)

463. *Ibid.*, I, xiv, 102.

*Et libella aliqua si ex parte claudicat hilum,*
*Omnia mendose fieri atque obstipa necessum est,*
*Prava, cubantia, prona, supina, atque absona tecta,*
*Jam ruere ut quaedam videantur velle, ruantque*
*Prodita judiciis fallacibus omnia primis.*
*Hic igitur ratio tibi rerum prava necesse est*
*Falsaque sit, falsis quaecumque a sensibus orta est.*

[It is as when a building is erected: if the ruler is false from the outset, or the set-square deceptive and out of true, if the level limps a bit to one side, then the building is necessarily wrong and crooked; it is deformed, pot-bellied, toppling forwards or backwards and quite disjointed; some parts seem about to fall down now: all will fall down soon, betrayed by the original mistakes of calculation; similarly every argument that you base on facts will prove wrong and false, if the facts themselves are based on senses which prove false.][464]

And meanwhile who will be a proper judge of such differences? It is like saying that we could do with a judge who is not bound to either party in our religious strife, who is dispassionate and without prejudice. Among Christians that cannot be.[465] The same applies here: if the judge is old, he cannot judge the sense-impressions of old age, since he is a party to the dispute; so too if he is young; so too if he is well; so too if he is unwell, asleep or awake.[466] We would need a man exempt from all these qualities, so that, without preconception, he could judge those propositions as matters indifferent to him.

On this reckoning we would need such a judge as never was.

We register the appearance of objects; to judge them we need an instrument of judgement; to test the veracity of that instrument we need practical proof; to test that proof we need an instrument. We are going round in circles.[467]

The senses themselves being full of uncertainty cannot decide the issue of our dispute. It will have to be Reason, then. But no Reason can be established except by another Reason. We retreat into infinity.[468] Our mental faculty of perception is never directly in touch with outside objects – which are perceived via the senses, and the senses do not embrace an outside object but only their own impressions of it; therefore the thought and the appearance are not properties of the object but only the impressions and feelings of the

464. Lucretius, IV, 513 (Lambin, pp. 309–311).

465. Both sides in the religious wars claim to be the one true Church, so no Christian anywhere can remain impartial.

466. Sextus Empiricus, *Hypotyposes*, I, xiv, 104–106.

467. *Ibid.*, 115–17.

468. *Ibid.*, II, vii, 89.

senses. Those impressions and that object are different things. So whoever judges from appearances judges from something quite different from the object itself.

If you say that these sense-impressions convey the quality of outside objects to our souls by means of resemblances, how can our rational soul make sure that they are resemblances, since it has no direct contact of its own with the outside objects? It is like a man who does not know Socrates; if he sees a portrait of him he cannot say whether it resembles him or not.[469]

But supposing, nevertheless, that anyone did wish to judge from appearances, he cannot do so from all of them, since (as we know from experience) they all mutually impede each other because of contradictions and discrepancies. Will he select only some appearances to control the others? But the first one selected will have to be tested for truth against another one selected, and that one against a third: the end will therefore never be reached.[470]

To conclude: there is no permanent existence either in our being or in that of objects. We ourselves, our faculty of judgement and all mortal things are flowing and rolling ceaselessly: nothing certain can be established about one from the other, since both judged and judging are ever shifting and changing.[471]

'We have no communication with Being;[472] as human nature is wholly 'situated, for ever, between birth and death, it shows itself only as a dark 'shadowy appearance, an unstable weak opinion. And if you should determine 'to try and grasp what Man's *being* is, it would be exactly like trying to hold 'a fistful of water: the more tightly you squeeze anything the nature of which 'is always to flow, the more you will lose what you try to retain in your grasp.

469. *Ibid.*, II, vii, 72–75. A similar argument appealed to St Augustine (*Contra academicos*, II, 7); cf. also Sextus Empiricus, *Against the Mathematicians*, II, 58–59.

470. *Ibid.*, II, ix, 88–89: the climax to Sextus' denial that appearances can be judged as probable, let alone true. It rules out dialectic as a means of telling truth from error (*ibid.*, 94) and continues suspension of judgement (95).

471. This Platonic assertion forces man to go beyond the transient flux of things and to seek the unchanging Reality lying behind it. From now to the last paragraph Montaigne transcribes, with minor adaptations, a very large borrowing from Amyot's translation of Plutarch: *Que signifioit ce mot E'i* (456H–357E); this is indicated here by continuous quotation marks: in the original no indication of any kind shows that this is a borrowing. (Even Marie de Gournay did not recognize it as such.) Departures from the original version by Amyot are indicated below. (Amyot's French version differs markedly from modern interpretations of the original Greek of Plutarch.)

472. Plutarch, 356H: with *true* Being . . .

'So, because all things are subject to pass from change to change, Reason is 'baffled if it looks for a substantial existence in them, since it cannot apprehend 'a single thing which subsists permanently, because everything is either com-'ing into existence (and so not fully existing yet) or beginning to die before it is 'born.' Plato said that bodies never have existence, though they certainly have birth, [C] believing that Homer made Oceanus Father of the Gods and Thetis their Mother, to show that all things are in a state of never-ending inconstancy, change and flux (an opinion, as he says, common to all the philosophers before his time, with the sole exception of Parmenides, who denied that anything has motion – attaching great importance to the force of that idea).[473]

[A] Pythagoras taught that all matter is labile and flowing;[474] the Stoics, that there is no such thing as the present (which is but the joining and the coupling together of the future and past);[475] 'Heraclitus, that no man ever stepped twice into the same river' – ([B]  Epicharmus, that a man who borrowed money in the past does not owe it now, and that a man invited to breakfast yesterday evening turns up this morning uninvited, both having become different people).[476] –  [A]  Heraclitus 'that no mortal substance 'can ever be found twice in an identical state because the rapidity and ease of 'its changes make it constantly disperse and reassemble; it is coming and 'going, so that whatever begins to be born never achieves perfect existence, 'since its delivery is never complete and never stops as though it had come to 'the end; but, ever since the seeds of it were sown, it is continually modifying 'and changing from one thing to another; just as from the human seed there 'first springs a shapeless embryo in the mother's womb, then a human shape, 'then, once out of the womb, a suckling child, then a boy, then, in due course, 'a youth, a mature man, an old and then a decrepit, aged man, so that each 'subsequent age to which birth is given is for ever undoing and destroying the 'previous one.'

[B]  *Mutat enim mundi naturam totius aetas,*
     *Ex alioque alius status excipere omnia debet,*

473. Plato, *Theaetetus*, 180E.

474. Not *Pythagoras* but *Protagoras*: cf. Sextus Empiricus, *Hypotyposes*, I, xxxii, 217.

475. Plutarch, *Des communes conceptions contre les Stoïques*, 586B–C. For Heraclitus, see Aristotle, *Metaph.*, IV, v, 1010a.

476. Plutarch, tr. Amyot, *Pourquoi la justice divine differe quelquefois la punition des malefices*, 264. (Some small changes to Amyot's French here, to accommodate the interpolations; grammar and clarity suffer.)

> *Nec manet ulla sui similis res: omnia migrant,*
> *Omnia commutat natura et vertere cogit.*

[For Time changes the nature of all things in the world; each stage must be succeeded by another, nothing remains as it was; all things depart and Nature modifies all things and compels them to change.][477]

[A] 'And after that we men stupidly fear one species of death, when we 'have already passed through so many other deaths and do so still; yet, as 'Heraclitus said, not only is the death of fire the birth of air, and the death of 'air the birth of water, but we may see it even more clearly in ourselves: the 'flower of our life withers and dies into old age; but youth ended in that adult 'flower, as childhood in youth and as that embryonic stage died into child-'hood; yesterday dies into today, and this day will die into tomorrow. Nothing 'lasts; nothing remains forever one.'[478]

To prove that this is so: 'if we remained forever one and the same, how is 'it that we can delight in one thing now and later in another? How can we 'each be *one* if we love or hate contradictory things, first praising them, then 'condemning them?[479] How can we have different emotions, no longer retain-'ing the same sentiment within the same thought? For it is not likely that we 'can experience different reactions unless we ourselves have changed; but 'whoever suffers change is no longer the same *one*: he no longer is. For his '*being*, as such, changes when his *being one* changes, as each personality ever 'succeeds another. And, consequently, it is of the nature of our senses to be 'misled and deceived. Because they do not know what *being* is, they take '*appears to be* for *is*.

'What is it then which truly IS? That which is eternal – meaning that 'which has never been born; which will never have an end; to which Time 'can never bring any change. For Time is a thing of movement, appearing 'like a shadow in the eternal flow and flux of matter, never remaining stable 'or permanent;[480] to Time belong the words *before* and *after*; *has been* and *shall* '*be*, words that show at a glance that Time is evidently not a thing which IS. 'For it would be great silliness and manifest falsehood to say that something 'IS which has not yet come into being or has already ceased to be.

'With the words "*Present*", "*This instant*", "*Now*", we above all appear to 'support and stabilize our understanding of Time: but Reason strips it bare

477. Lucretius, V, 828 (Lambin, p. 426).
478. Five words of Amyot omitted and a phrase adapted (357B).
479. Small omission from Amyot (357B).
480. Omission: Amyot, 357C ('like a sinking ship in which are contained generation and corruption').

'and at once destroys it: for Reason straightway cleaves *Now* into two
'distinct parts, the future and the past, as needing of necessity to see it thus
'divided into two parts.

'The same applies to Nature (which is measured) as to Time (which meas-
'ures her): for there is nothing in Nature, either, which lasts or subsists; in
'her, all things are either born, being born, or dying.[481]

'It would therefore be a sin to say *He was* or *He will be* of God, who is
'the only ONE who IS. For those terms are transitions, declensions and
'vicissitudes in things which cannot endure nor remain in Being.

'From which we must conclude that God alone IS: not according to any
'measure known to Time, but according to an unchanging and immortal
'eternity, not measured by Time, not subject to any declension; before Whom
'nothing *is*, neither will there be anything after Him, nor anything newer or
'more recent; but ONE, existing in reality, He fills Eternity with a single Now;
'nothing really IS but He alone; of Him you cannot say *He was* or *He will be*:
'He has no beginning and no end.'[482]

To that very religious conclusion of a pagan I would merely add one more
word from a witness of the same condition, in order to bring to a close this
long and tedious discourse which could furnish me with matter for ever. 'Oh,
what a vile and abject thing is Man,' he said, 'if he does not rise above
humanity.'[483]

[C] A pithy saying; a most useful aspiration, but absurd withal. For
[A] to make a fistful bigger than the fist, an armful larger than the arm, or
to try and make your stride wider than your legs can stretch, are things
monstrous and impossible. Nor may a man mount above himself or above
humanity: for he can see only with his own eyes, grip only with his own
grasp. He will rise if God proffers him –   [C]   extraordinarily –   [A]   His

481. Montaigne adds the words 'or born' (*ou nées*) and omits, 'intermingled with
Time' (357D).

482. The long borrowing from Plutarch ends here. The concluding words of the
treatise *On the E'i at Delphi* emphasize its connection with Montaigne's themes of self-
knowledge and the abasement of Man: 'And meanwhile it seems that this word *E'i* is
somewhat opposed to the precept *Know Thyself* and also in some ways accordant and
agreeable to it: the one is a kind of verbal astonishment and adoration before God, as
being Eternal and Ever in Being, while the other is a warning and reminder to mortal
Man of the weakness and debility of his nature' (358C).

483. Seneca, *Quaest. nat.*, I (Preface), cited by Sebond, tr. Montaigne, 186rº.

'88: humanity.' *There is in all his Stoic school no saying truer than that one: but* to
make . . .

hand; he will rise by abandoning and disavowing his own means, letting himself be raised and pulled up by purely heavenly ones.[484]

[C] It is for our Christian faith, not that Stoic virtue of his, to aspire to that holy and miraculous metamorphosis.[485]

484. '88: pulled up by *divine grace: but not otherwise.* (The closing words of the *Apology* until [C].)

485. *Metamorphose* may imply 'transfiguration': it certainly implies 'transformation' – the theme of the final pages of the last chapter (vol. III, chapter 13, 'On experience').

# READ MORE IN PENGUIN

In every corner of the world, on every subject under the sun, Penguin represents quality and variety – the very best in publishing today.

For complete information about books available from Penguin – including Puffins, Penguin Classics and Arkana – and how to order them, write to us at the appropriate address below. Please note that for copyright reasons the selection of books varies from country to country.

**In the United Kingdom:** Please write to *Dept. EP, Penguin Books Ltd, Bath Road, Harmondsworth, West Drayton, Middlesex UB7 0DA*

**In the United States:** Please write to *Consumer Sales, Penguin Putnam Inc., P.O. Box 999, Dept. 17109, Bergenfield, New Jersey 07621-0120.* VISA and MasterCard holders call 1-800-253-6476 to order Penguin titles

**In Canada:** Please write to *Penguin Books Canada Ltd, 10 Alcorn Avenue, Suite 300, Toronto, Ontario M4V 3B2*

**In Australia:** Please write to *Penguin Books Australia Ltd, P.O. Box 257, Ringwood, Victoria 3134*

**In New Zealand:** Please write to *Penguin Books (NZ) Ltd, Private Bag 102902, North Shore Mail Centre, Auckland 10*

**In India:** Please write to *Penguin Books India Pvt Ltd, 210 Chiranjiv Tower, 43 Nehru Place, New Delhi 110 019*

**In the Netherlands:** Please write to *Penguin Books Netherlands bv, Postbus 3507, NL-1001 AH Amsterdam*

**In Germany:** Please write to *Penguin Books Deutschland GmbH, Metzlerstrasse 26, 60594 Frankfurt am Main*

**In Spain:** Please write to *Penguin Books S. A., Bravo Murillo 19, 1° B, 28015 Madrid*

**In Italy:** Please write to *Penguin Italia s.r.l., Via Benedetto Croce 2, 20094 Corsico, Milano*

**In France:** Please write to *Penguin France, Le Carré Wilson, 62 rue Benjamin Baillaud, 31500 Toulouse*

**In Japan:** Please write to *Penguin Books Japan Ltd, Kaneko Building, 2-3-25 Koraku, Bunkyo-Ku, Tokyo 112*

**In South Africa:** Please write to *Penguin Books South Africa (Pty) Ltd, Private Bag X14, Parkview, 2122 Johannesburg*

# READ MORE IN PENGUIN

## A CHOICE OF CLASSICS

| | |
|---|---|
| Leopoldo Alas | **La Regenta** |
| Leon B. Alberti | **On Painting** |
| Ludovico Ariosto | **Orlando Furioso** (in two volumes) |
| Giovanni Boccaccio | **The Decameron** |
| Baldassar Castiglione | **The Book of the Courtier** |
| Benvenuto Cellini | **Autobiography** |
| Miguel de Cervantes | **Don Quixote** |
| | **Exemplary Stories** |
| Dante | **The Divine Comedy** (in three volumes) |
| | **La Vita Nuova** |
| Machado de Assis | **Dom Casmurro** |
| Bernal Díaz | **The Conquest of New Spain** |
| Niccolò Machiavelli | **The Discourses** |
| | **The Prince** |
| Alessandro Manzoni | **The Betrothed** |
| Emilia Pardo Bazán | **The House of Ulloa** |
| Benito Pérez Galdós | **Fortunata and Jacinta** |
| Eça de Quierós | **The Maias** |
| Sor Juana Inés de la Cruz | **Poems, Protest and a Dream** |
| Giorgio Vasari | **Lives of the Artists** (in two volumes) |

*and*

**Five Italian Renaissance Comedies**
(Machiavelli/The Mandragola; Ariosto/Lena; Aretino/The
Stablemaster; Gl'Intronati/The Deceived; Guarini/The Faithful
Shepherd)
**The Poem of the Cid**
**Two Spanish Picaresque Novels**
(Anon/Lazarillo de Tormes; de Quevedo/The Swindler)

# READ MORE IN PENGUIN

## A CHOICE OF CLASSICS

| | |
|---|---|
| Jacob Burckhardt | **The Civilization of the Renaissance in Italy** |
| Carl von Clausewitz | **On War** |
| Meister Eckhart | **Selected Writings** |
| Friedrich Engels | **The Origin of the Family** |
| | **The Condition of the Working Class in England** |
| Goethe | **Elective Affinities** |
| | **Faust Parts One and Two** (in two volumes) |
| | **Italian Journey** |
| | **Maxims and Reflections** |
| | **Selected Verse** |
| | **The Sorrows of Young Werther** |
| Jacob and Wilhelm Grimm | **Selected Tales** |
| E. T. A. Hoffmann | **Tales of Hoffmann** |
| Friedrich Hölderlin | **Selected Poems and Fragments** |
| Henrik Ibsen | **Brand** |
| | **A Doll's House and Other Plays** |
| | **Ghosts and Other Plays** |
| | **Hedda Gabler and Other Plays** |
| | **The Master Builder and Other Plays** |
| | **Peer Gynt** |
| Søren Kierkegaard | **Fear and Trembling** |
| | **Papers and Journals** |
| | **The Sickness Unto Death** |
| Georg Christoph Lichtenberg | **Aphorisms** |
| Karl Marx | **Capital** (in three volumes) |
| Karl Marx/Friedrich Engels | **The Communist Manifesto** |
| Friedrich Nietzsche | **The Birth of Tragedy** |
| | **Beyond Good and Evil** |
| | **Ecce Homo** |
| | **Human, All Too Human** |
| | **Thus Spoke Zarathustra** |
| Friedrich Schiller | **Mary Stuart** |
| | **The Robbers/Wallenstein** |

# BY THE SAME AUTHOR

**The Complete Essays**

Translated and edited with an Introduction and Notes by M. A. Screech

In 1572 Montaigne retired from public life and began the reading and writing which were to develop into 'assays' of his thoughts and opinions. Nobody in Western civilisation had ever tried to do what Montaigne set out to do. In a vivid, contemporary style he surprises us with entertaining quotations; he moves swiftly from thought to thought, often digressing from an idea only to return to it triumphantly, having caught up with it elsewhere, and in so doing leads the reader along the criss-cross paths of a journey of discovery. Montaigne set out to discover himself. What he discovered instead was the human race.

'Screech's fine version ... must surely serve as the definitive English Montaigne' – A. C. Grayling in the *Financial Times*

'A superb edition' – Nicholas Woolaston in the *Observer*

**The Essays: A Selection**

Translated with an Introduction and Notes by M. A. Screech.

Michel de Montaigne created a kind of autobiography so new and self-revealing, writes Michael Screech in his stimulating introduction, that 'we know the form of his mind better than that of anyone who wrote before ...'

A chapter *On Some Lines of Virgil* soon opens out into a frank and wide-ranging discussion of sexuality. *On Experience* sums up superbly his final thoughts on the right way to live. Other chapters touch on the great public issues of an age torn apart by religious and intellectual strife. All are united by the distinctive voice of Montaigne, a tolerant man, humane, often humorous, yet utterly honest in his pursuit of truth. There are few more stimulating personalities in literature.